S

ISBN 0 904491 62 5

A survey of streets,
buildings & former residents
in a part of Camden

Streets of Kentish Town

Thompson's map of the elongated
village of Kentish Town in 1801.
The road leading towards the
River Fleet at right angles to the
high road is Mansfield Place,
present-day Holmes Road

Compiled by Camden History Society

Edited by Steven Denford and David A Hayes

Designed by Ivor Kamlish

General Editor of Camden History Society Publications F Peter Woodford

Plan of the Walking Routes

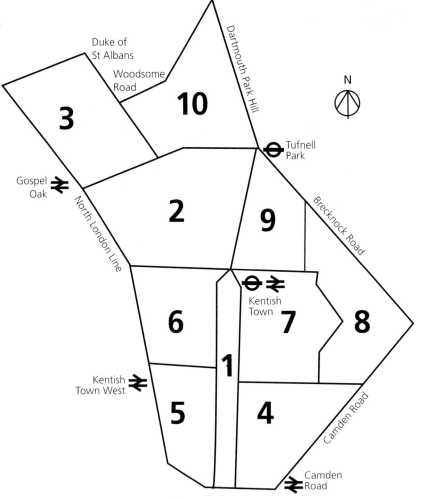

Duke of
St Albans

Woodsome
Road

Dartmouth Park Hill

N

10

3

Gospel
Oak

North London Line

Tufnell
Park

Brecknock Road

2

9

Kentish
Town

6

7

8

Kentish
Town West

1

5

4

Camden Road

Camden
Road

Contents

List of illustrations and maps   7

Historical overview   8

Note on key sources   12

Topographical notes   13

**Street names in this book
and their origins**   16

Route 1
Up & down Kentish Town Road
Circular walk from Kentish Town station   20

Route 2
Highgate Road to Fortess Road
Circular walk from Kentish Town station   31

Route 3
Grove, Green and Common
*Circular walk from railway bridge over
Highgate Road*   46

Route 4
The Camden estate
Circular walk from Camden Road station   59

Route 5
The Hawley–Buck estate
Circular walk from Camden Town station   71

Route 6
The 'Crimean' area and Holmes estate
Circular walk from Kentish Town station   83

Route 7
'New Kentish Town'
Circular walk from Kentish Town station   100

Route 8
Into the Torriano estate
*Circular walk from Brecknock Road/
Camden Road junction*   113

Route 9
Leighton Road to Fortess Road
Circular walk from Kentish Town station   123

Route 10
Dartmouth Park
Circular walk from Tufnell Park station   138

Sources   148

Index   150

List of maps and illustrations

Thompson's map
of Kentish Town, 1801 — 2

Part of Stanford's 1862 map of London — 6
No.115 Bartholomew Road — 11

Diagrams in Topographical notes
River Fleet in Kentish Town — 13
Manors and estates in survey area — 14
Railways in area — 15

Route 1
Kentish Town Chapel, 18th century — 24
William Stukeley, 1817 — 27
William Bruges, 1420 — 29

Route 2
Highgate Road, looking southeast, 1900 — 33
Read's Bottling Store, 1885 — 36
Highgate Road, looking northwest,
c.1900 — 39
Our Lady Help of Christians, 1917 — 45

Route 3
Kentish Town Panorama Panel 25 — 47
Leafy Highgate Road, c.1906 — 51
Girls in chemistry lab, Parliament Hill
school, 1920s — 53
1960s drinkers in the Bull and Last — 55
Kentish Town Panorama Panel 2 — 57

Route 4
Goad map (1900) of Rotunda
organ works and College Street
Board School — 64
Cain Place and Nag's Head — 65
Chestnut Row, 1860 — 66

Route 5
Kentish Town Congregational
Church, 1848 — 79
Castle Inn, c.1800 — 80
Young Nelson as a captain — 81
Free Christian Church, 1855 — 83

Route 6
Worker in Raglan Street works,
late 1920s — 85
Claudius Ash false-teeth factory, 1871 — 87
Aged Governesses' Asylum, 1849 — 92
Brinsmead piano factory, 1870 — 94

Route 7
National Schools, Islip Street, 1849 — 101
St Luke's Oseney Crescent, 1869 — 105
Sarah Doudney, c.1895 — 110

Route 8
Brecknock Road and Brecknock Arms,
c.1907 — 113
Highfields Works — 115
Sir Horatio Regnart — 120

Route 9
The Assembly House — 125
Philipp Gottfried's baker's shop, 1904 — 133
Ford Madox Brown, 1852 — 135
Dr Southwood Smith — 136

Route 10
The Lord Palmerston, c.1904 — 140
Edmund Clerihew Bentley, 1915 — 141
Washing-line posts with Gilbert Bayes
finials on York Rise Estate — 146

(Opposite) Part of Stanford's 1862
map of London showing plans for
the further development of Kentish Town.
The River Fleet is already underground
in the Inkerman Road area.

Historical overview

Kentish Town does not wear its heart on its sleeve. The casual visitor will look in vain for the normal evidence of antiquity: the medieval, if rebuilt parish church, the burial ground and perhaps a Tudor manor house or farm. The reader and explorer of the *Streets of Kentish Town* will have to peel away many layers of human activity to understand the history of this ancient settlement.

The oldest written reference to 'Kentisston' is in a land transfer deed of 1207. The origin of the name has been a subject of speculation. There are three main theories. One (which can be discounted) is that the name is derived from the Kingdom of Kent, because the ancient Kentish Law of gavelkind, under which an estate was divided equally among all the sons, was said to have prevailed for a long time in the locality. A second theory links the name with the Cantelupe family and the Manor of Cantelowes (see p 14), although the Cantelupe association with the area postdates the first appearance of the name. The third, most likely and more geographically apposite, derivation associates the name with the 'Ken-ditch',

meaning the 'bed of a waterway'.

For Kentish Town was initially a settlement near the River Fleet, whose Highgate tributary runs south beneath our survey area This river, now hidden from public view for over a century, is our oldest historical reference point. A mile downstream, on a knoll beside the river, stood the ancient parish church of St Pancras, thought to have been thus rededicated c.597 AD at the time of St Augustine's mission to England. Nearby was the site of the earliest, pre-Conquest, settlement in the parish. Thereabouts the Fleet was much given to flooding, a fact that nearly caused the demise of the old church, for the vicar and many of his parishioners scurried upstream to higher ground, there to consolidate the hamlet that became Kentish Town. This early village was probably at the southern end of the present-day 'High Street', near to the river but not too close to it, given its propensity to flood even here. The road through the village to the north then skirted the marshy ground in the bend of the river (see map on p 2) before crossing it at a bridge where Burghley Road now branches off Highgate Road.

The 13th century changed the face of 'Kentisston' in other ways. A royal decree of Henry III in 1218 ordered the clearing of Middlesex Forest, both for its timber and to create the arable and pasture lands needed to feed London's ever-increasing

population. So the fields were enlarged, and the first tavern appeared, as did a chapel-of-ease to spare the populace a 2-mile round trip to the old parish church. The latter was restored, remaining the mother church of a huge, elongated parish, stretching some 4 miles from the borders of St Giles and Holborn north to the heights of Highgate. Though distant from the parish church, Kentish Town was for centuries the parish's most populous part.

As the forest was pushed back, a field pattern emerged, the track up the valley was extended and the settlement became a roadside village. The growing City of London would offer it a guaranteed market for its crops for the next 600 years. Cattle 'on the hoof' for the London market are recorded by the 15th century, and Kentish Town would also have experienced and entertained merchants and military on their travels north and south. The famous state visit of the Emperor Sigismund in 1416 to William Bruges' substantial house in or near the village, together with references to other "goodly houses" and to the building of a new chapel in 1449, indicate that the community was by then well established and even prosperous.

The 16th century brought the first mention of the St Pancras Church Lands Charity, whose fields in Kentish Town provided the income to maintain both parish church and local chapel-of-ease. It also brought the Reformation, and the constant changes required by the swing of the ecclesiastical pendulum in those dangerous years. Good Queen Bess visited Kentish Town twice in 1568, occasioning free drinks for the poor. Eight years later she came again when 'Ye Queen's Grasse' dined in the village, and the Churchwardens paid out 20 pence for bread and drink. It was probably through such patronage that the place was 'discovered' as a pleasant location for a day's outing, or even as a country retreat. London's 'suburbs' were growing, and in 1580 Elizabeth became the first monarch to forbid further building within three miles of the City gates. In any case, increased traffic attracted criminals, and this hazard to life and limb probably discouraged building in Kentish Town until after the Civil War, followed by the twin disasters of plague and fire in 1665-6, when refugees from the City camped out in the surrounding fields. Even in 1718, the first recorded date of an Open Vestry meeting, Kentish Town was still an agricultural village. The Vestry (the 'St Pancras' Vestry) met at the chapel-of-ease and in local taverns. Pressures on this rural framework were now increasing. In 1725, the Vestry had to vote authority to the churchwardens and constables to prevent the illegal enclosure, by Cantelowes Manor, of the common lands at Kentish Town Green. Fifty years later, the village had become a country town with some "very fair houses", boarding schools, and

taverns with pleasure gardens. The air was "exceedingly wholesome".

A new, chastely classical chapel was built in 1784 (on a more northerly site) to replace the ancient chapel-of-ease, which had been sold to the farmer William Morgan, who promptly removed all trace of it. Substantial Georgian mansions were erected at the north end of the village, along Green Street (now Highgate Road) and bordering the old village green. A regular coach travelled to London from the Bull & Gate, and John Wesley and the young Horatio Nelson were regular visitors. Some of the houses remain today to remind us of this 'Golden Age', but, like the chapel, most have disappeared.

During the Regency, Kentish Town was mooted as a possible site for a new St Pancras parish church, but the urban inhabitants of newly populous Bloomsbury (in the parish's southern reaches) would have none of it. The New Church was built south of the nearby New Road (now Euston Road). Similarly, the 'Select Vestry' of unelected members (mostly wealthy landowners), which 'hijacked' local politics in 1819, also met in the south of the parish. Kentish Town had missed the chance of legitimising its rightful central place in the life of St Pancras. Thenceforth it would be a suburb, but still a very special one.

Until the late 18th century, Kentish Town was essentially a linear village of ribbon development along the main road.

By the 1790s, however, Mansfield Place (now Holmes Road) had struck west across the fields, providing access to Spring Place, a small industrial community with a brewery and tannery near the west bank of the River Fleet. The main road was administered then by a Turnpike Trust, and would remain so until the abolition of tolls in 1864. Road communication was improved in the early 19th century, when two new turnpike roads were opened, the present Fortess Road and Junction Road to 'Archway' (c.1814), and Camden Road, a decade later, to Holloway.

The Regent's Canal reached Camden Town in 1816, bringing industry with it. In the course of the century, numerous factories and workshops were established in the side streets and mews of Kentish Town. The area became for many years the home of world-famous manufacturers of floorcloth, false teeth, artists' materials, hats, church organs and pianos. Kentish Town, like Camden Town, was a great centre of the London piano industry, which had migrated north from its original location in the West End. "That healthful suburb dear to the heart of the piano maker" was how Kentish Town was described in *The Piano Journal* in 1901, at a time when every self-respecting household in the land aspired to possess a piano. Such industries required workers highly skilled in many different trades, and they in turn required homes.

By the later 18th century, London's insatiable demand for hay had led to the supplanting of milk production as the main activity in the fields, but it was not until the 1840s that houses were seen as a more profitable crop. Gradually, the fields on either side of the main road were given over to housing development, as the owners of various estates (see p 14) decided to capitalise on their assets. The relentless march of bricks and mortar was broadly northward, beginning in the 1840s at the southern end of the 'town', and mostly complete within a generation or so; although some roads in the northern part of our area were built up in later-Victorian times, while others on the Highgate borders appeared only in the 20th century.

The urbanisation of the area had begun in earnest with the Southampton family's decision in 1840 to develop their Tottenhall property in West Kentish Town (to the west of our area). Their original plans were for a spacious suburb of detached, or at worst semi-detached, villas. What actually appeared there was a mass of densely packed, inferior housing, later to become a notorious slum.

The owners of the later-developed estates to the east were anxious not to make the same mistake. Houses in eastern Kentish Town were generally more substantial and of greater architectural pretension, with the aim of attracting middle-class buyers. Some developers, however, felt obliged to lower

their sights, and the street layouts that eventually materialised were not always as spacious as those originally planned. Already, by 1860, the area was being described as "no longer genteel". Referred to disparagingly by the Grossmiths in *The Diary of a Nobody*, Kentish Town was scarcely a desirable address. Residents on its edges preferred to use such euphemisms as 'Highgate Rise'.

It is often said that what really depressed Kentish Town, as it began its suburban existence, was the coming of the railways (see p 15). But industry was already established locally, and the die was already cast when the first railway, the North London, cut through the area on its viaduct in 1850. Thus, although the effect of the railways on Kentish Town was considerable, it simply overlaid another layer of historical endeavour. As railway construction reached its peak, the last milk was exported from Kentish Town's pastures, and the River Fleet, by then an unhealthy sewer, quietly disappeared from sight, culverted underground.

By the end of the 19th century, Kentish Town was totally transformed. Apart from the cattle on their way to market and the slaughtering activity of the 32 butchers in the 'High Street', little reference to an agricultural past could be discerned. The main street evolved into a typical Victorian shopping area. Long-established shops were joined by new chain stores;

there was talk of a Library, and the Baths were completed. Elementary education was universal. New churches of various denominations had been built; new Anglican district churches became the focus of new suburban parishes, while the rebuilt chapel-of-ease at last gained parochial status in 1868.

The horse tramway of the London Street Tramways Co., which had arrived in Kentish Town in 1871, was electrified by the London County Council in 1909, two years after the opening of the competing Archway branch of the 'Hampstead Tube'. 1910 saw the opening of Kentish Town's first cinema. Edwardian Kentish Town seemed prosperous enough, but in the side streets it was often a different story. Houses originally designed for single middle-class families had been converted into flats. When World War I (WWI) came, it was no respecter of persons; air raids killed, maimed and destroyed. Between the Wars poverty survived amid the decaying streets, and we shall see examples of the pioneer rehousing that was then achieved. Some social housing schemes that were ready to start in 1939 were postponed as the Blitz arrived. Bomb damage was particularly severe in East and West Kentish Town, with more limited destruction in the 'High Street'. St Pancras Council lost no time, in 1945, in rebuilding on a large scale, with familiar if sometimes dull results. Ten years later, more adventurous schemes became policy, with differing degrees of success. Fifty years on, changing expectations have forced another look at the social housing stock, with expensive refurbishments of many blocks. Meanwhile, belated recognition of the qualities of the remaining Victorian houses has revitalised many formerly neglected areas.

Most of Kentish Town's former traditional industries have now closed. Competition from abroad, changing fashions, smokeless zones, and the need for more up-to-date premises have all contributed to this decline, and the service and media industries that have moved in do not possess the same élan. It is a similar story in the shopping areas. Kentish Town has felt the cold wind of competition from its brasher neighbour Camden Town south of the Canal, with the loss of prized local and other well-known names. But it still retains a 'local' feel. While many Kentish Town families can claim long associations with the place, we are reminded in our explorations of the many short-stay residents who have made it their temporary home. Today, the cultural mix is greater than it has ever been, and makes for a lively renewal of this long-established community. Application of lively talent is

also needed in the renewal of the physical framework. A first-rate environment will never be achieved if opportunities like the redevelopment of the Railway Lands, or the High Street, are implemented using third-class designs done on the cheap.

However, all is not lost. On sites too small or too awkward to attract the mediocrity merchants, attractive new buildings can be found. The ingenuity and care for detail involved in their construction show what can be achieved. Some are homes; others are for education or for fledgling new industries. These are the examples and the hope for the future; they are among the delights and discoveries to treasure as we explore the streets of Kentish Town.

Imaginatively designed
No. 115 Bartholomew Road (courtesy of
Workplace Cooperative 115)

Note on key sources

Those who wish to study the history of Kentish Town are fortunate indeed in having some key sources that provide detailed information on the area.

The first is a unique visual record of the village at the start of the 19th century. The *Kentish Town Panorama* is without comparison in London. It depicts the view along both sides of the main roads of the time, all in all some 4½ miles of scenery. The drawings of most of the buildings shown are the only surviving record of them. The *Panorama* was drawn by the artist James Frederick King (1781-1855), son of the 'accomptant' Thomas King. James, as a young man, lived at his father's house by the Castle Inn, before moving in 1837 to 3 Montague Place, at the northeast end of the 'High Street', where he lived until his death. His granddaughter saved the *Panorama* for posterity by selling it for a modest sum to St Pancras Council in 1930.

The *Panorama* consists of three rolls totalling 39 ft of pen and wash drawings with captions beneath. It was published in sheet format (uncoloured) by the London Topographical Society in 1986 with a commentary by John Richardson, who compared the drawings with the parish map of c.1800. He found that the *Panorama* was on the whole remarkably accurate, but there were several inconsistencies that led him to the important conclusion that it did not date from 1800. The watermarks on the rolls confirmed that it was drawn after 1848, in King's last years, from memory and possibly from sketches made throughout his life. We refer to King's *Panorama* throughout this book, and in Route 1 to another smaller *Panorama* by someone known only as 'H.G.', which came to light only recently. Roughly contemporary with King's work, it shows two views of a short stretch of the western side of what is now Kentish Town Road, as it was in 1788 and in 1846.

An equally fascinating source, this time a written commentary on the social make-up of the area which nevertheless conjures up many visual images, are the notebooks of Charles Booth, the compiler of the famous 'poverty maps' in the 1880s. Ten years later, he updated the maps and in Kentish Town he did so by walking each street with Inspector Tomkin of Y Division of the Metropolitan Police. Booth is not always a totally reliable commentator since his attempts to categorise the social make-up of a whole street at a time were inevitably somewhat broad-brush. His notebooks are now available to view on the Internet (see *Sources*, p 149) and we have quoted from them now and again throughout this book.

Our research has often drawn upon another well-known source about Kentish Town, Gillian Tindall's *The Fields Beneath*, first published in 1977. The work of a local writer, it tells the story of how a medieval settlement became part of the urban fabric of London. Unlike many more detailed historical accounts, it does so in a lively and engaging style.

Finally, a brief mention should be made of the poem *Parliament Hill Fields* by John Betjeman, to which we refer in some of the routes. This is an account of a tram ride he took as a boy, in 1913 or 1914, from Kentish Town up to his home at 31 Highgate West Hill. It is an imaginative reconstruction, combining historical accuracy with poetic licence, and evoking his own particular feeling for place.

Topographical notes

To help one grasp the complexities of Kentish Town's topography, we illustrate some major features in three diagrammatic maps of our survey area (not exactly to scale).

River Fleet

Culverted throughout the area by 1900, the Fleet's eastern (or Highgate) tributary runs south from its Kenwood source, via Highgate Ponds, before bending east and crossing under Highgate Road at its northernmost end (junction with Swains Lane). For a while it flows east of the latter, and in times past it formed several ponds around here. Turning south again, and bisecting Dartmouth Park, the stream runs today beneath York Rise, until reaching the Gospel Oak–Barking railway line, which it crosses in an iron pipe. Curvilinear Burghley Road traces the river's onward course to where it passes again under Highgate Road, at what was once Kentish Town Bridge. From here it cuts southwest, beneath the Midland Main Line to the modern Regis Road business park, where it was once joined by a minor tributary running south from the region of Gordon

House Road. The flow continues beneath the "Crimean" area west of the High Street, to a point where the pre-urban stream was bridged by a once much longer, L-shaped, Anglers Lane. Crossing under Hawley Road, the river veers south-eastward, via Old St Pancras and King's Cross, to join the Thames at Blackfriars.

In Kentish Town the Fleet's eastern arm met its western tributary flowing south from Hampstead. The location of the confluence is controversial. Various 19th-century maps show the western branch running through West Kentish Town (to the west of our area), the two tributaries meeting at Hawley Road. However, some 1830s maps suggest that, to enable the development of the area, attempts had by then been made to canalise the Hampstead arm, diverting it eastward along a straight, unnatural channel to join the 'Gordon House' stream that fed its Highgate cousin. The confluence of the two main tributaries is therefore placed by some at Regis Road.

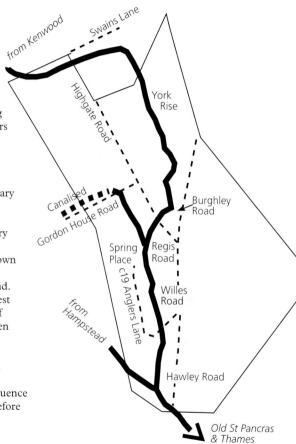

Manors and estates

St Pancras parish, of which Kentish Town formed a part, was granted in 603 AD by King Ethelbert to the Dean and Chapter of St Paul's. It was a large parish stretching some 4 miles, north to south, from Highgate Village to Fitzrovia and the borders of Holborn.

By the time of the Conquest, the parish comprised five manors. Tottenhall and Cantelowes, the two most northerly, were the chief contributors to the development of Kentish Town. Both manors were 'prebendal', endowing Canons of St Paul's, absentee landlords who leased land to others under a system known as 'copyhold'. A copyhold lease was one given by the lord of the manor (in this case the prebendary) during the lives of three named persons. Two copies were usually made, one for the lord and one for the tenant, who, provided he paid his rents and fines and met other obligations, enjoyed what amounted to hereditary tenure. The prebendal stalls in St Paul's Cathedral remain today to remind us of the existence of these manors. The main highway northward (now Kentish Town Road and Highgate Road) was the boundary between Cantelowes to the east and Tottenhall to the west. It split the village in two, placing each half under the jurisdiction of a different Manor Court.

By the 19th century, the manorial lands had passed into the hands of several landowners, who all, in the course of the century, capitalised on their assets, turning agricultural land over to housing development.

In our explorations we shall meet estates on the Cantelowes Manor land that were developed by the Torriano family, descendants of a City soap maker, and by two titled landlords: Marquis Camden, whose local estate, extending southward into Camden Town, had come into the possession of his father, the 1st Earl, on his marriage into the Jeffreys family, the previous copyholders; and the Earl of Dartmouth, who held both a large estate on the Highgate borders and a smaller property east of the 'High Street'. Adjoining the latter were two estates bequeathed by earlier owners to endow institutions, namely St Bartholomew's Hospital and Christ Church Oxford. The Cambridge college of St John's likewise held a large estate straddling Fortess Road; while a smaller property adjoining Fortess Road itself was managed by the Trustees of Eleanor Palmer's Gift Charity for the benefit of the local poor. All these lands were gradually converted into freeholds by the process of buying out the copyhold interest, a procedure only finally abolished in 1922.

The Tottenhall lands west of the main road had been acquired by the Fitzroy family when Henry Fitzroy, an illegitimate son of Charles II, married Isabella, Countess of Arlington. Henry's grandson, the soldier Charles Fitzroy, was able, in 1768, to convert his leaseholds into freeholds by special Act of Parliament, aided by his elder brother, the Duke of Grafton, then effectively prime minister. Charles became Baron Southampton in 1780, and the Fitzroys' local property was subsequently known as the Southampton Estate. Two local farmers (Holmes and Mortimer) developed their fields for housing, while the Hawley and Buck

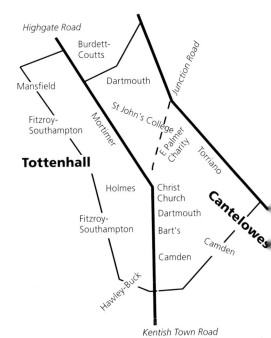

families were major developers of their Tottenhall land extending southeast into Camden Town. A small corner of Lord Mansfield's Kenwood estate also enters our story.

Railways

Running on viaducts and embankments, Kentish Town's earliest railways were the most visually intrusive. The North London Railway (NLR) from the East and West India Docks opened to Camden Town (now Camden Road) station in 1850, and was extended west to Chalk Farm the following year. Its offshoot, the Hampstead Junction Railway (HJR), owned by the London & North Western, struck north towards Hampstead Heath in 1860, with a station at Gospel Oak known as 'Kentish Town' until the opening 7 years later of a station in Prince of Wales Road, also originally called Kentish Town but renamed Kentish Town West in 1923. Silverlink Metro trains from North Woolwich to Richmond use the line today.

Running east from Gospel Oak is the elevated line nowadays carrying the Silverlink service to Barking. This line, the Tottenham & Hampstead Junction Railway (T&HJR), opened in 1868 as far west as a 'High Level' station above Highgate Road. 20 years later the track was extended to Gospel Oak, but only in 1940 was a connection laid there to the HJR, allowing access from the east to Hampstead and so

belatedly justifying the railway's name.

The line most affecting Kentish Town was the London Extension of the Midland Railway (MR), also opened in 1868. Although more obtrusive, it was often less visible, as its diagonal route across much of the area was in cuttings and tunnels (strictly, 'covered ways'). Today, with no smoke or steam to betray its presence, the line passes almost imperceptibly under the north end of the 'High Street' and through the residential streets to its east. Northwest of the main road, much of the line was visible, and it was here that a great swathe of land was taken by the Midland for its cattle, coal and locomotive depots. When, after WWII, steam traction ended, the coal trade contracted and rail freight was 'rationalised', the acreage of blighted land that eventually came up for disposal was enormous.

Behind its loco sheds, the Midland built a curve, linking its main line with the T&HJR, and as late as 1900 another (the Tottenham North Curve), running to a new Low Level station at Highgate Road, then continuing eastward in a cutting parallel its earlier elevated neighbour. The two Highgate Road stations were short-lived, both having closed by 1918. Each, like the Midland's Camden Road station (closed in 1916), was a victim of tramway competition.

The least visible of all the area's railways is the Underground's Northern Line,

opened in 1907 as the Archway branch of the Charing Cross, Euston & Hampstead Railway, with two stations in Kentish Town (one long since closed) and a third, just in Islington, at Tufnell Park. At all three sites, the characteristic oxblood-red tiles of Leslie Green's surface buildings pleasingly remain.

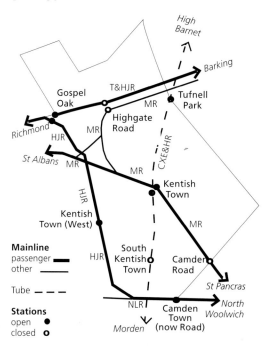

Street names in this book and their origins

(* = land owner in Kentish Town)

Alma
Battle of River Alma, Crimea (1854)

Anglers
Spot beside River Fleet
favoured by fishermen

Ascham
Roger, Elizabethan educationalist,
Fellow of St John's College*

Bartholomew
St Bartholomew's Priory & Hospital*

Boscastle
Name of first house built in road

Bramshill
Origin unknown

Brecknock
Abbey, Welsh home of
Elizabeth Jeffreys (q.v.)

Brecon
Elizabeth Jeffreys' home county

Brown's
Camden Town dairy, whose
cows grazed local fields

Burghley
Lord (William Cecil), C16
benefactor of St John's College*

Busby
Dr Richard (1606-1695), headmaster
of Westminster School and student
of Christ Church* College, Oxford

Camden
John Jeffreys Pratt, 1st Marquis*

Carker's
? Mr Corker (sic), local farmer

Carrol
From earlier Carrol Place,
but origin unknown

Castle
Former adjacent inn

Castlehaven
Elizabeth, Countess of, buried
in St Pancras Churchyard

Cathcart
General Sir George, killed
at Battle of Inkermann (q.v.)

Caversham
Rev. Dr Robert South (d.1716) of
Caversham (Berks.), bequeathed
local land to Christ Church, Oxford*

Charlton Kings
Torriano/Leighton family*
property near Cheltenham

Chetwynd
Charles, nephew of Frances,
wife of Earl of Dartmouth*

Church
Led to former Congregational
Church, now United Reformed

Churchill
Lord Alfred Spencer, partner of
Chetwynd (q.v.)

Clarence
William, Duke of, later William IV

College
St John's, Cambridge*

Countess
Lady Margaret (q.v.) Beaufort was
Countess of Richmond & Derby

16

Crown
Long-vanished public house

Dartmouth
William Walter Legge, 5th Earl of★

Dowdney
Sarah Doudney (sic), C19 writer

Dunollie
? Birthplace (near Oban) of street's builder

Evangelist
Cambridge College of
St John the Evangelist★

Falkland
Lucius Carey, 2nd Viscount (d.1643),
scholar of St John's College★

Farrier
A 'horse-doctor' supposedly
practised nearby

Fortess
Fortys or Fortess Field, local meadow

Frideswide
Saxon princess turned nun, patron
saint of Christ Church, Oxford★

Gaisford
Thomas (d.1855),
Dean of Christ Church★

Glenhurst
Arbitrary name suggested by LCC

Gordon House
Andrew Mensal, head of C18 boys'
school, kinsman of Duke of Gordon

Grafton
Duke of, head of Fitzroy family★,
holders of Tottenhall manor

(Little) **Green**
Adjacent Green Street
(Highgate Road)
led to Kentish Town Green

Greenwood
Thomas, local builder and
Bull & Gate landlord

Grove
Chestnut plantation once lay opposite

Hadley
Origin unknown

Hammond
Henry (1605-1660), Dean of Christ Church★
or Mrs Margaret, housekeeper to
Rev. South★ (see Caversham)

Hampshire
Origin unknown

Hargrave
John Hargreave (sic) Mann,
floor-cloth manufacturer

Hartland
Abbey, North Devon property of the
Buck family (see Hawley)

Hawley
Sir Joseph★, co-developer
of the Hawley Buck estate

Healey
Francis, local representative on Vestry
and Metropolitan Board of Works

Highgate
Hilltop village north of Kentish Town

Holmes
Richard, farmer, tanner,
brickmaker and coal-merchant

Ingestre
Charles Chetwynd★, Lord Ingestre

Inkerman
Battle of Inkermann (sic),
Crimea (1854)

Islip
Oxfordshire parish (1678-) of
Rev. Dr Robert South (see Caversham)

Ivor
LCC renaming, unexplained

Jeffrey's
Elizabeth Jeffreys,
wife of 1st Earl Camden★

Kelly
John, local builder

Kentish Town
From the locality

Lady Margaret
Margaret Beaufort founded St John's
College, Cambridge★ in 1511

Lady Somerset
Sarah, benefactress of St John's★

Laurier
Sir Wilfred, first French-speaking
Prime Minister of Canada (1896-1911)

Lawford
John Eeles, builder, and land
agent of Earl of Dartmouth★

Leighton
Sir David, married into
Torriano family★

Leverton
Thomas Leverton Donaldson,
Torriano estate land agent

Lewis
Lewis Buck, father of George Stucley
Buck, partner of Sir Joseph Hawley★

Lissenden
Meaningless 'pretty' name

Lupton
Roger, St John's College★ benefactor

Montpelier
Nearby Montpelier House
(Kentish Town once compared
to the French resort)

Mortimer
Mortimer's Farm adjoined

Oakford
Origin unknown

Oseney
Ruined abbey in Oxford,
property of Christ Church★

Ospringe
Property near Faversham (Kent)
endowing St John's College★

Patshull
Manor near Wolverhampton,
property of Earl of Dartmouth★

Peckwater
Quadrangle in Christ Church★
College, Oxford

Perren
Richard, Camden Town 'carpenter'

Prince of Wales
Albert Edward, future Edward VII

Prowse
Capt. William, fought under Nelson

Raglan
1st Baron (1788-1855), army
commander in Crimean War

Railey
Railey Works Co. had workshops here

Raveley
Land at Little Raveley (Hunts.)
endowing St John's College★

Reed's
William Reed, builder of Place

Regis
Regis family, proprietors of
local firm, Asphaltic

Rochester
Bishop of, father of Harriet Murray,
wife of 2nd Marquis Camden★

Royal College
Veterinary college near far end of street

Ryland
Probably a builder

St Pancras
Teenage martyr (d.304 AD),
patron saint of historic parish

Sandall
South Yorkshire property of
Earls of Dartmouth★

Sanderson
Wallpaper manufacturer?

Spencer
see Churchill

Spring
Water source feeding River Fleet

Torbay
South Devon variant on earlier Exeter

Torriano
Joshua Prole Torriano (fl.1783)★

Twisden
Cordelia Twysden Molesworth
married into Dartmouth family

Wesleyan
Site of Wesleyan chapel

Willingham
Either builder of Terrace or from Cambs.
property of St John's College★

Willes
Lt-General James, marines
commander in Crimean War

Wilmot
Possibly builder, or from family name
of *Earls* of Rochester (q.v.)

Wolsey
Cardinal, founded what became
Christ Church★ College, Oxford

Woodsome
Dartmouth family★ property
near Huddersfield

York (Mews)
Frederick, 'Grand Old' Duke
of, brother of George IV

York (Rise)
Parallels Dartmouth Park
Hill, once York Road

Up & down Kentish Town Road

Circular walk from Kentish Town station
For modern map see back cover

Kentish Town, historically, is a linear settlement which is older than it looks. **KENTISH TOWN ROAD,** its backbone, is more than an undistinguished Victorian shopping street. As well as being the Village Street of the much older agricultural settlement, it was an early route northward out of London through Highgate, and a turnpike road from the 18th century until 1864. At Kentish Town several layers have to be removed before we get to the fields beneath. This walk begins the process. It starts at Kentish Town Underground station. We shall proceed south to the entrance of the historic village on one side of the street and return to our starting point on the other. To get a better view of the buildings described we walk down the east side and return up the west side, describing the opposite side as we do so.

Whether we descend from a bus or glide up from the depths of the Northern Line by escalators (first installed in 1932), we need to get our bearings – so turn right and proceed to the shelter of the glazed canopy over the railway bridge spanning the Midland mainline and Thameslink

tracks below. This ornate metal structure was once part of Elstree station and was erected here after the Kentish Town main line station was rebuilt in 1982. Adjacent to it is an old drinking fountain erected by the Metropolitan Drinking Fountain and Cattle Trough Association. It is a pink granite pillar some 7 ft high variously inscribed "In memory of Joseph Payne, June 1870" and "The memory of the just is blessed (Proverbs 10:7)". The allusion to justice supports the assumption that the dedicatee was the philanthropic judge Joseph Payne, Deputy Assistant Judge at the Middlesex Sessions, who was a stalwart of the Ragged School movement. A very popular and witty man, his funeral was attended by a great crowd, including children from the Kentish Town Ragged School.

From the canopy, look over the road towards Hampstead Heath. This is the view that the graphic historian of Kentish Town, James Frederick King (p 12) would have had from his house on this very spot at what was then No.3 Montague Place.

This Route explores the main street and traces its story from when it ran across farmland. Kentish Town's story is firmly rooted in the activities, needs and skills of an agricultural community whose main street in 1739 contained two shoemakers, a corn chandler, baker, haberdasher, general shop, wheelwright, coachmaker, farrier, stonemason, cooper, 'Morgan the Blacksmith' and a seller of asses' milk.

West side
(viewed from opposite)

Turn back south along the same (east) side of the High Street, observing the side opposite. The first block of buildings now contains **Nos.317-347 Kentish Town Road**. Before the turnpike was abolished in 1864 and individual terrace names were suppressed, it was called York Place. This was a long terrace of some grandeur when Kentish Town enjoyed a reputation as a healthy place for retirement as well as a favoured location for boarding schools. It dates from 1794. At first, all houses were respectably tenanted, some with those 'living on their own means'. One such in 1805 at No.9 York Place was Samuel Sewell Esq. When he died in Kentish Town in 1821, a codicil to his will suggested that his wife had been a natural daughter of King George II and had passed on "a portion of the late King's wearing apparel". Christopher Haedy, Steward to the Duke of Bedford, was living at No.5 in 1805. Haedy drew up the plans for the development of the duke's Fig's Mead Estate or Bedford New Town in 1834. In the 1860s at No.7 York Place, now **No.337** (and occupied by Chicken Express), lived Cornelius Varley (1781–1873), a watercolour painter and inventor who in 1811 patented his Graphic Telescope, a device with telescopic lenses enabling artists to draw objects some distance away. He was the younger brother of the better-known painter John. His son Samuel, a telegraph engineer, was living with him.

The front gardens of York Place remained free of shops until the 1890s. At **No.339**, Bishop & Hamilton carried on their stationery and bookselling business from 1894 to 1979. In the 1920s, it seems, Mr Dunn the hatter enjoyed a cigar and chat here each morning, after checking on the window display at his shop at **No.343**. Woolworth's at Nos.**329-335** arrived in 1924. Previously at Nos.329&331 was the emporium of 'fancy draper' Charles Hardwick, the 'Bon Marché' store that features in Betjeman's poem *Parliament Hill Fields* (see p 31). King records a much earlier bakery on the site of **No.319**, "where dinners were drest", and a butcher's shop at **No.317**. More recently, this butchery would be continued by George Kimber from 1907 to the late 1960s.

South of York Mews (p 99) are the mixed buildings of **Nos.293-315**, with limited architectural pretensions. This stretch was once known as Mansfield Place (as was the next turning ahead) and formed the main-road frontage of Richard Holmes' estate on Southampton land to the west. Holmes was a farmer, besides operating a tannery and a brickfield, and describing himself as a "dealer in coals" at the Old Bailey trial in May 1784 of Edward Hudson, who was sentenced to be transported for stealing 8

hempen coal sacks and some poultry from Holmes' yard. Nos.305-315 are on the site of Richard Holmes' paddock and large wooden barn. His main residence, a trim late-18th-century house, was next door on the site of Nos.301&303. A neighbour of the Holmes family in Mansfield Place in 1805 was John Bluck, an artist and engraver who exhibited at the Royal Academy. He is best known for his aquatints for the publisher Rudolph Ackermann.

Today, the Iceland supermarket occupies Nos.301-305, rebuilt in 1932 for Marks and Spencer, who remained until 1981. Earlier buildings on this site housed one of Kentish Town's first cinemas, the Electric Alhambra, which flourished 1911–1918. It had a 500-seat auditorium, with a tearoom and separate 'family' entrance from Holmes Road. At Nos.297&299 stood, until 1840, Image House, an imposing building set back from the road, owned by Benjamin Capper, a coal merchant. He let it to a school for young gentlemen. By 1900 Nos.293-299 had become the property of Herbert Beddall, a well-known local draper. He rebuilt his store on the corner of Holmes Road (p 83) in 1900 to an imposing design which has now given way to an anonymous curtain wall. In the 1930s, No.299 became the then essential component of a shopping street, a Lyons Teashop. Today an eatery of a different stamp, namely McDonalds, occupies the site.

South of Holmes Road is that portion

of Kentish Town Road formerly known as Old Chapel Row. The corner building, now **O'Reilly's**, is a colourful public house; admire the decorated façade and the ornamentation at roof level. The first pub on the site was called the Star & Garter. When it was rebuilt in 1885 it became the Old Farm House. This may have been a reference to Holmes's Farm house on the opposite side of Holmes Road, whose ruins had then finally been removed. The Old Farm House only became O'Reilly's in 2001, and the former name is still inscribed above; and on the side wall, its date of rebuilding.

Until 1864 the wooden Tollhouse and Bar stood opposite the Star & Garter. In 1851, the tollhouse keeper was one Robert Everet, who lived with his wife and children in a house in Old Chapel Row. Toll evasion was a continual problem, and an additional tollgate, barring Holmes Road, had to be installed in 1855.

A few doors down, at **No.281**, are the premises of Dawson and Briant, long-established jewellers with the only Listed shopfront in Kentish Town. **Old Dairy Mews**, at No.277, now shelters eight minimal brick town houses behind its metal gates in a quiet enclave. Before 2000, this was a busy and noisy milk depot, latterly for First Express dairies. They had replaced the Vicarage Farm Dairy, which in the early 20th century had a shop here containing glazed china milk pails covered in butter muslin and a statue of a Negro boy holding a china basket heaped with real eggs. It was the site until 1848 of the vicarage of Kentish Town, a substantial mansion behind high walls and barred gates, which was demolished when the clergy moved to a new house closer to the re-sited parish church in Highgate Road (p 34). In its place, William MacLaren built four houses called Vicarage Row.

In Old Chapel Path, a turning off the main road, lived the eminent attorney William Clulow, John Wesley's friend and legal adviser. In 1784 he had drawn up the 'Deed of Declaration' for Wesley to sign, and on 3 November 1787 Wesley records their discussions on the best way for the Methodists to license their meeting places, as required by the "execrable Conventicle Act". During his later years, John Wesley visited his friends in Kentish Town to finish his writing and to enjoy the quiet of the country. His last visit was on 19 January 1791, six weeks before he died. Another resident of Old Chapel Path was the undertaker William Page, who in February 1793 gave evidence against 19-year-old James Clarke for stealing 25 yards of printed cotton from the linen shop of Frances Brookes, which was run from part of Page's house. Clarke was sentenced to death.

Between Old Dairy Mews and Crown Place Nos.265-275 Kentish Town Road have been badly mauled. **Nos.273&275**

have been rebuilt in utilitarian style and are now occupied by Lloyds TSB. At the end of 2003 two small shops, Nos.269&271, were demolished in favour of a most unsuitable building. **Nos.265&267** are the current premises of estate agents Salter Rex, in 2004 celebrating 150 years of activity in Kentish Town. They moved here in 1977 from their previous 'Gothic' office at No.311, where they had been for over a century.

CROWN PLACE – now severely truncated, see p 84 – was originally Crocker's Place, after Crocker the owner at the beginning of the 19th century. It was subsequently known for a time as Strawberry Place. **Nos.259-263**, now occupied by solicitors Walter Jennings, was one of the historic inns of Kentish Town. Formerly known as the Green Dragon, and first licensed in 1751, it became the King's Arms in 1785, a name it retained until closure in 1969. Robert Crocker, a retired Bow Street officer and licensee, developed the land at the rear with stables and a skittle ground. In 1823, his successor was the more appropriately named James Merry. Later, small houses were built here, and in 2004 the space is being transformed again. The side view of the former tavern suggests that much of the older building has survived. South of the King's Arms, James King's *Panorama* shows a terrace of six cottages and a larger house, followed by the Tudorish façade of an old inn, which

King refers to as the White Lion and Bell. This is Kentish Town's mystery tavern. King claims that it was swept away in 1811 and replaced by three houses (Nos.239-243) erected on the site by Mr Gambee. The inn's name, though, never appears in any parish or (post-1721) licensing records. Later research suggested that King's memory may have been faulty, and that the tavern was actually the Red Lion, a house frequented by the Vestry in 1724, which lost its licence in 1762, and which had shared a rear access from Crocker's Yard. However, in a recent article (by Patrick Nother in *Camden History Review* 28), Rev. Randolph Yearwood, a 17th-century vicar of St Pancras, is quoted as having given his address in 1666 as "the White Lion in Kentish Town" – which suggests that a tavern of that name, with or without a 'Bell' suffix, did indeed exist locally at that time. From here to Anglers Lane, the *Panorama* shows a neat row of private houses with gardens. Today, the houses are a mixture of later-19th-century and post-WWII rebuilding. **No.233** is still the recognisable double frontage of James Mann's house at No.3 Old Chapel Place, and **No.241**, also with a wider frontage, marks the site of the 'mystery tavern'. The present structure dates from the 1860s.

Until 1881, when the Vestry made a proper junction, Anglers Lane (p 85) emerged from beneath an arch in the last house of the terrace. On the corner, and now a **Nando's** restaurant, is the former Jolly Anglers, a tavern referred to in the Vestry minutes of 1725 as the Compleat Angler. The Social Villagers (p 124) sometimes met here. At the far end of Anglers Lane was a favourite fishing place on the River Fleet, and the side wall of Nando's now bears an inscription about this, taken from John Richardson's *Kentish Town Past* (see quotation, p 90). Next door at **No.225** King records another butcher's shop, that of a Mr Hale; the Hale family were in business here from at least 1766. An 1823 Directory lists the business here as in "Great Green Street", an alternative name for the whole of the main road through the village (i.e. what is now Kentish Town Road and Highgate Road).

Beyond the butcher's was a paddock and then a large 18th-century house, known as Old Chapel House. This was a stately town house with a pedimented entrance, described as a boarding establishment for young ladies. The last proprietor, in 1841, was Mrs Sarah Sams, who had 5 staff and 25 pupils. The house was then converted into two shops, becoming part of Old Chapel Row, as can be seen in the 1846 view on the recently discovered *Panorama* of a stretch of the west side of Kentish Town Road, drawn in the mid-19th century by someone known only as 'H.G.'. This panorama shows two views: of the road in 1788 and in 1846. Across a lane leading to stables beside Old Chapel House in

both panoramas is the farmhouse with outbuildings that farmer William Morgan built for himself in 1784. This farmhouse, which was replaced by two houses, **Nos.207&209**, in 1863, contained wainscot panelling from the old chapel and reused gravestones as paving slabs. Today nothing remains of the chapel built by Robert Warner in 1456 on land given by him in 1449, or of the adjacent burial ground, although it is said that old walls were still visible in 1870.

It is here, at the heart of 18th-century Kentish Town, that we confront the crisis of identity from which the place has suffered for over 800 years. This chapel was a chapel–of–ease, without parochial status. The parish church was further south, at Old St Pancras (now on Pancras Road), where the first settlement was. However, by the reign of King John (1199−1216), and probably because of the persistent flooding of the River Fleet, most of the population had moved north to drier Kentish Town. There is a tradition that the first chapel in Kentish Town was founded by the episcopal brothers Cantelupe and dedicated to St John the Baptist. Walter de Cantelupe was Bishop of Worcester from 1236 to 1282 and his brother Thomas was Bishop of Hereford from 1275 to 1282. Thomas was canonised in 1306. Another kinsman, Roger de Cantelupe, was Vicar of St Pancras from 1242 to 1249. So it seems likely that services began in this first

chapel in one of the early decades of the 13th century and that the Vicar moved up into a new house in the village some years later. Although many of the services would be held in Kentish Town, the authorities were loth to abandon the venerable parish church, so Kentish Town remained a mere chapel-of-ease until the mid-19th century.

The site of the first chapel is not known, although links with William Bruges' house (see p 30) and also a house belonging to the Ive family near the site of Kentish Town station have been suggested. We are on firmer ground by 1449, when Robert Warner, local landowner and member of the Grocers' Company, presented a site, now Nos.207-209, for the building of the new chapel. Of this second chapel of 1456, there are a few drawings (**Fig 1**, p 24), a record of its enlargement in 1633 and a note of its size (53 ft by 26 ft); also the comment in 1779 that "being a very ancient structure it was greatly decayed….It was dangerous for the inhabitants to attend divine service therein". Just before demolition, an eyewitness described it as "a small, low, heavy-looking structure which was fitted with oak and had a very sombre appearance; it contained a gallery and some curious carving". The Trustees bought a new site, just north of the Bull and Gate, and the new chapel was consecrated in 1784. Meanwhile, the Old Chapel was sold at auction for £150 to William Morgan, a transaction which landed the Trustees before the Court of Arches in 1788 for "converting consecrated ground to secular use". The Trustees eventually retrieved the lease and the freehold was sold in 1926.

In 1800 William Morgan and Richard Morgan were farming 140 acres on either side of Kentish Town Road. Formerly cow pasture, it had now become grassland to satisfy London's increasing demand for horse-fodder. The Morgans' successors at Nos.207&209 would become just as important to the economic life of the town, but in a totally different sphere. Drapers Charles and Alfred Daniels opened their first shop here in 1865; known as 'The Little Wonder', it had expanded by 1913 to include most of the block between Anglers Lane and Prince of Wales Road ahead.

After 1926, **Nos.217-223** were rebuilt to provide a single store but **Blustons** at Nos.213&215 refused to budge and are still there, with a shopfront that also deserves Listing, as an example of a style now rarely seen. They are only the second firm to occupy this building, taking over in the 1920s from George Arnold, pawnbrokers, who had been here for half a century. The Daniels brothers' store suffered severely in WWII but rejoiced in belated war-damage repairs in 1952, its 87th anniversary. When the family sold the store in 1954, it was as if an era had ended. Today, we can note the impressive scale of Nos.207-211, where the **Owl Bookshop** has been a candle of culture since 1974 (having been started across the road in the previous decade), and the later, stone-faced Nos.217-221, which are now occupied by Somerfields supermarket.

An earlier tenant here was the pianoforte maker Alexander Eason, whose showrooms were at No.217; in 1867 he was advertising locally made 5-octave harmoniums in mahogany for £5. At **No.197** was Salmon & Glickstein, which claimed to be the "largest tobacconists in the world"; they had 140 shops. Family members were co-founders of J Lyons & Co, which opened up shops across the country. A newcomer in 1913 was the Palace Cinema, designed

1 Kentish Town Chapel (18th-century watercolour, before 1770)

24

by the young John Stanley Beard. It replaced the Garden Cinema in adjoining Prince of Wales Road (p 77). Used as a recruiting station in WWI, it was taken over by Gaumont in 1929 and finally closed in 1959. The distinctive entrance in Kentish Town Road has gone, but some traces of decoration remain on the flank wall in Prince of Wales Road.

Before the 1840s, Prince of Wales Road – now a major artery – did not exist, except for a short section built off Kentish Town Road in the early 19th century and called Grafton Place. On the south side of the junction, the four houses of Southampton Terrace (later Nos.181-187) were built in 1819. In the southernmost lived Thomas Bird, the Parish Surveyor. These houses had been demolished shortly before WWI. In the next decade the North Western Polytechnic (p 76) was built on the site. Within the last few years, its building has been sensitively converted into flats with a Pizza Express restaurant at street level, providing a much needed 'quality corner' at this important junction.

As you continue to walk down the east side of Kentish Town Road, note on the pavement opposite a single Victorian Gothic stone gatepost and the remains of original iron gates. These stand at the entrance to **CHURCH AVENUE**, formerly the wide tree-lined approach to the Kentish Town Congregational Church, built in 1848, and before that the road to

the parish pound (see p 78). The expansion of the GULliver Telephone Exchange turned this pleasant urban space into a dark corridor. The diminutive building at the side was the Kentish Town Post Office until 1959. The houses containing small shops, **Nos.163-177**, were built in 1848 on the site of Clarke's Farm, as Hawley Place: this was land belonging to the Hawley–Buck estate (see Route 5). Note the remains of stucco decoration.

Beyond Clarke's farm was another farm house, known by the mid-1840s as Gambee's Cottage, which was demolished to make way for Kelly Street (then Church Street), laid out in 1848. After Kelly Street are **Nos.149-161**. **No.157** was formerly one of several oil shops (where once essential household items such as paraffin were sold) in Kentish Town Road that were run by Salmon's, who had another store at No.387. Roughly on this site King shows a small detached house with an entrance to gardens alongside. This may be the house Lady (Emma) Hamilton is said to have stayed in after Lord Nelson's death; Denyer located it about here and said the gardens were noted for their beauty. No.149, on the far corner is now the funeral directors **Levertons**, but was formerly the premises of Frederick Richards, undertakers here since 1913.

South of Castle Road is another historic centre of Kentish Town. The grey-painted building at **No.147**, currently the Bullet cocktail lounge, was until 2002 the Castle

pub, built in 1849 as a replacement for the famous Castle Inn (p 80), which was set further back from the highway and had a pleasure garden leading west to the river. Next door, and also set back, was Nelson's uncle's house, where the Admiral came, or so it was jocularly said, to "keep an eye on the Fleet", and another contender for Emma Hamilton's possible Kentish Town domicile (p 81). After it is the unmistakable oxblood tiling by Leslie Green for the Underground Group. This was South Kentish Town station of the Hampstead Tube, opened on 22 June 1907 and closed on 5 June 1924 due to a lack of power created by a strike at Lots Road Power Station in Chelsea, and not re-opened except as an air raid shelter in WWII. South Kentish Town was originally to be called 'Castle Road'. The station was the inspiration for John Betjeman's story about the passenger who alighted here after the station had been closed.

Cross at the forked junction and, ignoring Royal College Street (which approaches from the left), continue along the east side of Kentish Town Road. **CASTLE PLACE**, opposite, formerly a street of small terraced houses, is now merely an alley leading into Castle Road. On the corner, a single-storey Kentish Town café and two similar annexes have been built in the former garden of **No.133** and are currently painted dark red. This ancient house (No.133), originally divided into two, appears on the 1801 map and on King's *Panorama*. We are now at former Providence Place, once known as "the entrance to the village", where the vacant frontage shown by King is now filled up with small shops. **Nos.119-127** are surviving 2-storey examples dating from 1824. **Nos.111-117** have been rebuilt, with 3 storeys and gabled fronts. Providence Place is a reminder of the earlier days of the village, but the condition of the properties suggests that redevelopment here cannot be long delayed. At the end of the terrace, **No.99** was the former Clarence public house, renamed Dillons in 1999 and closed three years later. In 2004 it was being rebuilt within the original external walls.

After Farrier Street are sixteen houses and shops originally called Moreton Terrace, from Moreton House near Bideford, a Buck family home (we are still in Hawley–Buck territory). The Terrace was built between 1835 and 1844 and Nos.75-79 were destroyed in WWII. **Nos.75&77** were rebuilt in utilitarian fashion for Chamberlaines Cycles. On the corner of Hawley Road, the Moreton Arms, built as such in 1842, became the Duck in 1988 and **Quinn's** in 1994, currently colourful in yellow and blue.

Beyond Hawley Road lies the railway viaduct which now marks the gateway to Kentish Town and marches across the triangular **Camden Gardens**. The viaduct was constructed by the East and West India Docks and Birmingham Junction Railway (later the North London Railway), which reached Camden Town in 1850. During its construction, one Sunday morning in late 1849, seven of the completed arches collapsed, although the arch over the main roadway survived and there was no loss of life. A much later accident, on 9 January 1962, when two goods trains collided at the junction, was not so fortunate. Five loaded wagons crashed down into the road and twelve people were injured.

This section of Kentish Town Road was commonly known until the early 19th century as Water Lane, from the propensity of the River Fleet to overflow its banks (in 1826 to a width of 65 ft). Built here, on the west side of the road and shortly before the coming of the North London Railway, were Moreton Villas, a group of stuccoed Classical houses, some of which survive as precious archetypes of the early Victorian developer's dream house. The semi-detached pairs nearest Hawley Road at **Nos.57-63** are the earliest, dating from 1837. Like detached **No.55**, they are Grade-II Listed. **No.51**, beyond, has added Tudor details and a later shopfront. With its back premises beside the railway viaduct, No.51 has successively housed the offices of United Collieries, the stained-glass artists J Binder & Co., a post-WWII banana merchant, and more recently a local newspaper, the *Camden & St Pancras Chronicle*. The southernmost houses of Moreton Villas, numbered 8, 9 & 10, and built in the early 1840s, were soon demolished to make way for the railway.

The remaining stretch of Kentish Town Road, south of the railway bridge, lies in Camden Town.

East side
(viewed from opposite)

Now carefully cross over to Quinn's for the return to Kentish Town station, walking up the west side of the street while looking at the east. The corner of Jeffrey's Street and Kentish Town Road is nicely turned with a stuccoed block leading into a 4-storey brick terrace, originally known as Jeffrey's Terrace. The name derives from Elizabeth Jeffreys, wife of the first Earl Camden, the ground landlord. It is not known why from the first an apostrophe was introduced. The houses were built from 1809 to 1814. An advertisement for one of these in 1813 stated that the Terrace commanded extensive prospects of the surrounding countryside "although only 2 miles off the stones. Stages pass the house nearly every hour". Flooding was not the only hazard in this area: in the early 19th century householders used to fix bells to their shutters as a warning of intruders.

At the corner of Farrier Street (p 67) is **Atunbi House** (opened 1993), on the site of one of the blocks of artisans' dwellings that once lined both sides of the street.

Beyond, **Nos.104-108** are now Camden Studios, but were built as a warehouse for George Arthur Dunn's, clothiers and hatters, which occupied this site from 1895 until 1984. These premises were the central depot from which orders were distributed to over 100 branches. Dunn's made its reputation when almost every man wore a hat, and the firm found it hard to survive in an almost bareheaded world. James Wigg's medical practice in **No.112** went to Bartholomew Road (p 111) in 1973. **No.114** on the corner has recently become offices for the surveyors Ringley's. The building dates from 1884, when the low timber buildings of Cain Place, which had frontages on both Kentish Town Road and Royal College Street behind, were swept away. At the same time a drinking fountain, long since demolished, was erected at the corner to commemorate one Jabez Inwards, at the instance of Mr M G Ling of the Central Temperance Association.

Across from here, Rochester Road (p 62) enters, at what was once Chestnut Row, so called from the two chestnut trees sheltering the old cottages that stood here and which were said to have been planted by Lady Hamilton when she stayed in Kentish Town. On the southern corner of the road in the late 19th century was the Rochester Hall school (p 65) and facing it was the Church of St Barnabas. King shows, on the site of the church, dairyman Walter's rather insanitary cowshed, which

was replaced by four houses called Camden Row. These made way in 1884 for the church of St Barnabas, one of the later Anglican Parish Churches to be created in St Pancras. The church, with seats for 600, was designed by Ewan Christian. Its foundation stone was laid in October 1884 and the church was consecrated by Frederick Temple, Bishop of London on 18 July 1885. The site cost £2,350 and the building £5,000. The church was declared redundant and closed down in 1956. The following year it was taken over by the Greek Orthodox Church as its **Cathedral of St Andrew & St Barnabas**. Behind are extensive Church Halls, built in 1970, including a short-lived cinema called The Venus. This showed mainly art-house films and was the last cinema in Kentish Town when it closed in 1975.

Beyond Bartholomew Road stands the **Abbey Tavern**, with striped brickwork and decoration. In 2004 it was restored and reopened for business. The pub was built in 1861 as the Albany, its first proprietor being Robert Thurston. It had changed its name to its present one before WWI. The terrace to which it is attached was originally Bartholomew Place, built in 1807-08 on the estate bequeathed to St Bartholomew's Hospital in 1667 by William Cleave, Haberdasher of London. The terrace kept most of its gardens until 1870 and had unobstructed views, to the rear, over Holloway and Islington. It

displaced a nursery ground and orchard, worked by a gardener called Allam. Earlier, the 18th-century antiquarian, Dr William Stukeley (1687–1765) (**Fig 2**) had a rural retreat here, on which he built a 'Druid's Walk' and 'Eve's Bower' and his own Mausoleum. He was Rector of St George The Martyr (Queen Square), a keen amateur archaeologist and the first

2 Dr William Stukeley (G Kneller pinx, Audinet sculpt), published 1817

secretary of the Society of Antiquaries. His enthusiasm considerably exceeded the accuracy of his conjectures; he is best remembered locally for sketching out a supposed Roman camp, 'Caesar's Camp' at the Brill by St Pancras Old Church. He was enthusiastic about the charms of living in Kentish Town − "extremely convenient for keeping my horses and for my own amusement … an half-hour's walk [from Bloomsbury] over sweet fields. … 'Tis absolutely and clearly out of the influence of the London smoak, a dry gravelly soil, and air remarkably wholesome". Stukeley's assessment of the local soil was as erroneous as his theories on Stonehenge, that in Kentish Town being typically clay.

In June 1824, soon after her return from Italy, Mary Shelley (1797−1851), the creator of *Frankenstein*, moved with her 4-year-old surviving son Percy Florence, into No.5 Bartholomew Place. Here they lived briefly with (or near) Jane Williams, whose common-law husband Edward had drowned with the poet Percy Bysshe Shelley. Mary's later letters to Jane display very strong feelings for her: e.g. "Often leaving you at Kentish Town I have wept from the overflow of affection". From the windows of No.5 they watched the passing of Byron's funeral procession. Mary, however, did not like Kentish Town, which she thought to be "an odious swamp".

Crossing Prince of Wales Road, continue up the west side of the High Street, viewing the buildings opposite. No.158 was latterly the home of the Mornington Building Society, Kentish Town's own co-operative, founded in 1868. Its meetings were held in the British School Room, on the same site, which had opened on 26 June 1807 as the first Congregational Church in Kentish Town. When the New Chapel opened in Kelly Street in 1848, the old building continued in use as the Kentish Town British School until 1909, when all the pupils were transferred to the new Torriano School (p 118). It was also used for community meetings. Here, in 1849, 400 people attended the Annual General Meeting of the Kentish Town Literary Society. The church finally sold the old building in 1927, but alterations to convert it for commercial use simply enveloped the old frontage, which is still virtually intact behind the façade; the old School Room has a fine hammer-beam roof.

The building had become known as Trafalgar Chapel, the houses to the north having been built as Trafalgar Place in 1806-7. Of these, **No.166** was in the late 19th century a base for the piano maker John Rintoul (whose works lay behind) and **Nos.174-178** have been rebuilt and now house the Kentish Town Job Centre. A darker side of Kentish Town's history was enacted here in 1786 when Joseph Richards, a youth of 18, was hanged for the murder of Walter Horseman, opposite the home of his victim. Before being "turned off", he desired to see the widow of the deceased, but she was gone to London.

Another resident of Trafalgar Place was Olivia Serres, otherwise known as Princess Olive. She had been born Olivia Wilmot, the daughter of Robert Wilmot, a house painter and embezzler, in Warwick in 1772. She had a talent for painting and studied art with John Thomas Serres, George III's marine painter, whom she married in 1791, exhibiting her paintings at the Royal Academy. She divorced Thomas Serres in 1804 and then made ends meet by selling her paintings and her writings, in which she was given to making outrageous claims e.g. that her uncle, Rev. Dr James Wilmot, had written the *Letters of Junius*. Between 1807 and 1815 she managed to make the acquaintance of some members of the Royal Family and then wrote to the Prince of Wales seeking financial support because, she alleged, she was his cousin. In a memorial to him when he became King in 1820 she declared that she was the daughter of the Duke of Cumberland (brother of George III) by his first marriage to a daughter of James Wilmot. She claimed that when George III had learned the truth he had given her a yearly pension of £500 for life and created her the Duchess of Lancaster, which, she said, entitled her to the income of the Duchy. Her claim was supported by documents. She assumed the title Princess Olive of Cumberland, placed the royal arms on her carriage and announced her parentage in several letters to the newspapers and in pamphlets. On her imprisonment for debt in 1821, she appealed to the public for contributions, placing posters reading "The Princess of Cumberland in Captivity!" all over London. In 1823 her case was taken up in Parliament but was denounced as unfounded by Sir Robert Peel. She died in 1834 but her claims were continued by her eldest daughter, 'Princess Lavinia' (p 82).

The east side of Kentish Town Road beyond this point remained open grassland for another 50 years. Patshull Road, on the Dartmouth estate, was laid out in 1864. The next block of shops was called Wolsey Terrace, because we are now on the edge of Christ Church estate (p 100); Cardinal Wolsey was the founder of the Oxford college. The terrace was built in 1860-61. Most of the houses were rebuilt in 1963 with a rigid horizontal façade and roof line, ignoring the gentle rise in the street. Only the tavern on the southern corner remains, currently decked out in red and yellow. Now called **Auntie Annie's Porter House**, it was built as the Wolsey Tavern, a name retained until 1993. Kentish Town was famous for butchers. At one time, of the 32 in this street, three were in this terrace. Many slaughtered their meat on the premises via a mews at the rear, a convenient feature of these later Christ Church properties.

Beyond Gaisford Street the next terrace,

3 William Bruges, Garter King of Arms, 1420: "from an illuminated manuscript in the Museum at Oxford"

completed in 1862, was again briefly called Wolsey Terrace until the whole road was renumbered in 1864. The heavy Victorian façade is intact, save for **Nos.210–216**, which were destroyed in WWII and rebuilt in 1959, to give a more spacious Post Office. At **No.204**, the locally based grocers Walton, Hassell & Port maintained a presence for nearly a century, closing in 1969. But the field beneath contains traces of some of the most important historic buildings in Kentish Town.

The first is Morgan's Farm. The Morgan family occupied this site for many years before moving away in 1831 (see p 102). King shows a gabled Elizabethan house with extensive outbuildings, with three cottages and a blacksmith's shop. The earliest recorded owner was Sir William Hewett, clothworker, who was Lord Mayor of London in 1559-60. Christ Church came into possession in 1735. The farm buildings were not finally demolished until 1860. On a triangular site bordering the road, a pound for stray animals stood until 1832; next to this in 1775 the Vestry erected a 'cage' to contain disorderly persons.

To the north of the farm, the *Panorama* records a favourite location of such ballooning pioneers of the 18th century as Lunardi and Blanchard, but does not mention another building, with an unusual L-shaped moat, clearly visible on Thompson's 1801 map. This is probably because the ruins of this structure by then formed a part of Morgan's Farm. The moat is believed by some to mark the site of Kentish Town's most important medieval structure, the house of William Bruges (1375−1450), first Garter King of Arms (**Fig 3**, p 29). An alternative site in St Pancras Way has its champions. In 1416, Bruges entertained the Holy Roman Emperor Sigismund during a state visit to England. The assorted nobles, clerics and their retainers ate nine pigs, seven sheep, one hundred pullets, one hundred pigeons, thirty capons and twenty hens, hares, rabbits, kids, salmon, eels, crabs, oysters, wild boar and red deer. Today, **Nos.240&242** stand on the site. In this third section of Wolsey Terrace, Nos.230-254 were damaged in WWII and **Nos.250-254** were rebuilt in 1954. A long-term tenant is Barclays (formerly the London & South Western Bank) at **Nos.230-234**.

The last terrace in the walk lies to the north of Islip Street. The public house on the corner, the **Jorene Celeste**, was originally the Oxford Vaults and later, until 1985, the Oxford Tavern. It then became the Vulture's Perch, said to have been taken over at one time by the entrepreneur Richard Branson with a view, not pursued, to creating a chain of Virgin pubs. Jorene was a fashion model in the 1930s and her grandchildren decided to honour her memory by naming their hostelry after her. **Nos.262-266** were rebuilt in 1964 to give Kentish Town its first purpose-built Public Library. At the end of the terrace stands Kentish Town station and the end of our journey. Opened in 1907 as part of the Hampstead Tube, it replaced the remaining houses of Inwood Terrace built in 1816.

We cross the main road carefully to the glazed canopy replacing the old station building of the Midland Railway. This, opened in October 1868, was removed in 1981 and access was altered to provide shared booking facilities with the Underground. Originally a busy station, the traffic it later lost returned with the introduction of electrified Thameslink services. As a final poignant reminder of the vanished trades that formerly flourished in the back premises of the High Street, observe, high on the north wall of the station, the faded sign "Crowe, Trellis and Joinery Works". This advertised timber merchants whose yard was at adjacent No.280 from 1911 to 1940. Just across the road is the famous Assembly House (p 124), an opportunity to relax before catching the train or bus home.

Highgate Road to Fortess Road

Circular walk from Kentish Town station
For modern map see inside back cover

When the Bon Marché was shuttered, when
  the feet were hot and tired,
Outside Charrington's we waited,
  by the "STOP HERE IF REQUIRED",
Launched aboard the shopping basket,
  sat precipitately down,
Rocked past Zwanziger the baker's,
  and the terrace blackish brown,
And the curious Anglo-Norman parish church
  of Kentish Town.

John Betjeman's poem *Parliament Hill Fields* recalls a tram journey he took as a child from Kentish Town up Highgate Road. The verse quoted refers to the first part of this Route, which begins opposite Kentish Town station. Turn right out of the station and stopping under the large iron canopy enjoy the splendid view towards Parliament Hill Fields in the distance, the only surviving remains of rural Kentish Town. The canopy stands atop a wide bridge that carries the road over the railway here. By the Assembly House pub (p 124) ahead, cross over busy **KENTISH TOWN ROAD** and pause.

The tram stop to which Betjeman refers was in the middle of the roadway; trams ran to Parliament Hill Fields from Euston Road or Moorgate, until replaced by trolley buses from 1938, and eventually by the motorbus. We might deduce from the poem that Charrington's was at this spot, beside the Midland Railway line. However, this appears to be poetic licence. From 1922 Charrington's did have a coal yard at No.49 Kentish Town Road at the edge of our area (p 72), but the poem is set in the previous decade, just before WWI. In 1914 the coal merchants *George Hickling & Co.* were at No.351 just south of the railway bridge, at the present junction with Regis Road. Hickling's was still there in the 1960s, its shop front having a long narrow window displaying a miniature train, with trucks filled with nuggets of coal, as described in an earlier stanza of the poem.

Now turn right and head north, taking the left-hand fork (Highgate Road) at the junction ahead. A few steps farther on is a row of shops ending in a terrace of three stuccoed houses surmounted by a scrolled decoration. In 1904 **No.383**, now a café, was Fred's Dining Room, while **No.385** was Albert Zwanziger's bakery. To avoid persecution during WWI, the family changed its name to Cordingley. First taken over by Maurice Cohen, a pastrycook, and a fish-and-chip shop by the 1920s, No.385 is still a 'fish bar' today. Next to this, **No.387**, now Top to Toe beauty salon, was an oil shop advertised as "Salmon's Oil, Colour, White Lead and Varnish Stores". Two giant oil jars were affixed to the façade. The firm also had shops at No.157 and No.314.

The shops here are what remains of a terrace called New Chapel Place, built opposite the Assembly House in the 1790s. The numbering ran northward from No.10 to No.1, which was next to the pub (now at No.389). It was here that Joseph Salter (p 67) set up shop in 1854 when the building explosion in Kentish Town was getting underway. His firm of estate agents, Salter Rex, moved a few years later to No.311.

Some say that the **Bull & Gate** has been here from Tudor times, and that its original name was Boulogne Gate, commemorating the capture of the French port by Henry VIII in 1544. Dismissed by many students of inn-signs, this theory was popularised by George Steevens (1736–1800), a Hampstead resident once described as "a mischievous wit in literary matters". The Bull & Gate was first recorded in 1715 and was certainly one of the 11 Kentish Town hostelries licensed in 1721. It was by the Bull & Gate that in 1730 W Yates, B Fink and H Morris robbed Squire Greenwood and Mr Sutton, and then terrorised the village before escaping, but they were apprehended and later hanged at Tyburn. King in his *Panorama* states that the Social Villagers (p 124) had meetings at the Bull & Gate, and the *Epicures' Magazine* in 1815 stated that the pub was the "rendezvous of politicians". The pub was rebuilt in 1871 – note the date high up on the façade and the painted stucco bull and farm gate. In the 'Venue' attached to the pub (formerly a snooker hall), rock bands have been appearing live since the early 1980s; the Bull & Gate is an important part of London's underground music scene. In the late 19th century the pub was a well-known horse-bus terminus, and by the side of it is an unnamed cobbled yard that once led to stables of the London General Omnibus Co., but which now leads to a storage facility of Jaques Samuel Pianos, which calls itself London's largest piano company.

HIGHGATE ROAD begins past the pub. The road itself dates from about 1700, having evolved from the ancient track heading out of London. The route is mentioned as early as the 15th century in Court Rolls but is likely to be even earlier. Until the mid-19th century the road was known as Green Street, as it led past Kentish Town village green (Route 3). It officially became Highgate Road in 1864, six years before the numerous Places and Terraces built along it were renumbered and combined.

This route to Highgate Cemetery is still taken by funeral processions, none larger than that accompanying the body of the famous bare-fist fighter Tom Sayers of Camden Town in 1865. Some 10,000 people were said to have witnessed his enormous funeral cortège.

Continuing north, the first terrace of Georgian houses is the remnant of Upper Craven Place, shown on Thompson's 1801 map and built by Thomas Greenwood in the late 18th century. This is probably Betjeman's "terrace blackish brown". Above the doorway of **No.3** is the very lifelike head of a grinning, bald and bearded old man, with something of Gladstone about him, although in the early 20th century this was the HQ of the local Conservative party. Thomas Greenwood, who was also the landlord of the Bull & Gate, lived at **No.5** (then Upper Craven Place) before moving into a house on the site of the Forum ahead, where he died in 1810. Next door at present-day **No.7** was the Craven House School for Girls, which remained here until 1860. No.5 (and later Nos.5&7) served for much of the 20th century as the Foresters' Hall, home to the local 'court' of the Ancient Order of Foresters, founded in 1834 from an earlier fraternity, the Royal Foresters, which survives today as the Foresters' Friendly Society. The now demolished large end house of the Terrace was home in 1817 to Andrew Mensal after his retirement from the Gordon House Academy (p 47). The house was owned, but not occupied, by James Frederick King.

Look to the right, noting the corner shop at the junction of Highgate Road and Fortess Road, now a minicab office. Beyond, on the same side and lying back from the road, is the rear of the Tally Ho pub on the corner of Fortess Walk (p 44). The whole of this site was once part of a paddock surrounded by the houses of former Willow Walk. Here, facing Highgate Road, King's *Panorama* shows an early "Police Station", actually no more than a sentry box. Willow Walk disappeared in about 1814, when Junction Road (now Fortess Road) was built (see p 137), and thereafter the adjacent stretch of Highgate Road was known as Junction Place.

Back on the west side, the present **Forum** was built over much of Upper Craven Place. It opened in 1934 as the Forum Theatre, although it was a cinema, seating 2,175. Like the earlier Palace (p 24), it was designed by John Stanley Beard, in Art Deco style. The interior, by Beard's partner, W R Bennett, still boasts a series of friezes depicting Roman battle scenes. Rumour has it that they were paid for by Mussolini, who donated money to make the place suitable for a rally by Oswald Mosley. From 1937 onwards, Mosley's party, the British Union of Fascists, was banned from marching through East London where it drew its largest support, but it held a large march from Kentish Town to Trafalgar Square in July 1937. The cinema was taken over by the ABC chain in 1935 and closed in 1970. The Forum then became a dance

4 Highgate Road, looking southeast, c.1900. On the right, the Christ Apostolic Church (Betjeman's "curious Anglo-Norman parish church")

and bingo hall before it was reborn in 1985 as the Town and Country Club, a popular live music venue. That role has continued since it reverted to its original name in 1992, and today it is renowned for its Indie, rock and soul concerts. The building is Grade-II Listed.

Cross Greenwood Place (p 35) to the front of the **Christ Apostolic Church**, which is likewise Listed. The original building here was erected in 1784 to replace the old Kentish Town Chapel (p 23); it was designed by James Wyatt in a neo-Classical style, with a Tuscan portico. A growing population soon outgrew the chapel, which was enlarged in 1817 and again in 1843-45 when, to the designs of J H Hakewill, the stunted twin towers were added and the church's appearance was changed to Romanesque, Betjeman's "curious Anglo-Norman". The new church was a major reconstruction rather than a complete rebuild, as the Vestry had decided that the winning design of a competition held in 1842 was too expensive to execute. The result was described by *The Ecclesiologist* as "the very meanest and most contemptible of churches".

While this horror was being built, a temporary church – a pioneering prefab – was erected on the opposite side of Highgate Road, on a site lent by the landowner, St John's College, Cambridge. It was designed by Peter Thompson, who received government funding in

the 1840s to manufacture prefabricated churches and schools, often for export to the growing Empire. It took only a month to construct. Built of wooden panels on brick foundations, with a tower surmounted by a belfry and windows of 'vitreous glass', the church was covered in asphalted felt. It could accommodate 500 adults and 300 children.

The rebuilt chapel of ease became a District Chapelry in 1851 and a parish church in 1868, when 22 new parishes were carved out of St Pancras. Although by this time the building had long been known as St John the Baptist Church, the dedication is believed to have never been officially sanctioned. Declared redundant by the Church of England in 1993, 'St John's' stood empty until occupied by a group of ecological activists. Since 1996 it has been the HQ of the UK branch of the international Christ Apostolic Church, founded in 1935 and with around 40 churches in London that minister primarily to the capital's African community.

Pause now to observe again the opposite side of Highgate Road, and the latest (1972) incarnation of Kentish Town **Fire Station**. An early precursor, the Old Engine House, stood a little to the south in Junction Place. Its Victorian successor was erected off the west side of Fortess Walk, where a solitary red-painted gatepost survives. The present

station stands on much the same site, but expanded and now accessed from Highgate Road. Its frontage lies on a stretch of road once called Woodland Place, which was replaced by a row of Victorian shops, only one of which remains, at **No.28**. This was used as dining rooms in the early 20th century (**Fig 4**, p 33), and in the 1990s by the Greater London Pensioners Association. It is at present a carpet shop.

Also on the fire station site stood the earliest Methodist chapel in Kentish Town, built in 1778 by Thomas Walton for use by itinerant Methodist preachers. It was converted to a private dwelling in 1828, when the chapel was replaced by another in Leighton Road (p 127).

Beyond the fire station and its prominent practice tower is an old building boldly labelled "Piano Workshop". It stands at the end of a mews-like turning called **No.30A** containing several old industrial buildings and leading to a piano warehouse, one of the few remaining in the area. Before WWI, No.30A housed organ builders Henry Dyer & Son and a piano-key maker, John Murray. One of the buildings was occupied in the early 1920s by piano makers Noakes & Co., and then for a couple of years from c.1926 by the Piano Workers Guild Ltd. This was formed in response to a decline in the piano industry that decade, presumably by piano makers fearful for their livelihoods. By 1931 another piano maker, Bamberg, Rudolf,

Ernest & Son had moved in. Six years later, piano manufacture appears to have ceased at No.30A, though in fairly recent years the old premises have become the London showroom of a modern firm, the Piano Works Company.

Continue just past the church to view Nos.19-37, the Highgate Community Mental Health Centre, ("the **Highgate Centre**"), run by Camden Social Services and offering psychotherapy-oriented day care. It covers the site of the terrace of ten Georgian houses of Lower Craven Place, built by John Greenwood, which on its northern side abutted the River Fleet. The writer Douglas Jerrold (1803–1857) lived in the terrace in 1839-40, during a short-lived period of affluence following the success of his play *Black-eyed Susan* and shortly before he helped found *Punch* magazine in 1841. The houses were demolished in the 1960s.

Now backtrack and turn right along the south arm of U-shaped **GREENWOOD PLACE**. It was built in the late 18th century as Prospect Row, and once really did have a prospect – of open fields across the valley of the River Fleet towards Hampstead. The view from the end of it today shows the vast extent of the Kentish Town railway lands, which stretched to and beyond the blue hangar-like UPS building in Regis Road (p 99), away to the left. Turn right, past the rear of the former parish church, which survives

from the Wyatt building of 1784. This north–south stretch of street was known as Prospect Place until in the 19th century it was combined with Prospect Row to form Greenwood Place, named after Thomas Greenwood, the builder. Charles Booth, walking in the area with Inspector Tomkin in 1898 to update his poverty map, noted ramshackle cottages here, all soon due to come down, as the street was in the hands of the Midland Railway.

Pass the **Greenwood Centre**, opened by Jock Stallard MP in 1973 as a training centre for the 'mentally handicapped', part of which is now occupied by the Camden Society, set up in 1985 to promote a better standard of living for people with learning disabilities. The Society's offices, and **Deane House** beyond, stand on the site of the bottling stores of Read Brothers Ltd, export bottlers of ale, stout and porter. The magnificent building (**Fig 5**, p 36), designed in 1885 by Theodore K Green, remained in use by Read's until just before WWII. It stood alongside the railway line and was served by a siding. Its castellated and turreted tower formed an impressive backdrop for many posed locomotive postcards in the age of steam.

In 1898 Booth records no houses in Greenwood Place, but Read's 'brewery' nearby and 12 houses fronting Highgate Road (quite substantial properties built in 1813 as Francis Terrace); within a year the houses had been demolished and replaced

by the large 'steam cabinet works' of Maple & Co. Maple's was a high-class furniture manufacturer, with its main shop in Tottenham Court Road and factories and warehouses in various parts of Camden.

Turn right along the second arm of Greenwood Place. On the right, **No.19,** now A&A Self Storage, began as Maple's timber yard and sawmill, later becoming their Exhibition Works, a base for the firm's sideline as an exhibition furnisher. More recently, as Lensham House, the building was home to the Family Policy Studies Centre until its closure in 2001. To your left are the two main blocks of Maple's factory – depository on the left, furniture making on the right. When Maple's moved out c.1970, clothing manufacturers moved into what became Evandoré House (still so labelled). It now forms part of the **Highgate Business Centre**, where several film and theatre companies are based.

Re-emerging into **HIGHGATE ROAD**, notice almost opposite a nautical-looking Camden Council housing block. Known as **Elsfield**, rendered in white with blue railings, it was designed by Bill Forrest and dates from 1972. It replaced houses known until the 1860s as Burghley Terrace. Elsfield stands on the corner of Burghley Road (p 42), which joins Highgate Road directly opposite us. It was here that the Highgate arm of the River Fleet passed under the main road at Kentish Town

Bridge. In 1487 this was called the Handeford Bridge. The river formed a pond here, which in 1825 was said to have swollen during flooding to a width of 13 ft.

Turn left and continue north beside the 5-storey building fronting Highgate Road at Nos.39-51. In this Maple's factory furniture of various kinds, including beds and mattresses, was made. By the early 1970s, the 'rag trade' had colonised much of the block, which took its name, **Linton House**, from gown makers Norman Linton & Co. Current occupants include the Expressions Dance Centre (opened 2004) and Anchor Care Alternatives, which provides care workers for people in their own homes.

On the right-hand (eastern) side, in the debased-Georgian-style buildings at **Nos.54-56**, is Irish Centre Housing accommodation that was built in 1989 on the site of 18th-century Bridge House (No.58), unnecessarily demolished a year before. The gardens of Bridge House led down to the River Fleet. Water carters once repaired to Bridge House to refresh themselves after collecting water from the pond by Kentish Town Bridge. No.58, by Edwardian times, housed the John Apps Laundry. After WWI it became the rubber factory of the false-teeth makers Claudius Ash & Co. (p 86). In the early 19th century the other houses on this stretch of the road were called Woodland Cottages, named from the adjacent Woodland House, built in 1795 and a school until Victorian times. Just past the Irish hostel is **COLLEGE YARD** (College Mews until 1937), through which ancient College Lane, which we traverse later (p 41), debouches into Highgate Road. Beyond, Fleet House at **No.62** (preserving the name of the nearby buried river) once housed a succession of piano repairers, including, in the 1960s, the firm of J S Tozer that we shall encounter elsewhere (p 90).

Remaining on the left-hand side of the main road, we now cross **CARKER'S LANE**. This ancient footpath once led across fields and through watercress beds to Gospel Oak. King's *Panorama* labels it as a "near cut to Hampstead". He showed it as Corker's Lane, and there was indeed a farm in the area run by a Mr Corker. The lane was cut off by the coming of the

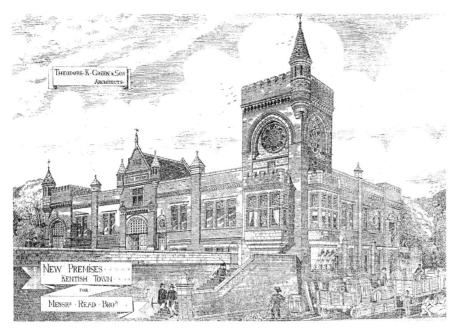

5 Read's Bottling Store (The Builder, 7 Feb 1885)

railway. In 1898 Booth noted only one house in Carker's Lane, lived in by a foreman at Read's bottling stores.

The old industrial building with an entrance in Carker's Lane, and lining the west side of **HIGHGATE ROAD** ahead at **Nos.53-79,** replaced the original houses of Fitzroy Place, built in 1799 on land owned by the Fitzroys (see p 14). The block was once part of a large wallpaper factory owned by the Shand-Kydd family. Dating from c.1908, their Kentish Town factory lay initially behind the 'Fitzroy Place' houses, but these later succumbed to demolition as the works expanded. Born out of the Arts & Crafts Movement, the Shand-Kydd firm once rivalled Morris & Co. in the production of high-quality, hand-stencilled wallpaper. By 1968, "wallpaper millionaire" Peter Shand-Kydd had sold up, and departed to try his hand at sheep farming in Australia. (He would later return to Britain, becoming the second husband of Frances Shand-Kydd, the mother of Diana, Princess of Wales.)

The redundant factory was quickly colonised by carpet dealers. As the International Oriental Carpet Centre, it housed a score of carpet merchants trading in products from various parts of the Middle East and Asia. After a decade or so the IOCC closed, although the carpet trade did not desert Highgate Road. Several carpet dealers still occupy individual shop units along its length. The refurbished factory turned warehouse is now named **Highgate Studios**. In the 1980s the TV presenters Tariq Ali and Darcus Howe had their 'Bandung Studios' here. Here today is the Highgate Children's Centre offering day care and education for children up to 5; while numerous neighbours include Avenues Publishing, Trapeze Learning (offering private tuition to schoolchildren), an Ocean furniture store and an LA Fitness centre.

Without crossing the road, notice opposite **Nos.64-70**, a collection of Listed 19th-century houses. Small double-fronted No.64 was home for many years until WWI to the builder Nathan Cansick. On the far corner of Lady Somerset Road a wooden camel guards the entrance to The Orientalist, a shop at **Nos.74-80** selling Middle Eastern merchandise.

Next, turn left into **SANDERSON CLOSE**. The derivation of its name is a mystery. Did the naming authorities, aware that a wallpaper factory once adjoined the site, lazily borrow the name from the best-known wallpaper firm of the day, once a rival of Shand-Kydd?

Walk down to the red-brick industrial buildings at the foot of the hill. These are the remnants of the Midland Railway's locomotive sheds, now put to different use. The Midland Railway's passenger engine depot opened here in 1867-68. This was the company's only London depot before goods engines were relocated in the late 19th century. Originally two sheds were provided, but one of these was demolished when the line was widened in the 1890s, and in 1898 two more sheds were built. Shortly before WWI the Kentish Town site was servicing, storing and repairing as many as 140 steam locomotives, as well as goods and passenger rolling stock. Many railway employees lived in nearby streets. In the 1950s the sheds were re-roofed after wartime bomb damage, but they became redundant after the introduction of diesel traction and closed in 1963. What remains of them now includes **Hiview House**, the registered office of the major contracting firm J Murphy & Sons.

Turn right into the **Carrol and Sanderson Close Estate**, this part of which was built over the northern extremity of the locomotive depot. Designed for Camden Council by Yorke, Rosenberg & Mardall, the estate dates from c.1976. The path running through it at the foot of the hill (Sanderson Close) is secluded and tree-lined. The houses here have a jagged skyline of sloping roofs. There are wooden pergolas and a landscaped play area in front of an old brick railway wall.

Beyond the play area, turn right and by the wall at the far end ascend steps, left. Pause at the top to view two railways, running parallel at different levels, one high on an embankment and the other in a deep cutting. Now carrying Silverlink's Gospel Oak to Barking service, the high-level line began as the Tottenham & Hampstead Junction Railway (T&HJR), which opened from Tottenham to Highgate Road on 21 July 1868. A short extension westward to Gospel Oak opened 20 years later but, despite the line's name, no permanent connection was laid to the Hampstead Junction line (via Hampstead Heath) until 1940. The low-level line was opened by the Midland Railway in 1900, reaching here from Kentish Town Station via the 'Tottenham North Curve' – which swept round to the west of the engine sheds – before continuing east, parallel to the T&HJR, which it eventually joined, in Islington, at Junction Road Junction [*sic*]. Passenger traffic continued to use the Midland line until the 1960s; the Barking service from Gospel Oak commenced on 5 January 1981.

To your right observe a paved ramp leading to Highgate Road. This follows the line of Carrol Place, which before the coming of the Midland Railway was a short turning off Highgate Road. Originally named Pleasant Row, it was built by Richard Mortimer on his farmland in 1810, and joined up with the southern end of Mortimer Terrace (p 46), which is now truncated north of the railway lines. Booth, in 1898, recorded that nearly all the houses in Carrol Place had been bought up by the Midland and pulled down, and that the remaining cottages were doomed.

Do not walk up the ramp, but turn right

and walk alongside the block **Nos.1-32 CARROL CLOSE** and a short service road for the Estate. Follow the road as it turns left into **HIGHGATE ROAD**. Here, on the right at **No.95**, with buff bricks and glazed penthouse, is the modern Silver Lodge. It was built on the site of the Aldenham Boys' Club which, plagued by hooliganism, closed in the 1980s. The club was founded in 1911 as the Aldenham Club for Young Men & Lads, next to Kentish Town Church, with assistance from Aldenham School (Herts.). In its early years a cricket match between local boys and pupils at the public school was a highlight of the club's sporting calendar. The members of the pop group Madness used to hang out here in the late 1970s before they achieved fame.

On the site of the service road in the 19th century lay the entry to a large house called The Retreat, occupied from the 1850s by Edward Weston, the proprietor of Weston's Music Hall in Holborn, later the Holborn Empire. In 1863 he transformed the house and grounds into public pleasure gardens, which he claimed extended over 7 acres and were lit by 100,000 gas jets. Music, dancing, fireworks and balloon ascents were proposed. Sampson Copestake of neighbouring No.11 Fitzroy Place won a lawsuit to prevent the licensing of Weston's Retreat for music, dancing or the sale of spirits, so that only beer or wine could be

sold. Described in the press as "a flowering garden of beautifulness", the pleasure gardens were, however, not a success – their age had passed – and Weston was probably quite relieved when the land was needed by the Midland Railway. Within 3 years he was forced to close, and (in his own words) "beat a Retreat". He received compensation, and then established (and became the proprietor of) the 'Old Bedford' music hall in Camden Town. A few years later a railway superintendent was living in The Retreat, which in the 1890s was demolished to make way for the enlarged Midland locomotive depot.

Now turn right and take a few steps past No.95 to view on the opposite side the **Vine**, Elizabethan-style, with a big half-timbered cornice, and at present a 'gastropub'. A pub was first built here in about 1730 and called the White Horse, but by 1751 it had become the Vine. In the 18th century it had a garden and skittle ground. On King's *Panorama* it is claimed that the earliest regular daily coach service from Kentish Town to London started from the Vine in 1778, with two coaches departing each day. No.82 lies on the site of the coach office for purchase of tickets, and the inn's stabling block would have extended southwards as far as present No.74 on the corner of Lady Somerset Road. The inn was completely rebuilt in 1899, and the half timbering dates from 1934. The only original bit of the inn is the archway to the right of the forecourt.

For a while the archway led to the Green Street Races, as well known in their day as Epsom. Run by John Wiblin, the pub landlord, they were held on land owned by St John's College, Cambridge in two 'Race Fields' that ran from Burghley Road to Little Green Street (p 40), and which included most of what is now the Ingestre Road Estate. The races were started in 1733 and were still being advertised in 1739, when Wiblin gave the name of his pub as the Two Running Horses and of the racetrack as the "Little Newmarket Course". The records of an Old Bailey trial of 1736 show Wiblin asserting that a nearby public house known as the Whittington & Cat (no doubt a rival establishment) harboured "people of ill fame". The archway led behind the pub to a footpath that crossed a bridge over the Fleet and continued to Islington. Next to the archway today is the red-brick **Media House** (No.82), the HQ of Zierler Media, an international TV advertising agency. To the left of the Vine are **Nos.94&96,** a stuccoed pair with a mansard slate roof, by the side of a yard crammed with architectural bric-à-brac.

6 Highgate Road, looking northwest, c.1900 (courtesy of Corporation of London, London Metropolitan Archives). Erstwhile Blenheim Terrace on left. Note tramlines and railway bridge ahead

We now turn left and continue north along **HIGHGATE ROAD**, past the flats at **Nos.97-119,** where among the ground-floor shops is the local Post Office. The block dates from 1976 and supplanted a row of houses known until the 1860s as Blenheim Terrace (**Fig 6**). The new development entailed the demolition of No.109, whose owner unsuccessfully fought Camden Council to prevent it pulling his house down, claiming it had been in his family 'for 250 years'; it does seem to be shown on early-19th-century maps.

Fortunately, the houses opposite, on the right-hand side of Highgate Road, built as Fitzroy Terrace in 1815 and consisting of six houses (**Nos.98-108**), have survived. Note the Sun fire insurance mark on No.102. Five further terraced houses to the left, **Nos.110-118**, were built later in the 19th century. A plaque at No.110 bears a heraldic shield. These houses were once Nos.1-5 Gospel Terrace, and it was in one of them that Kentish Town's first Catholic chapel, St Alexis, was opened in 1846. It was a private foundation, the work of Rev.

Hardinge Fiorenzo Ivers, a descendant of Thomas Ives [*sic*], who in 1252 was granted leave by Henry III to enclose part of the highway outside his Kentish Town mansion. Ivers travelled widely in Europe, saving some Jesuits in Lisbon from death at the hands of a vicious mob. Invited to Rome, he was made a hereditary Count of the Holy Roman Empire by Pope Gregory XVI. Having entered the Catholic priesthood, he returned to Kentish Town in 1845, where he established a chapel and a Free School for the local poor in one of his own Gospel Terrace properties. Plans were made to build a Gothic church on the site, with seating for 1000. The foundation stone was laid in 1849 by Prince John, the Spanish Infante, as the Archduchess of Austria was indisposed. Building work was apparently begun, but a bitter dispute between Ivers and Cardinal Wiseman led in 1854 to the latter's suppression of the St Alexis Chapel and his expulsion of Ivers, who eventually died destitute in 1868, in College Lane behind the former chapel. Its role had by then been assumed by a new Catholic chapel in Fortess Road (p 44).

The next three cottages date from the 18th century and are set back behind long front gardens. Cross over to them by the zebra crossing shortly before the railway bridge. **No.120**, in Edwardian times, housed the local branch of the Society for Organising Charitable Relief and Repression of Mendacity. The last

house in the group, **No.124** may be, much altered, the small dwelling with attached factory shown on King's *Panorama* as Mr Macdonald's Wax Chandlery. The factory burned down spectacularly in the early 19th century. The owner's surname was actually McDonogh, who cannot be traced with any certainty after 1805, when the rate book records commence.

Walk towards the railway bridge ahead. This carries the former Tottenham & Hampstead Junction line (see pp 37–38). Opened in 1868 was Highgate Road (High Level) station, entered through the arch that still exists under the bridge – occupied now by M&A Coachworks, whose "good lettering" beneath the bridge is praised in *The Buildings of England*. Just before the bridge the road is carried over another railway bridge, below which is the Midland Railway's later, parallel line, in a cutting and disappearing eastwards into a tunnel. A Low Level passenger station opened in 1900. Weary locals could then catch a train from Highgate Road to Southend for a day out, until both High and Low Level stations closed, in 1915 and 1918 respectively, victims of tramway competition. In the early 1960s the Low Level station was occupied by Darcars Ltd, a family-run, one-stop garage that is still operating at the site.

The reader can break away from this Route if desired and continue under the railway bridge up Highgate Road,

following circular Route 3, to the north end of the original village of Kentish Town and back again. If your feet or time do not allow of this, turn back southward, then left up cobbled **LITTLE GREEN STREET**, containing eight 18th-century cottages, some bow-fronted, and once shops selling (for example) ribbons and coffee. The name dates from the time when Highgate Road was known as Green Street. The buildings were put up from 1777 on former common land, permission to enclose which had been granted as early as 1723.

At the top of the rise is a pair of decayed timber gateposts, reminiscent of the wild meadow that survived here until the late 19th century. Ahead lies the red-brick and concrete **Ingestre Road Estate.** Walk a little way into the Estate, along **INGESTRE ROAD**, its main access route, between council houses at **Nos.1-10** and a block named **Calver** on your right. The ground on which the Estate was built has an unusual history, having been developed for housing only well after WWII. Stanford's 1862 map of London shows a planned straight road marching across it, with a crescent attached, but this never materialised as the Midland Railway bought the land here just a few years later. It was not until 1896 that the company built an ugly 3-storey block of 'Enginemen's Lodgings', to provide overnight accommodation for footplatemen from outside London working trains to and from the capital, hauled by engines stabled at the nearby locomotive sheds. The Lodgings, on the site of Calver, later became an LMS Staff Hostel. Further east, beyond a leafy copse, the Midland also built an Electric Generating Station, served by a siding off the T&HJR. This later became a boiler works, and then the Harbar Works of William Cooke & Co., which made "iron strip and bar". The building was bombed during WWII.

The former Race Fields to the south remained largely a wilderness and a haven for wild flowers until laid out as allotments between the wars. Trespassing children played here, dubbing their playground the 'Kentish Town Alps'. In the 1960s, the copse area, here to the east of Little Green Street, was transformed into a more official children's playground, promoted by the local community campaigner Tammo De Jongh (see p 43). Variously nicknamed 'Tammoland' and 'The Magic Land', the playground survived until 1968, when the bulldozers moved in.

The next block on your left is **Grangemill**, while facing you beyond it is **Fletcher Court**, more or less on the ironworks site. Behind it (not visible from here) lies **Wardlow**, near the site of the original Ingestre Road from which the name of the Estate was borrowed, and which is now buried under Acland Burghley School (p 147). That road, in

turn, was named after the benevolent Charles John Chetwynd, 19th Earl of Shrewsbury and Viscount Ingestre. His concerns about working-class slums led him to develop estates for the poor in both Soho and Kentish Town. To the right is the centrepiece of the estate, still (in 2004) a Council-run care home for older people. Beyond are further blocks called **Hambrook Court** and **Tideswell**, and the Ingestre Community Centre opened in 1973 at the far south end of the Estate. The Community Centre provides a youth club, playgroups and classes in yoga and karate. All but two of the residential blocks are named after places in the Derbyshire Peak District. The exceptions honour Major George Fletcher and Sergeant Stephen Hambrook, two Royal Engineers who dismantled a large unexploded wartime landmine discovered during the building of the Estate in 1969.

Return to the gateposts at the entrance to the Estate. We are now in **COLLEGE LANE**, today a narrow footpath, and once an ancient cart track, running parallel to Highgate Road along the waste (or common) land of the village. The lane was named after St John's College, Cambridge, which owned the land. It continues to our right as a tunnel under the railway, and past the site of St John's Farm, which the old track once served. We, however, turn left and southwards. The lane is quaint and lit by old-style lamps,

flanked on the right by small cottages opening onto it, facing bushes that mask the Ingestre Road Estate on the left. Some of these cottages were built at the same time as Little Green Street but others are later, including **No.22**, Railway Cottage, which bears the date 1840. Diminutive **No.16**, Hope Cottage, is set back, as is its neighbour, **No.17**. **Nos.12&13** were constructed in 1881-86 by the local builder Nathan Cansick. On the façade of the latter is a faded DIY war memorial, dated 1914–1918 and honouring several soldiers from College Lane who perished in WWI. The war memorial was erected after St Pancras Council decided to honour the dead not with a stone but by renaming a local Outpatients Department. No.8, the last house in the row, is modern.

On the left side can be seen the derelict club house of the British Railways Staff Association, which from the 1950s was a thriving Working Men's Club for rail workers and their families. Controversially closed c.1998, it looks forlorn, and the weeds are now taking over, concealing its entrance. Beyond on our left is rendered **No.30**, designed by Martin Goalen, and with triangular windows echoing its steeply sloping roof. It is home to Academy Projects, an architectural firm specialising in new buildings and renovation work at archaeological sites. On the right we pass the old footpath leading to the Vine, which we saw earlier, and which once continued eastward across fields. This section of College Lane ends by **Nos.1&2,** a charming pair of cottages with matching tiny triangular front gardens. Peter Straub, the American writer of 'horror' novels, was living in College Lane c.1972.

Crossing over Lady Somerset Road, continue into the southern stretch of College Lane. There are no houses fronting the lane, but some of the walls bear witness to older buildings, the outlines of previous doors and windows being quite visible. College Lane now ends in College Yard (p 36), but we retrace our steps to **LADY SOMERSET ROAD**, where we turn right.

Shown as 'planned' on Stanford's 1862 London map, the road was developed on land owned by St John's College, Cambridge who had acquired it from the Platt family, one of whose number had attended the College. The road took its name from Sarah, Lady Somerset, a benefactress of the College, who bequeathed land in Wiltshire and Cambridge in 1692. This wide, tree-lined road has tall 3-storey terraces (with basement areas), double-bayed on the ground and first floors. A resident in 1985, at **No.52** on the left, was John Willis, son of the playwright Ted Willis and then head of documentaries and current affairs at Yorkshire Television.

Just ahead of that house, turn right along **EVANGELIST ROAD**. Like neighbouring roads, it was built on land belonging to the Cambridge college of St John the *Evangelist*. Until 1908 it was called St John the Evangelist Road. Staggered in deference to a bend in the road, the houses have a medieval look to their porches, with very thin columns supporting stilted arches. The plasterwork of **No.3** is not painted, which gives it an original feel, as does its door glass.

Join **BURGHLEY ROAD**, cross over and turn left up its far side. The road was named after another benefactor of St John's College, Lord Burghley, Chancellor to Queen Elizabeth I. It curves north-eastward, following the line of the River Fleet. **No.16** is set back, a post-modern block with a pyramid-shaped roof. It is a care home run by the Bridge Housing Association. It replaced (c.2000) the neo-Gothic vicarage, built in 1863 by Henry Baker FRIBA, of Kentish Town parish chapel, later church (p 34). At its entrance is a very ecclesiastical looking **No.18** with a bizarre tower. The carving on the capitals on the next few houses is very fine. Across the road, **Nos.23-39** is infill Camden Council housing, built after wartime bomb damage. Before the last block note the large modern window of the building behind; this is the rear of No.25A Lady Somerset Road, a studio house by Rick Mather, built in 1977-79.

Burghley and Lady Somerset Roads traverse the neighbourhood in an X-formation, meeting at the crossroads ahead. Continue ahead up the former as it climbs the hill and curves eastward. The houses here are smaller, forming continuous terraces on either side. Notice how the basement areas we saw in the road's earlier-built lower half have given way, in this later-19th-century uphill stretch, to small front gardens. At **No.60**, halfway up on the right, were the lodgings from 1945 to 1947 of Kwame Nkrumah, the future first Prime Minister of Ghana, then enrolled as a PhD student, both in anthropology at LSE and in philosophy at UCL. He served as vice-president of the West African Students' Union in Camden Square. A flat at neighbouring **No.64** was occupied in 1990 by the actor Sylvester McCoy, best known as the seventh incarnation of television's *Doctor Who*, and who appeared here in the voters' list under his real name, James Kent-Smith. **No.89,** near the top of the opposite side, was home c.1973 to Robin Hicks, the producer of BBC Radio's *Farming Today*. In her autobiography, the TV presenter Joan Bakewell mentions a flat in Burghley Road where she used to meet Harold Pinter at the time of their liaison.

Around the corner to the left is the roadway giving access to the eastern end of the Ingestre Road Estate. On its left, a new building was rising (in 2004) on the triangular site of a former factory at No.91A Burghley Road. Marked on the

1952 OS map as a "pan factory", this actually belonged to the London Fan & Motor Co., makers of ventilating *fans*!

We are now on land shown on an 1829 map as Rakish Hill ('rakish' in the sense of 'sloping'). Burghley Road continues ahead to meet Dartmouth Park Hill, with the white-painted wall of Acland Burghley School (p 147) on the left. Opposite at **Nos.88-98** is another 1950s Camden Council infill housing block, this time with the design feature of a central stairwell. Beyond, at **Nos.104&106**, is the recently restored entrance to Burghley Yard, which led in the late 19th century to the stables of the London General Omnibus Company. One of the units in Burghley Yard was designed by and is home to the architectural practice of Van Heyningen and Haward (see p 143).

Retrace your steps and turn left down **OAKFORD ROAD**, a short, straight road of smaller late-Victorian terraces. The derivation of its name is unknown. Booth in 1898 recorded that none of the houses were in single ownership, but were nevertheless mainly occupied by "clerks and the better class of artisans". At the top end of the street, more post-war flats occupy **No.41**. At **No.34** on the right-hand side, note the colourful tiled porch, possibly original. Further down on the left, at **Nos.7-11**, is brick infill housing with balconies, erected by Camden Council after WWII on a bomb-damaged site. Near

the bottom on the right, **No.2A**, reached under **No.2**, is "The Yard", occupied until the 1970s by the organ builders Temple Wright.

We now regain **LADY SOMERSET ROAD** at its eastern end. Note the differing styles of building, and in particular the rather ugly, large terraced houses– or linked pairs – with mansard roofs, dormers and Tudor-style drip moulding above the windows. They were built in the 1880s. **No.10**, just to your left, is home to the Graigian Society, a team of non-Christian 'monks', who live a unique green lifestyle, campaigning through creative graphics, animation and drama to protect the natural environment and lead people to spiritual fulfilment.

At **No.13,** almost opposite, lived Tammo De Jongh (d.1996), the eccentric portrait painter and mystic. A vigorous campaigner for the local community, he was a founder member of the St Pancras Civic Society, and of his own 'Positive Movement', which defined its philosophy as "pro-human-beings and anti-machine". To launch the Movement in February 1971, a model elephant 12 ft high was wheeled through the streets from Lady Somerset Road to Rhyl Street School in West Kentish Town. His painting, *The Twelve Faces of Humankind*, was used on the cover of King Crimson's 1970 LP, *In the Wake of Poseidon*. Shirley Frost, who lived at the same address, was the founder of another

local campaigning group, Mothers in Action. Living next door at **No.11**, in the 1970s and '80s, was the artist and art-book publisher, Telfer Stokes.

Turn left up Lady Somerset Road, which soon rounds a bend to emerge into **FORTESS ROAD**, along which we turn right, concentrating here on its near (west) side. In Route 9 we shall consider the road's opposite side, and its genesis c.1814 as a new turnpike road, initially named Junction Road.

On the near corner is the **Junction Tavern,** which is listed in the 1874 Directory. The earlier OS map of 1870 does not mark this building as a pub, and also shows the five houses north of the junction as the northern limit of building in the road at that time. The Tavern is now a 'gastropub', with an attractive conservatory and garden running along Lady Somerset Road. To the south of the pub the present **No.95** was first known as Bellina House, when it was a school kept by the wife of a retired missionary, P Litten Randall.

Three doors south, Ivy Lodge (No.4 Bellina Villas) was occupied by 45 nuns, the Sisters of Marie Auxiliatrice. The Sisters arrived in this country in 1870 as refugees from the Franco-Prussian War and came to Ivy Lodge from Southwark in 1871. The order was founded in 1864 to help relieve the poverty brought about by the French Industrial Revolution and was first based in a hostel in Toulouse, where some of the Sisters living in Kentish Town in 1871 had been born. In England, the sisters were asked to help the match girls during their dispute with Bryant & May. The English branch of the order was founded by Marie Dominique Mazzarello (1837–1881) and ten houses were set up in England, but only two remain. Sister Marie was made a saint in 1951 and the Sisters in the Muswell Hill branch recently celebrated the 50th anniversary of her beatification.

Living at No.3 Bellina Villas in 1852 was Joseph Cundall (b.1818), the publisher, book designer and pioneer photographer. Later he was sent to Bayeux by the Government to make the first photographic record of the (so-called) Tapestry. Set in spacious gardens that sloped down towards the west, the Villas were replaced between 1870 and 1894 by a mixture of houses with industrial units built on the lower ground at the back. The arrival of the latter marked the end of this area as a desirable neighbourhood.

On the north corner of the terrace **No.91** is home to the Hellenic Book Service, with knowledgeable staff for those interested in Greek culture. At the start of this century, **No.91A** housed the short-lived Centre for Men's Development, which provided counselling, physiotherapy and other classes.

Next turn right down an unnamed alley between **No.81** and **No.75**. The drive

was built to access the industrial units behind the shops. Down it on the right is **No.79**, now home to the design agency Whitewater Graphics. From 1903 to 1911, Nos.79-81 housed the publishing and supplies department of the Salvation Army before their removal to Judd Street. By 1916, **No.77** (at the far end) was a factory of the piano makers T G Payne & Co (cf. p 136), whose premises embraced Nos.75-81. By the 1930s, as times changed, No.79 was occupied by Fullotone Gramophones Ltd. Demolished No.75 (on the south side) served in Edwardian times as stables of The Omnibus Proprietors Co. Ltd.

Turn left into **Bellina Mews**, a 1990s development replacing an old furniture factory erected in the grounds of Bellina Villas. Walk across the car parking area and leave through the line of bollards. Look ahead to four mews houses, originally built as stables. This is **Fortess Yard**, built at the same time as the industrial buildings. Beyond the mews houses are the grounds of the former vicarage whose entrance is in Burghley Road. Walk up Fortess Yard – a private road – to regain Fortess Road, emerging between Nos.61A and No.65.

Divert briefly to the left to look at the fine fiddles in the window of **No.67**. The flourishing firm Frederick Phelps (Violins) Ltd moved up the road here in 1988, two years after separating from its parent company, Phelps Pianos Ltd. Turn back

southward to **Nos.49&51**, where the latter firm was founded in 1895 by Frederick Phelps to make and sell pianos. Still at the same address, it was one of the few firms to survive the decline of the piano industry in the 20th century. In 1988 Phelps Pianos became part of the Markson Piano Group, and the Markson Music Centre is also based here, offering piano tuition, seminars and master classes and a "Creative Space" for musical events and art exhibitions.

Up for sale in 2004 was double-fronted **No.41**, built about 1860 as the presbytery of the erstwhile neighbouring Roman Catholic chapel, Kentish Town's second. After the suppression of the first – Father Ivers' private mission in Gospel Terrace (p 39) – a new temporary mission chapel, known as Our Lady Help of Christians, was opened in Fortess Road in 1856. Three years later a permanent church (**Fig 7**) was opened, designed by E W Pugin (1834-75), son of the more famous A W N Pugin, pioneer of the Gothic Revival. In 1969 the Catholics swapped this building with the Wesleyans, moving to Lady Margaret Road (p 128) where they now worship. Latterly the Kentish Town Methodist Church, the Fortess Road premises were demolished in 2003 and are now (2004) a building site.

Walk on to where **FORTESS WALK** intersects, running down to Highgate Road. Before Fortess Road was built c.1814 (as Junction Road), Willow Walk was a small lane off the east side of Highgate Road encompassing three sides of a sizeable field named Little Paddock (not to be confused with the much larger 'Little Paddock' further south and to the *west* of the main road shown on Thompson's 1801 map). King's *Panorama* has an excellent view of it. Junction Road cut straight through the paddock, isolating the northern arm of Willow Walk from its other two sides, which now lay east of the new road, and whose fate is described in Route 9 (p 137). The northern arm of Willow Walk retained that name until 1937, when it became Fortess Walk. Before moving, notice on the near corner an 18th-century building painted battleship grey that has somehow managed to survive.

Continue past the **Tally Ho** pub. The 1870 OS map indicates that this was considerably smaller when first built c.1863, with a large triangular open space on its south side. By 1890 the pub had been extended over this area. Note the coloured band of tiling at waist height. The Tally Ho was a rival in flamboyance to the nearby Assembly House (p 124), after the latter had been rebuilt in 1898 as a Victorian gin palace. During the 20th century the pub was developed along Willow Walk so that it now also has a frontage in Highgate Road, with a car park and a garden. Its future is in doubt after a planning application was submitted in 2004 to redevelop the site.

Upon reaching the traffic lights at the junction ahead cross over to the east side of the road and walk south past the Assembly House pub, over Leighton Road to reach Kentish Town station and the end of our walk.

7   The altar of Our Lady Help of Christians Church in 1917 (E W Pugin)

Grove, Green and Common

Circular walk from railway bridge
over Highgate Road
For modern map see inside back cover

This circular walk explores the area around the old village green at the northern end of Kentish Town village. We start from the bus stop north of the railway bridge that carries the Silverlink Metro service from Gospel Oak to Barking above **HIGHGATE ROAD**. Immediately north of the railway bridge, on the west side, is **No.137**, Southampton House. This handsome double-fronted house, with a delicate fanlight above the door, was built in 1820 by James Patterson and served as the Southampton House Academy, a private school for boys. Its headmaster was Rev. John Bickerdike who was here until 1849. In 1828 he charged 24 guineas per annum and advertised that his first two wishes for his pupils were "the fear of God and bodily health". The playground was lost when the railway was built in the 1860s. Next door is the **Southampton Arms**, built out over the front garden of an early-19th-century terraced house. The names of both buildings derive from the fact that land on this side of the road was on Lord Southampton's estate, although the pub sign incorrectly displays the arms of the *City* of Southampton.

Turn left into **WESLEYAN PLACE**. In the 18th century there were regular Methodist meetings of farm workers at the Gospel Oak tree across the fields. The Mortimer family, who farmed the land hereabouts, offered a farm building to the Methodists, who later converted it into their Green Street Chapel. Wesleyan Place, laid out by Richard Mortimer in 1810, marks its location; the congregation moved to Bassett Street, West Kentish Town, in 1864. The Place has a collection of early-19th-century houses. Especially noteworthy are **Nos.1A and Nos.2-4**, a terrace of four stuccoed houses in Greek Revival style. In May and June 1820, the poet John Keats (1795-1821) lodged at No.2, where he suffered haemorrhages from his lung.

Wesleyan Place ends in a buff-brick modern housing estate developed in the late 1980s. Just before it the turning left is **MORTIMER TERRACE**, its name recalling the Mortimer farm. It now leads to coachworks but when first built in 1810 it led south, and beyond the line of the railway, into Carrol Close (then Pleasant Row). The ratepayer of **No.13** in 1820 was the poet, political writer and man of letters Leigh Hunt (1784-1859). As Keats's condition deteriorated, he moved into his mentor Hunt's overcrowded house to be cared for. Here he could look out over the fields of Mortimer's Farm towards his beloved Hampstead. Keats wrote, "I read the greatest part of the day and generally take two half-hour walks a day up and down the terrace which is very much pester'd with cries, ballad singers, and street music." He moved back to Hampstead in August 1820, before his final journey to Italy. Charles Rossiter (1827–1890) later lived at former No.9. A prolific artist who specialised in genre subjects, he exhibited at the Royal Academy from 1852 until 1890. His best-known work is *To Brighton and Back for 3/6*, which is in the City of Birmingham Art Gallery. His wife Frances (née Sears) and his son Francis were also artists. By the end of the 19th century the prospect once enjoyed by Keats was very different: coal drops lined the whole west side of what remained of the Terrace, fed from the adjacent railway by a 'travelling crane'.

Return along Wesleyan Place to **HIGHGATE ROAD** and turn left. The short stretch to the junction with Gordon House Road ahead was earlier called Grove Place, where in 1867 there was another boys' school, Grove House, run by the ominously named Rev. Thomas Tough. Cross at the traffic lights and pause to take in the delightful sylvan prospect up Highgate Road. On this west side once lay The Grove, a series of Georgian mansions set well back from the main road (then

Green Street) and facing what was Kentish Town's linear village green. A chestnut plantation previously occupied the site. Around 1800 The Grove was by far the wealthiest part of Kentish Town village. Today, only No.175 (p 51) remains of this enclave, and that house was built later, in 1818. Many of the 18th-century mansions were pulled down in early Victorian times, to be replaced by Victorian villas, all in their turn now gone.

Just west of the corner ahead of you, at the extreme southern end of The Grove stood the Gordon House Academy, once one of the most famous schools of Kentish Town. It appears on King's *Panorama* (**Fig 8**), and King was himself a pupil here in 1788 when the headmaster, Mr Cooper,

fell dead "of apoplexy" while teaching. Cooper's replacement, Andrew Mensal MA (1764–1841) of King's College, Aberdeen gave the school its Gordon House name. Born in Huntly (Aberdeenshire), he was offered a living by his kinsman, the Duke of Gordon, but decided instead to tramp barefoot to London to seek his fortune. As headmaster, he was said to have walked with his pupils, once a week, to St Chad's Well near present-day King's Cross, to drink its waters, as a means of "keeping the doctor out of the house". He retired in 1817. The school continued over the next 20 years. In 1839 a College for Civil Engineers was opened here and stayed for about 2 years. In the 1840s Gordon House was occupied by the architect Simeon

Thomas Bull (1789–1847), a pupil of George Gwilt. In the later 19th century it was home to a succession of doctors. John Betjeman recalled Gordon House in the early 20th century as being "grim behind its high grey walls".

Next door was to have been a large building, the Emmanuel Hospital, a home for the blind, which burned to the ground in March 1779 before it had opened. The proprietor, Mr Lowe, was arrested on suspicion of arson and put in Liverpool gaol, where he poisoned himself. His body

8 Kentish Town Panorama: Panel 25 from left-hand side to 6. Includes Wesleyan chapel, Gordon House Academy, the ruins of Emmanuel Hospital, and south end of The Grove.

"was ordered to be buried in the crossroads with a stake driven through his body", a rather extreme end for an early insurance fraudster. The ruins of the building are shown on King's *Panorama*. They were replaced by an attractive late-18th-century villa called Ravenswood, which in the 20th century (until WWII) housed the "Medical & Surgical Nursing Home and Nurses' Co-operation [sic]".

Beyond, King's *Panorama* shows two semi-detached properties and what appears to be an imposing early-18th-century house, owned in the early 19th century by a solicitor, John Rose. The *Panorama* has this as the former home of J Suckling, an uncle of Lord Nelson, although no such uncle seems to have existed. The house may have been owned by another uncle, William Suckling, as the latter insured a "messuage, barn, orchard and a garden" in Green Street in 1778, which he left to his widow on his death in 1798. However, while the name Green Street was latterly used for what became Highgate Road in 1864, at an earlier period it was sometimes also used for the whole of the main road through the village (i.e. Kentish Town Road and Highgate Road), so this may refer to William Suckling's house next to the old Castle Tavern (p 81). Mr Rose's house was empty from 1825 to 1842, when it was demolished and a row of villas was built upon its frontage. These included Linden House (at No.1 The Grove),

Haddo House and Bathurst House (No.4), where James Coxeter, the benefactor of the Highgate Road Baptist chapel, lived. Haddo House became a "Home for Working Boys in London" in 1934; its name probably derives from Haddo House (Aberdeenshire), a home for 250 years of the Gordon family. Now covering the site of all these buildings is the **Haddo House Estate**, dating mainly from 1963-65 and designed by Robert Bailie for St Pancras Borough Council. **Haddo House** itself is the 8-storey block of flats facing east, with prominent glazed external staircases, which was featured in architectural journals across the world at the time.

Now turn left along **GORDON HOUSE ROAD**. Named after Mensal's academy, this once ran west, as Gordon House Lane, through Southampton farmland to a convergence of many paths and tracks near the Gospel Oak tree. Widened in 1880, it was renamed as a Road four years later. The first building on the south side (to your left) was once the Gordon House Works of Samuel & Spencer, makers in 1904 of "brewers' signs". Next door stands a simple red-brick chapel, in Early English style, dating from the mid-19th century. The red bricks on its frontage are known to have come from the kiln in Kiln Place, Gospel Oak. Until after WWII the chapel was the local branch of the Catholic Apostolic Church, the Irvingite congregation migrating here

from temporary premises in Prince of Wales Road (p 90). By 1955 the building had become a "daughter church of Kentish Town Parish Church", but subsequently it was not maintained. By 1967, when the Greek Orthodox church began negotiations to acquire it, the church was partially roofless and very dilapidated.

It was restored through donations from the Greek community, and used for conferences and educational purposes until 1971, when services began. The freehold was bought in 1975 and it is now the Greek Orthodox **Church of St Anargyre** (Cosmas & Damianos). Next door is a new infill building, **St Anargyre House**, with an insistent pattern of round-headed windows. This was built in 1996 and includes a large hall for community events plus, since 2002 (when another storey was added), hostel accommodation. There follows a long row of late-19th-century housing with mansard roofs. The poet Tom Pickard was living in Gordon House Road in 1986, then newly appointed as writer in residence to two Sunderland shipyards.

The Haddo House Estate continues opposite. Set back from the road are the two blocks of **Wheatley House** and a block called **Ravenswood**, the latter lining Glenhurst Avenue (p 50) and named after the demolished mansion mentioned above. Facing Gordon House Road, and very noticeable, is **Clanfield** (of 1971), with a bizarre sloping façade and railed balconies at a similar raked angle.

Directly opposite Clanfield, before the railway arrived in the 1860s, a well-established tree-lined footpath led past the foot of the gardens fringing Mortimer Terrace and the grounds of The Retreat (p 38) southwards across the fields to meet Carker's Lane (p 36).

The north side of Gordon House Road remained relatively open well into the 20th century. A garden nursery run by Julius Barko in Victorian times, and later by William Thomas, survived here until at least 1927. A factory was then built at Nos.32&34, serving as the Heath Works of paper merchants D O Evans & Sons, and later of the wallpaper manufacturers John Line & Sons. From 1965 it was occupied by the musical-instrument makers Rose-Morris. Now known as **Spectrum House**, it has a renovated courtyard that is home to a number of firms, but primarily Hawkshead Retail Ltd. At the entrance to the yard beyond Spectrum House are two tall bollards, one inscribed "George IV", suggesting relocation from another part of Camden, the Regent's Park Crown Estate. The yard leads to the SAS Martial Arts Academy and Health Institute, established in 1986. The Kwikfit garage beyond is part of the **Gordon House** business estate.

On the south side, the 1920s 5-storey block with a green pantiled roof is called **Heathview**, although its view of Hampstead Heath is now blocked by the 1970s brick-built flats at the corner of Lissenden Gardens, to which we now cross. Beyond Heathview is a triangular piece of what appears to be wasteland, abutting the railway line. This is actually part of the **Wesleyan Place Nature Reserve**, managed by the London Wildlife Trust and accessed from Mortimer Terrace. Originally a buffer zone to keep the coal dust from the railway off the houses in Gordon House Road, the land is held in perpetuity by a covenant for that purpose. When the land was purchased by the developers Mark Fitzpatrick, local residents successfully lobbied Camden Council to grant the London Wildlife Trust a 10-year lease on part of the site; the rest was used to build the modern flats in Wesleyan Place we saw earlier. The lease ran out in 1997, but has since been renewed annually. Approximately 1 ha. in area, the reserve consists mainly of mature mixed woodland, divided into four sections with different habitats, including 'mini meadow areas' and a pond with wild flowers. The fast-diminishing London sparrow has been spotted flitting among its trees. The site is open once a month.

On the north side, beyond the flats, is the "Gospel Oak Entrance" to Parliament Hill Fields. The lower reaches of the Hill were once known as Salisbury Plain. In the 1840s the Southampton Estate proposed laying out this area with streets and houses, but a concerted campaign eventually led in 1889 to the acquisition of Parliament Hill Fields by the Metropolitan Board of Works as an extension to Hampstead Heath.

Just beyond the entrance is the Parliament Hill Fields Lido, built in 1937-8 by the LCC. Now Listed Grade II, it is but a shadow of its former self. The LCC opened 13 similar open-air pools across London, but this is considered an outstanding example. Fountains at each end, popular with younger swimmers, acted as water aerators.

Ahead lie Gospel Oak Station and two railway bridges carrying the former Tottenham & Hampstead and Hampstead Junction lines across Gordon House Road. We, however, return to and turn left along **LISSENDEN GARDENS**. The 1970s, brick-built flats to your left are known as **Salcombe Lodge**. They stand on a site that was originally a nursery, later replaced by the Defoe Garage, then Lissenden Motors, and finally the Lissenden Works of the British Vacuum Flask Co. Notice in the side wall an old plaque bearing a hand pointing to the Church Lands, which refers to a field of nearly 4 acres (now partly taken by the running track on Parliament Hill Fields) once owned by St Pancras Church but exchanged with Lord Mansfield in 1875 for a field further south in Gospel Oak.

Passing **Chester Court**, look right along **GLENHURST AVENUE**, which was completed in 1912. The name was chosen simply to be attractive to buyers. Referring to Glenhurst Avenue, John Betjeman would later write: "I remember thinking how beautiful the new bits of Metroland Villas were, and my father telling me they were awful".

LISSENDEN GARDENS is lined by tall red-brick Edwardian mansion flats, described by Betjeman in his poem *NW5 and N6* as "red cliffs". Erected from 1900 by the Armstrong family, they were meant to be the latest in fashionable apartments and to encourage a new style of living for Londoners, which never really took off. 'Lissenden' is thought to have been a another 'pretty' invented name. Lissenden Mansions, which begin on your right, we shall encounter later at their far end.

Parliament Hill Mansions are on the left. Over the doorway to **Nos.21-30** is a plaque to Richard Henry Tawney (1880–1962), "economic historian, Christian Socialist and founding father of the Welfare State". The plaque is one of three erected in 2003 by the Lissenden Gardens Tenants' Association, under the Lottery-funded 'Awards for All' scheme. Flat 28 was home for five years after WWI to Tawney and his wife Annette, whom he had married in 1909. In 1916, on the first day of the Somme offensive, Tawney was severely wounded in the chest and abdomen by machine-gun fire, and lay in no man's land for many hours before being rescued. He lived with pain and discomfort for the rest of his life. He was president of the Workers' Education Association and Professor of Economic History at the London School of Economics, and an important contributor to British socialist thinking.

Haydn Wood (1882–1959), the violinist and composer of light music, lived in Flat 25 in 1916. His tune for *Roses of Picardy*, which was published that year, was an immediate hit and earned him a fortune. Flat 40, further up, was home c.1973 to lute maker Stephen Gottlieb and his wife Jane Dorner, a freelance editor. (Sir) John Betjeman, the future poet laureate, was born at Flat 52 on 28 August 1906, in the year that the estate was completed. He was only a baby when his family moved out of NW5 to smarter N6 at No.31 Highgate West Hill. Was it from here or there that he heard "the old North London puff and shunt"? Farther along at Flat 90, Walter Wood (1866–1961), a prominent writer on military history, lived in 1910. Another resident was the German-born Sabine Loeffler (1919–2005), who founded the Lissenden Gardens Tenants Association in 1972 and that year spearheaded the campaign to save Parliament Hill Mansions from redevelopment, persuading Camden Council to buy the blocks and modernise them. A public meeting was held in the tennis courts in the small square at the north end of Lissenden Gardens. The tennis courts must once have been another attraction for prospective buyers of the 'right class'; they were used in 1908 by the Parliament Hill Lawn Tennis Club.

Turn right past **The Cottage**. This once housed the Estate Office and was occupied for many years by Armstrong family members such as Douglas Cave Armstrong, who was listed here in 1926. Beyond The Cottage, turn left and up steps to view, at **Nos.42-51 Clevedon Mansions**, the second of the recently erected plaques, this one dedicated to the composer Martin (Fallas) Shaw OBE (1875–1958), "the quiet revolutionary of English music", who occupied Flat 50 for a few years before WWI. He is best remembered for his music for the hymn *All Things Bright and Beautiful* (1915). In 1908 he became organist at St Mary's, Primrose Hill, whose vicar, Percy Dearmer, became Shaw's ally in his lifelong campaign for better church music. Favouring medieval plainchant and Tudor melodies, Shaw compared sentimental Victorian hymn tunes to overripe bananas. Alice Zimmern (b.1855), the German-Jewish Girton College graduate, suffragist and champion of female education, died in 1939 at Flat 45. She had lived in Lissenden Gardens since Edwardian times, when she had occupied No.41 Parliament Hill Mansions.

Follow Clevedon Mansions as they

round the corner into the northern arm of L-shaped Lissenden Gardens. The actor George Merritt (1890–1977), who appeared in over 120 films over four decades, more often than not in the role of a policeman, was living here in Flat 4 in 1967, in which year he made TV guest appearances in both *The Avengers* and *The Prisoner*. Flat 11 was home in 1983 to James Hanley, the Dublin-born novelist and friend of John Cowper Powys, who a decade earlier had lived at Flat 51

in **Lissenden Mansions**. The latter's northeast end now lines the opposite side of the street. Along on the right, at **Nos.11-20**, is the third 'Awards for All' plaque, to the painter Anthony Green, a distinguished Royal Academician with an international reputation who occupied Flat 17 for 50 years (1939–1990), until he and his family moved to the country.

The Nordoff-Robbins Music Therapy Centre lies behind **Nos.1-10** at **No.2** Lissenden Gardens in a converted former

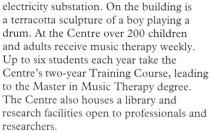

electricity substation. On the building is a terracotta sculpture of a boy playing a drum. At the Centre over 200 children and adults receive music therapy weekly. Up to six students each year take the Centre's two-year Training Course, leading to the Master in Music Therapy degree. The Centre also houses a library and research facilities open to professionals and researchers.

In front of the Centre is the sole remnant of the houses in The Grove. This double-fronted house dating from 1818, now **No.175 Highgate Road**, was formerly No.5, Clifton Lodge. In the mid-1970s it was converted into flats, and is now owned by the Nordoff-Robbins Centre. Notice how this house, like others in The Grove, was set well back from the main road. Neighbouring houses, pulled down in the building of the Lissenden Gardens estate, included No.6 (Ivy House), still occupied in 1900 by Alfred William Armstrong, whose family developed the mansion flats; and Clevedon House at No.8, which lent its name to Clevedon Mansions. For several years after his marriage in 1847, the latter was home to the poet, essayist and British Museum librarian Coventry Patmore (1823-1896), best known for *The Angel in the House*, a poetic treatment of married love. His attractive and talented

9 Leafy Highgate Road, looking south towards railway bridge, c.1906.

51

wife Emily, eventually the mother of six, also wrote, under the pseudonym Mrs Motherly. Patmore later recalled a "small party" at The Grove, where there were only three guests: Ruskin, Tennyson and Browning.

Just to the north of Lissenden Gardens once lay the 18th-century mansion occupied by Thomas Cartwright Slack, a wealthy sugar baker, who founded the National School in Monte Video Place (p 67). On King's *Panorama* his sad fate is related – in 1815 he and his servant perished in a house fire attempting to save his young son, who was rescued by the courageous Lewis Wiber. The latter was rewarded with £600 from a subscription raised by local inhabitants. Slack's neighbours lived in a row of large Georgian houses whose sites are now taken by Parliament Hill School (see below). In one of them was Miss Hanwell's Establishment for Young Ladies, which King says was "of long standing for respectability and excellent management".

Retrace your steps and turn right to regain **HIGHGATE ROAD**, by the K2 telephone box on the corner, shaded by a chestnut tree that is probably a remnant of the former plantation (**Fig 9**, p 51). Opposite is the splendid Grove Terrace whose Grade-II Listed houses are set back behind a vestige of old Kentish Town Green. We shall visit it later (p 56).

Turn left up the west side of Highgate Road and pass the campus of **Parliament Hill School** (PHS), which opened here in September 1914 as a County Secondary School for Girls, after its move from Ingestre Road (p 148), where it had been founded in 1906. Akin to a grammar school, with an entrance examination and a well qualified staff, PHS gained a high reputation for teaching in both arts and science (**Fig 10**). By 1934, any girl not awarded her School Certificate by the age of 16 was required to stay on for a further year. In 1956 Dame Edith Evans opened a range of new school buildings. 425 pupils were then joined by 394 more girls from local schools; a roll of 1,350 was planned. PHS still retains much of its former prestige, designated now as both a 'Beacon School' and a 'Technology College'. To the north is the voluntary-aided **William Ellis School**. Founded in October 1862 as the Gospel Oak Schools in Rochford Street, this moved to Allcroft Road two years later when its first site was needed by the Midland Railway, and then here to Highgate Road in 1937. William Ellis (1800–1881) founded some ten schools, all of which used a method that eschewed learning by rote, but only this one survives. During WWII both schools formed part of the North London Emergency Secondary School. Today the PHS girls and William Ellis boys share a joint sixth form.

The William Ellis driveway follows the line of 19th-century Grove Farm Lane.

A little way along it, off its south side and thus on the PHS site, stood a large house called The Gothic, home to Sir James Williams (according to King) and later to Thomas Glover. By Edwardian times it had been renamed Gothic Hall and was occupied by Rev. A S Kroenig-Ryan, the vicar of St Martin's (Gospel Oak), and his wife who ran a ladies' school in their home. In front of the house King shows a hollow tree, used until 1794 as a "high-water fountain mark", from which water gushed whenever the Hampstead Ponds reached extreme high-water level. Fifty years later, the New River Company unsuccessfully sank a 533-ft well here; and in 1855 a very deep bore of some 1300 ft also produced no water. However, a New River Company reservoir, labelled as the "Artesian Well Water Works" on Stanford's map of 1862, and shown as "disused" by the end of that decade, lay beside the main road just to the north of Grove Farm Lane. A track bounding this site on the west, and known in 1869 as Driftway, is now the pathway leading diagonally into Parliament Hill Fields from the Hampstead Heath entrance, next left. In February 2004 a huge hole appeared near here in Highgate Road, accompanied by flooding, probably linked to the various earlier water features in this area.

Opposite The Gothic, on the north side of the Lane, and so on the William Ellis site, was the farmhouse of Grove Farm, described by King as 130 acres farmed by Edward Austin. In 1884 William Boucher, "dairyman and grazier", was still grazing his cows on the slopes of Parliament Hill. The land here was known well into the 1830s as The Common, as was the adjacent stretch of Highgate Road. The land by then lay in the southeast corner of Lord Mansfield's Kenwood estate. Based near here in 1906 were the Mansfield Rifle Club and the Mansfield Bowling Club; the latter retained its name when, presumably

to make way for the PHS, it relocated to Croftdown Road, which lies opposite.

After another 100 metres, and beyond the old reservoir site, we pass another entrance to Hampstead Heath, leading to the Parliament Hill Fields cafeteria and the bandstand from which Betjeman recalled hearing "silver music". The path lies on the line of a lane known in 1869 as Churchland Way, which led west to the St Pancras Church Lands (p 49). The present stretch of Highgate Road, bordering the

Heath, is lined with plane trees, whose bobbles the young John Betjeman longed to touch as he travelled on the open-topped tram on his way home to Highgate West Hill. The café at the present bus terminus at the foot of the hill was used as a waiting room for LCC trams in the 1930s.

Cross over to the **Duke of St Albans** pub (on the corner of Swains Lane, Highgate). This is the last (or the first) building in Kentish Town and a pub has been here since the mid-19th century, when it was owned by Watney, Combe & Reid. It was rebuilt between 1953 and 1955 along with the northern part of St Alban's Villas (Nos.10-14 on this side of St Alban's Road ahead and No.9 on the road's southern corner).

The Villas took their name from the pub, and indirectly from a sometime occupant of Holly Lodge, just up the hill in Highgate. In 1827 the 9th Duke of St Albans became the second husband of Harriet Mellon, a former actress of Irish peasant stock, and 24 years his senior. Her first husband had been Thomas Coutts, an elderly wealthy banker who lived at Holly Lodge and from whom, on his death, she inherited a fortune. The Duchess of St Albans herself died in 1837, leaving her estate to a granddaughter of

10   Parliament Hill County Secondary School: girls in chemistry laboratory, 1920s

her first husband, Angela Burdett, who was ennobled in 1871 and whom we remember as the philanthropic millionairess Baroness Burdett-Coutts (1814–1906). In 1850 the latter purchased the Kentish Town House estate whose western boundary fronted Highgate Road here.

This estate lay on land that was known in the 15th century as Deaconsfield and two centuries later as Dicas Field. It was copyhold land of Cantelowes Manor, once owned by William Bruges and later by the Ive family. In the 16th century John Draper, citizen and brewer of London, had his home here. In about 1777 the London solicitor, Gregory Bateman, built himself a grand mansion called Kentish Town House. It had an ornamental water garden fed by the River Fleet. Building costs apparently ruined the lawyer – the house was nicknamed 'Bateman's Folly'. A few years later, it was occupied by Robert Milligan, promoter of the West India Docks, who may have enlarged it, and then by Philip Hurd, a rich lawyer and bibliophile who was here until 1831. He kept deer in the grounds and ran an up-to-date dairy and piggeries. The house was demolished in 1850 shortly after Lady Burdett-Coutts purchased the estate, which adjoined her Highgate properties. St Alban's Villas were then laid out as was St Alban's Road, but we defer discussion of this and other roads developed on the Burdett-Coutts estate until the forthcoming *Streets of Highgate*.

Return south down Highgate Road, crossing over St Alban's Road, and pass **Nos.1-6 Oak Court**, linked, semi-detached villas with pilasters and heavily rusticated ground floors, before pausing at a pair of mid-19th-century semi-detached houses, **Nos.1&2 St Alban's Villas.** These eight houses together were originally numbered 1-8 St Alban's Villas. No.2 was once home to Paul Robeson (1898–1976), the Black American singer, actor and political activist. He lived here from 1938 until the outbreak of WWII, with his wife Essie (Eslanda). The international superstar was at that time much involved locally, as patron of the West African Students' Union in Camden Square, and performing gratis at the left-wing Unity Theatre in Somers Town as an ordinary member of the cast. At No.4 St Alban's Villas lived Thomas Idris, Mayor of St Pancras 1903-04 and founder of the famous soft drinks company whose works were in Royal College Street, Camden Town and in Whitcher Place (p 61).

Beyond is the imposing building of **La Sainte Union** (des Sacrés Coeurs), a convent school founded in Camden Street in 1861 by nuns sent to London from the Order's headquarters at Douai in Northern France. Outgrowing their cramped Camden Town premises, they purchased Charlton House in 1864, converting it into a Roman Catholic boarding school for girls. A north wing was added in 1869, and a south wing in 1892, when the original façade was also renewed, creating the building we see today. Note the crucifixion in the cartouche above the first entrance, the Holy Family scene by the main door, the two bleeding hearts in roundels, and the 2nd-floor Diocletian window surmounted by a broken pediment containing a statue of Christ. During WWII many of the girls were evacuated to Bath, though some stayed behind. A barrage balloon hovered above the school, which suffered some bomb damage. The 7 acres of grounds originally acquired with Charlton House were used in the late 19th century not only for vegetable gardening but also to keep cows, pigs and poultry. They also offered plenty of room for later expansion, including the building in 1956 of a new junior school (behind), now named Debrabant Wing, after Jean Baptiste Debrabant, who founded the Order in 1828. LSU today is a voluntary-aided RC comprehensive school for girls, specialising in science.

Charlton House had been home to Henry Bessemer (1813-98), the inventor and pioneer of efficient steel production, who in 1846 took a 14-year lease on two earlier buildings on the site, which he renamed Charlton House after the village in Hertfordshire where he was born. In the larger of the two houses had lived the sugar merchant John Ernest Grobb and his descendants, while the adjoining smaller house had been home to the Browell family, before the then famous actor Joseph Shepherd Munden (1758–1832) took up residence in 1813. He was a leading light in village life and chaired a Harmonic Society which met in the Assembly House.

He was said to have turned miserly, which may explain why he moved to this smaller house from the much larger **Croft Lodge**, beyond La Sainte Union, of which it is now a part.

Croft Lodge is a large, double-fronted late-18th-century house, remodelled and extended in the mid-19th century. It is shown on King's *Panorama* as occupied by the thespian Kemble family; they may have stayed there as friends of Munden. In 1912 the convent school bought Croft Lodge and adapted it for use as classrooms and sleeping accommodation. During WWII it was occupied by the RAF. As one Sister recalled, the airmen's training included pretending to shoot at the nuns in the school garden.

Croft Lodge gave its name to Croftdown Road, crossing which we reach the flats of **Highcroft** on the far corner. This was built on the site of Sidney House, shown on King's *Panorama* as a "pretty Villa" but incorrectly labelled as the house of the actor Joseph Munden, who (see above) actually lived in Croft Lodge. In the 1950s Sidney House was home to a member of the Shand-Kydd family (p 37), before it was demolished to be replaced by the present block. A few steps farther on are the remains of an old wall, bowing and in poor condition, which may well be part of the garden wall of old Sidney House. It stands beside a 3-storey terraced row called **Nos.1-3 Hillside**, built in 1884. Next to this is the 19th-century incarnation of the **Bull and Last** pub (**Fig 11**), which was licensed in 1721 as Ye Last. In 1763, a patrol left here at 7 pm each evening for

11 1960s drinkers in the Bull and Last, with a mural drawn from an 1820 engraving.

Great Ormond Street, to escort pedestrians along roads then haunted by highwaymen and footpads. The derivation of the pub's name is unclear. Some suggest that this was the last inn on the road north before the steep climb to Highgate, although a Cow & Hare hostelry, predating the Bull and Last, once stood at the very foot of Highgate (West) Hill. Or was it, perhaps, the last port of call for the waggoners and drovers from the country before they reached London?

Pause here at the corner of **WOODSOME ROAD**, for which see Route 10. This western end of the road was begun in 1870 over the outbuildings of the Bull and Last pub across from us. In that year **Nos.1A-5A** were built by Robert Smerdon. All these houses were in use as shops until quite recently. A resident of **No.2A** was the rock guitarist Gary Moore, and the radio and TV presenter Chris Evans lived at **No.16**.

The only business remaining in the next block on the main road is **No.31 GROVE TERRACE**, now a fitness centre. A basement stretches under No.31 as far back as the alley behind (old College Lane).

The houses beyond, lying obliquely to Highgate Road, stand by the site of a preparatory school run in 1799 by Miss Browell, a member of the Browell family who lived on the site of La Sainte Union that we passed earlier. For nearly half a

century from 1826 the school was run by Angelica, and then Sophie, Mainstone. It has been written that the school was demolished when these houses were built c.1870. In fact, the original building survives behind as **No.28** and its 17 windows facing the Terrace (as depicted on King's *Panorama*, **Fig 12**) can be viewed from the alley running from Grove Terrace to Woodsome Road (part of the old cartway which continues south as College Lane, see p 41). It is possible that this building is of even greater antiquity, as there is a building shown on roughly this site on the 1638 map of "the River of Wells").

We now reach the impressive main stretch of **GROVE TERRACE**, set back from Highgate Road. Many of its houses retain their wooden doorcases and Doric columns, radial fanlights and panelled doors; and some their cast-iron balconies. The railings and lampholders are also Listed, and even the manhole covers are worth a look. In 1772 the Dartmouth estate obtained permission to enclose the common land fronting the highway (this was later bought by St Pancras Borough in 1903). The developers of Grove Terrace, an urban terrace in the countryside, were thus able to provide rights of way to the main road. The first houses, Nos.18-27 at the north end, were built by 1780, erected and owned by John Cheeke, a carpenter of Drury Lane, who later owned the Bull and

Last pub nearby. They were first known as Cheeke's Row. Cheeke died in 1794 and his widow married Richard Cooke, a stonemason who completed Kentish Town Terrace (as it was known until the mid-19th century) soon after 1800. Nos.1-5 at the south end were the last to be built. Cooke himself lived grandly at the largest house, **No.14**, until he moved to premises at the rear of the terrace. A later occupant (1862–1865) of this house was Ford Madox Brown (see also p 135).

The furniture maker Thomas Seddon (c.1793-1864) died at his home at **No.27**. He was the father of the painter of the same name who was a close friend of Ford Madox Brown. **No.24** was home to Ken Loach (b.1936), the left-wing TV and film director who created *Cathy Come Home* and *Up the Junction*; he was living here in 1970, the year of his second feature film, *Kes*. At **No.23**, up until the 1980s a regular sight to be seen was that of Mrs Pollyrodgers and her daughter coming and going through the front door on horseback. Presumably this was the only way they could get to the stable in their garden. At **No.22** the engraver Charles Grignion the Elder (1717–1810) lived from 1799 until his death in 1810. He had a long and extensive career as an engraver, studying under Gravelot and employed by Hogarth. Most of his work was book illustration. He fell on hard times as an old man and a subscription was raised to support him and his family in 1807; his destitution was one of the reasons behind the foundation of the Artists' Benevolent Fund in the year he died. Grignion was living in the area before moving here – he was a St Pancras churchwarden and as such was cited in the 1788 lawsuit that the Vestry won against the Trustees when the latter sold off the site of the old Kentish Town Chapel for secular use. His wife Mary was robbed on the Hampstead stagecoach in January 1773; at the Old Bailey trial of the highwaymen involved, she said "I have been robbed so often lately that I was not frightened at the time", a reminder of the danger of travelling to and from Kentish Town in the 18th century.

Beyond No. 22 a leafy, gravel path leads to garages and, over to the left, **GROVE TERRACE MEWS**, secluded 1950s houses. At No.1 Grove Terrace Mews the architect Michael Powers, who designed the choir school in the shadow of St Paul's Cathedral, was living in the 1980s. Next to the path, **No.21** has a covered balcony. The first occupant of **No.18**, from 1793 to 1816, was William Inwood (c.1771–1843), the architect of many churches, including the New St Pancras Church on Euston Road. At **No.12** in the 1960s and '70s lived the Labour MP (Sir) Kenneth Robinson, Health Minister under Harold Wilson, perhaps best remembered for initiating the first post-Wolfenden debate on the legalisation of male gay sex. **No.6** was home in 1954-67 to the artist Kate Beard.

Nos.1-5 were the last houses to be built, as South Terrace. At **No.5** from 1937 lived the painter Mark Gertler, born (1891) in Spitalfields of Jewish extraction and later a member of the London Group. Depressed by long illness, a failing marriage and a poorly received exhibition, he gassed himself in his studio at No.5 in 1939.

Continue past Dartmouth Park Road into a stretch of footway, part of the College Lane–Grove Terrace continuum, once known as South Grove and now officially Grove End. Past Lynton Villa and Cumberland Villa (**Nos.154&152 Highgate Road**) is Grove End House at **No.150**, a splendid Grade-II-Listed, late-18th-century villa. This was one of three houses purchased in 1874 by James Coxeter (1813–1902), a maker of surgical instruments and artificial limbs who lived not quite opposite, in The

12 Kentish Town Panorama: Panel 2 from 4 ("a pretty villa once occupied by the comedian Munden") to 6 (beginnings of Grove Terrace). 5, the Bull and Last.

Grove. Grove End House was home from c.1884 to the stained-glass painter John Burlison (cf. p 106). It was built over the site of two imposing properties shown in King's *Panorama*. One of these mansions belonged from 1761 to the Woodfall family; Henry Woodfall was the proprietor of the *Morning Advertiser*. His widow Mary died here in April 1782.

Ahead, on the southwest corner of Chetwynd Road, stood the second of Coxeter's acquisitions, Grove End Villa. This he donated to the London Baptist Association, who demolished it and in 1878 erected in its place their **Highgate Road Chapel**. Built in Kentish ragstone, it was designed by the cousins F C Satchell and R C Edwards. Note its large Decorated west window, and the row of side windows in similar style. In 1974, the chapel, still Baptist, was affiliated to the Fellowship of Independent Evangelical churches and has latterly also housed the delightfully named Tadpole Nursery. It contains a 6-ft-deep marble baptism pool, but at the time of writing there are plans to redevelop the building to include 12 residential units.

Cross over Chetwynd Road to the chapel and walk down **COLLEGE LANE**, a continuation of the footpath encountered in Route 2 (p 41). South of the Chapel is an early-19th-century detached house known as **Grove End Lodge**, the third of James Coxeter's purchases. This became

the Manse of the Highgate Road Chapel, as well as serving in Edwardian times as a Home & Institute of the YWCA. South of this, in 1799, stood a short-lived French academy, run by a Monsieur Jollie, who regularly had his pupils dress in French uniforms and then drilled them in military style. The academy was probably in the building that came to be known in the 19th century as St John's Park House, which then housed another school and which was pulled down after 1850. In the 16th century the land on which it stood was part of the Cholmondely estate; Sir Hugh Cholmondely (d.1601) owned a house in Green Street, which may well have been here.

The Council flats of present-day **Denyer House** were built in the 1930s at the same time as the York Rise Estate (p 147) behind them. Councillor C H Denyer was Mayor of St Pancras in 1934-35 and the editor of *St Pancras Through the Centuries*. In 2000, part of the Madness video for *Drip Fed Fred* was filmed, with Ian Dury, in a 'bunker' behind Denyer House. The block covers the site of a large house known as St John's Farm House, which had 19 acres of land. This marked the northern limit of the estate owned by St John's College, Cambridge, that extended from here to Leighton Road and east to Brecknock Road. King shows the house as occupied by William Minshull, "a county magistrate of high respectability",

who leased or owned much of the land locally and to whom a monument was erected in Kentish Town Church. The building had previously been occupied in the 1790s by Meyer Cohen, a wealthy Jewish stockbroker. He was the father of the eminent historian Sir Francis Palgrave (1788–1861), who was born here in Green Street. As a child, he translated *The Battle of the Frogs and Mice*, then erroneously attributed to Homer, from the Latin version into French, which his father had published as "par François Cohen de Kentish Town, âgé de huit ans" in 1797. Upon marriage, he adopted his mother-in-law's maiden name. He was deputy keeper of the reorganised Record Office, and local historians have him to thank for thwarting official plans to destroy the decennial returns by census enumerators. His antiquarian interests led him to edit with scrupulous accuracy, and publish, a number of historical records, and he greatly promoted the study of medieval English history. Palgrave died at his house in Pond Street, Hampstead.

From Denyer House walk the few paces west to Highgate Road. We are back at our starting point, with buses running south down Highgate Road or west along Gordon House Road.

Route 4
The Camden estate

Circular walk from Camden Road station
For modern map see back cover

Beginning at Camden Road station, this circular walk takes us through the northernmost part of the Camden estate in the former manor of Cantelowes, which came to the Pratt family through the marriage of Charles Pratt (1714–1794), 1st Earl Camden, to Elizabeth, daughter of Nicholas Jeffreys. The estate was not developed until the 19th century and most of the streets were then listed as being in Camden Town, although today this area is considered by many to be a part of Kentish Town.

If alighting from a Silverlink Metro train at **Camden Road station**, walk down to street level (you can also approach the station by walking from Camden Town Tube station up Camden Road). The railway line, intended as a link to the Docks from the main London & Birmingham line terminus at Chalk Farm, was authorised in August 1846 by the East and West India Docks and Birmingham Junction Railway Act. The line, with its improbably long name, was eventually opened in 1850 and was alternatively known as 'The Camden Town Railway'. It was renamed the North London

Railway, once a further link had been made into the City, in 1853 – the same year the 'Camden Town' station here, a small wooden building built on the site of watercress beds, was renamed Camden Road.

When the line was widened, the station was replaced by the present building, which opened on 7 December 1870 and reverted to its original name, Camden Town. Designed by Edwin Henry Horne in a restrained Italian Romanesque style, it is the only survivor of several similar stations by him on the North London line. The station was again given its current name, Camden Road, in June 1950.

Under the railway bridge (round to the left) is an old drinking fountain set in the wall, now very much disused. It was erected in 1870 when a larger, freestanding fountain a few steps away in Camden Broadway – a neo-Gothic affair designed by the stained-glass artists Clayton and Bell – was removed. Camden Broadway was the name once given to the triangular space we reach across Royal College Street under a second, now defunct, railway bridge. The Broadway was formed by the junction of two main roads: Great College Street (as Royal College Street was then known) and Camden Road. A third road, Brecknock Street, when first projected, would have formed the straight, northern side of a larger triangular space. As developed,

Brecknock Street ended in Great College Street, at the point now covered by the large doors (just past advertising hoardings) of former station offices. The offices were built when the viaduct and the station were enlarged in 1870; Brecknock Street was then diverted to emerge in Camden Road by the side of the station at the start of our walk and renamed Bonny Street. The offices were used from 1930 for half a century by the tobacconists A Brilliant and more recently as a café bar, which has closed.

Cross over **ROYAL COLLEGE STREET** to the buildings opposite. The only houses in Camden Broadway were this still extant terrace of four, built in the early 1840s and from the first containing shops. In the 1850s to the left alongside them was built Broadway Terrace, of which two houses (**Nos.190&192**) remain. These houses were all renumbered as part of Great College Street in 1866. From the 1890s the long-established firm of piano manufacturers Eungblut (by then amalgamated with Rogers) had a base at **No.186**, expanding as far as **No.180** after its main works in Plender Street were destroyed by fire in June 1905. The firm was taken over by the Kemble Piano Group (now part of Yamaha) in the 1930s. **No.188** was the offices of the *St Pancras Gazette* in the late Victorian and Edwardian periods.

To your right turn the corner and

continue up **CAMDEN ROAD**. Authorised by an Act of 1824 and begun a year later, this was built as part of a turnpike road linking the West End with the Great North Road. It was known initially as the 'New Road to Tottenham', and for a while as the 'Holloway Road'. The villas and terraces that soon lined it were not officially numbered as part of Camden Road until October 1864, after tolls had been removed. In 1872, the rails of the London Street Tramways Co. arrived in Camden Road, and were extended along its whole length during that year; the service was electrified in April 1909.

The first row of terraced houses on this (west) side, **Nos.57-73**, originally Nos.13-21 Brecknock Place, was completed in the 1840s, and the houses appear to have always been used as shops. The name Brecknock recalls Brecknock Priory (in Powys), the home of Elizabeth Jeffreys, wife of the 1st Earl Camden. Note the iron balcony on the first floor of **No.65** and the Irish bar called Father Ted's at **No.69**. The last house in the row, **No.75**, was originally No.13 Brecknock Crescent. This was the first building in an adjoining row of houses which used to face the King's Road, now St Pancras Way (ahead), in a shallow arc. This can be discerned by walking past the low addition housing a café (**No.75a**) and looking back at the edge of the building. King's Road was the medieval lane from Gray's Inn to Kentish Town.

By the corner of St Pancras Way is the post-war **Bernard Shaw Court**. It lies on the site of Nos.14-28 Brecknock Crescent (subsequently Nos.163-187 King's Road), and a fence at the rear preserves the old curved line. This northern arm of Brecknock Crescent was built in the early 1840s by the builders John Cumberland and John Greenwood. In 1851 Charles Mackay (1814-1889) was living at No.21 with his family and two servants. He had worked as a journalist with Dickens at the *Morning Chronicle* and had recently moved back to London from his native Scotland to join the *Illustrated London News*, whose editor he later became. At this period Mackay was assisting Mayhew in looking at the condition of the working class in England and Wales and was writing poetry about cholera outbreaks. His poetry was set to music by his friend Henry Russell and one song sheet, *The Good Time Coming*, sold over 400,000 copies.

Just past this junction Camden Road continued to run through open fields until the 1840s when George Pratt, 2nd Marquis Camden, began to develop a new suburb called Camden New Town. The Kentish Town Act of 1813 had empowered the 1st Marquis to sell building leases throughout his local estate. Over the next 30 years, individual plots of land were progressively leased through Lord Camden's agent, Joseph Kay, to various speculative builders. Most of the estate

was sold off by the 4th Marquis at the end of WWI. Here we explore the southwest corner of the 'New Town', which lay mostly on the eastern side of Camden Road, and focused on Camden Square.

Cross over St Pancras Way, and look left along it to a large 1930s block, **No.100 St Pancras Way**, which stretches behind to Rochester Place and is now home to Camden Council's Environment Department. The main entrance is stuccoed, with an anthemion frieze. The block was built over semi-detached villas called Camden Cottages, erected here in the early 1820s and quite select at the time. No.100 was the main London works of scientific instrument makers Hilger, founded by the German optical technicians Adam and Otto Hilger in 1874. The firm moved here in 1902 when they were based at the then No.75a Camden Road (site of present No.79), slowly acquiring properties behind it facing King's Road and Rochester Place. Before WWI they developed methods for spectrochemical analysis and processed synthetic crystals in house. They forged many international links and sold equipment worldwide. By WWII the company had a reputation as one of the foremost optical and precision instrument makers in the world. In 1948 they amalgamated with the metrology instrument manufacturer E R Watts and became known as Hilger & Watts. The company moved to Margate in 1968.

Continue along Camden Road, past **No.79**, a rather ugly 1960s block housing the HQ of Camden Social Services and offices of the Camden Primary Care Trust. Beyond Rochester Place are 3-storey yellow-brick flats, **Nos.81&83**, built in 1980. These cover the site of four original villas, including former Nos.77&79, taken over by Hilger in the early 20th century for another of their works, and the original No.81, which from 1917 to 1920 was home to the painter Walter Sickert; a certain Dick Whittington was living here before WWI.

Walk past the Nissan dealer that stands at the foot of a low-rise tower block (**Nos.85-89**) and cross over Rochester Road. We now come to red-brick **Cherry Tree Court**, a sheltered housing scheme built in the early 1980s and run by Circle 33 Housing Association. Many of its 23 places are taken by Greek Cypriot residents. We then pass two pairs of original semi-detached villas **Nos.95&97**, and behind a tall brick wall, **Nos.99&101**, before reaching the gated entrance between **Ann Stephenson House** and **Denys Holland Lodge**. Here turn left to go into a quiet enclave of brick and concrete buildings, which are halls of residence of University College London (UCL). Facing us is **Ifor Evans Hall** (1968), named after the then provost of UCL and to the left the more recent **Neil Sharp Block**: this and Ann Stephenson House fronting Camden

Road each provide accommodation for around 300 students.

Returning to Camden Road, turn left past the fence that encloses the back of a red-brick building, part of the Camden School for Girls (p 123). This was built over the site of No.119, Tower House, a once impressive detached villa with its own coach entrance to the side and large gardens behind. The original semi-detached stuccoed pair beyond at **Nos.123-125** has Ionic porches and is Listed. The architect H H Bridgman was living at No.125 during the 1870s and 1880s when designing a number of buildings in the Camden Town area, including the Mother Redcap (now renamed the World's End) and the St Pancras Workhouse in the King's Road.

Now retrace your steps to the wide Rochester Road, turn right along it and shortly right again into the eastern arm of cobbled **ROCHESTER MEWS**. Before 1886 the road was often called Rochester Road Mews. Here there is a selection of interesting mews houses. The end house, **No.20**, is an architect's conversion completed in 1994. A two-storey workshop on the site was demolished, the party wall was underpinned, and a new basement was built before a replica of the original house was constructed above, complete with a cedar-clad roof terrace.

This arm of Rochester Mews now ends at the UCL buildings we saw earlier but

once continued parallel to Camden Road as mews. Left of the gates a private road runs beside the buildings of **Max Rayne House** (begun in 1968 and extended in 1980) whose name recalls the property tycoon and philanthropist (d.2003) who studied law at the college. Opposite Max Rayne House are three small buildings erected in the mid-1990s on land taken from the gardens of houses in Rochester Road. The private road was once Whitcher Place, named after John Whitcher of Camden Road, who in 1864 took a 60-year lease on a plot of land (the present site occupied by UCL) then described as "garden ground, coach house and stables". When first developed in the 1860s the site was laid out as Whitcher & Searles Nursery; its four glasshouses can be seen on the 1870 OS map. Shortly before 1900 the ground was covered over with a laundry and other industrial buildings; and, until 1933, a bus garage of British Automobile Traction Co., whose green 'British' buses ran on the busy Route 24 (Pimlico to Hampstead Heath). Idris, the firm famed for its sparkling mineral water, leased a factory at Nos.1-8 from 1899 and took over the laundry building as well in 1905; they were here until WWI. A yard at No.6 was leased in 1936 to the tile manufacturers W B Simpson & Sons, whose earlier work had included the fitting out of the Holborn Restaurant.

Return to the corner of Rochester Road.

Rochester Mews continues opposite, but we turn right into the Rochester Conservation Area, designated in 2001, which comprises Rochester Road and Terrace and parts of both Wilmot Place and Rochester Place. All the roads here were first laid out in the 1840s. The Rochester name derives from the marriage of Harriet Murray, daughter of the Bishop of Rochester, to George Pratt, the 2nd Marquis Camden.

ROCHESTER ROAD dates mainly from 1848. The four houses on our left are slightly earlier (1846-47) and were collectively called Rochester Villas until renumbered as **Nos.56-59** in 1886. George Joseph Evans, the Victorian wood engraver, lived at No.57 from 1895 to 1901. The houses on the right-hand side at this end of the road are tall, boasting quite grand stairways up to the entrances, with stucco surrounds, and some have original iron balconies and railings, particularly delicate on **Nos.6&8**. No.6 houses the Woodentots Montessori Nursery, established in 1989, with room for 12 children at any one time. The school uses teaching methods developed by Maria Montessori in early-20th-century Rome, which aim to bring out the personality of each child and let them develop at their own pace. The first resident of **No.9** was Edward Hacker, registrar of births and deaths and a line engraver of animal subjects. He was the father of the London painter Arthur Hacker RA (1858–1919), who was born at this address.

At its far end, Rochester Road joins Kentish Town, but access from the latter has been blocked off so that it is relatively quiet. Dominating the road is a large public central park, recently re-landscaped, complete with a children's play area and plenty of trees and flowering shrubs. The buildings facing the park are a mixture of terraced and semi-detached houses with the occasional detached house, and all have well-stocked front gardens. The central section on the right, **Nos.17-22**, is a row of post-war housing. Behind it is another children's playground laid out over a garage that was built at the end of Whitcher Place in the interwar period. **Nos.23-32** are five original houses grouped in pairs. The former house at **No.33** was built in 1851 by Charles Crane (p 67) but was replaced with unsympathetic 1950s infill, its façade now heavily disguised by a climbing plant. Containing flats, it has for some time had the alternative name of The Leys.

At this point cross over the road and turn left along **ROCHESTER TERRACE**, which enters Rochester Road at an angle by the side of the park. The houses in this street are slightly later, dating from the early 1850s and developed primarily by the builder John Darlington. At this end there are a few post-war houses and apartment blocks, but the road comprises mainly large three-storey Victorian semis, stuccoed on the ground floors and all facing the park. At **No.9** there is a blue plaque dedicated in 1986 to 'Father' Henry Willis (1821–1901). Willis built no fewer than 2000 organs during his career, including those at the Great Exhibition of 1851 (later used in Winchester Cathedral); St George's Hall, Liverpool; the Royal Albert Hall; and St Paul's Cathedral, as well as many smaller ones for country churches. Locally, a Willis organ can be seen at St Luke's (p 105) and there is a magnificent specimen at St Dominic's Priory, Southampton Road. His factory (p 64) was behind his house, in Rochester Place, which we shall visit later. From 1898 he was nicknamed Father Willis (in imitation of the 17th-century organ builder Father Smith) when he was assisted by his two sons. The firm of Willis & Sons, although no longer family-owned, is still building organs. Italianate **Nos.5&6** are the only examples of this style in the Conservation Area. The engineer Eugenius Birch (1818-84), who lived at No.6 in the 1850s and 1860s, was the most celebrated designer of Victorian seaside piers. The ill-fated West Pier at Brighton is his most famous creation, but he designed no fewer than 13 others in England and Wales, some still extant, such as Eastbourne and Bournemouth. He developed a screw piling technique that was widely copied for other piers during the 1860s. Birch also designed the first recreational aquarium in England, which opened in Brighton in 1872. Mike Brearley OBE was living in Rochester Terrace at the time he captained the England cricket team (1977-1981). He was the first to lead England to five wins in an Ashes series.

Rochester Terrace ends in **WILMOT PLACE**. This was the first street in the Conservation Area to be finished, this end dating from 1846. Bebbington says the road was named after the builder responsible for its development, although most of the land here was leased by John Darlington. Wilmot was coincidentally the family name of the *Earls* of Rochester. In this leafy section of the road there are several pairs of large semis with brick pediments overlooking the park. Note the ironwork balconies, very floral on **No.9** directly opposite. These houses are shown as Wilmot Cottages on the 1851 census but were soon afterwards numbered as part of Wilmot Place itself. Inspector Tomkin, walking around the area in 1898 with Charles Booth, told the latter this was "a wonderful quiet neighbourhood". The road, into which we turn to our right, was begun in 1840 as a turning out of the King's Road (now St Pancras Way) ahead. Three houses were constructed on this north side in that year. They stood beyond the corner of Rochester Place, at which we pause; only **No.3** survives. The buildings at this end of Wilmot Place are now mainly business premises but **Nos.19-30**, on the south side, form an intriguing modern reworking of a Victorian terrace, using old bricks and with the addition of a glass-fronted upper storey and large curving concrete panels. On its St Pancras Way frontage it incorporates the façade of the 1830s Sussex Cottages.

The south-eastern section of **ROCHESTER PLACE**, to our left, is an early street dating from the late Georgian period, when it ran behind the gardens of Camden Cottages and fringed open country towards Holloway. It was not however fully developed as a mews with buildings until the 1860s. Now it is an uninteresting back road full of business premises. Look along it to **Nos.26&28**, on the corner with Rochester Mews, which are occupied by Cosprop, its sign prominently displayed. Cosprop is a leading costumier to the film, theatre and television industries. Founded in 1965 by the Oscar-winning costume designer John Bright, the firm specialises in the hire of original period clothes and the making of authentic reproductions. Its 1960s building covers the site of Clarendon Cottages and Clarendon Yard, developed in the late 1840s and which Booth wrote in 1898 was occupied by "a poor class of omnibus employees".

The north-western arm of Rochester Place, into which we turn (right), was laid out later to serve as a mews behind Rochester Terrace. This cobbled street has an interesting selection of houses with a mix of light industrial and residential uses; buildings with coach doors spring from the narrow footway. **Nos.36&38**, a concrete-faced block on the right, was until recently Soul II Soul Studios, a warehouse bought in 1990 by the soul star Jazzy B for conversion into recording studios and the base for his Soul II Soul collective, which had global chart success with *Back to Life*. **Nos.61&63** opposite was another workshop of Hilger, from the 1930s until 1968. The turning left is Reed's Place, its entrance framed by four bollards, each bearing the initials 'SPPM' (for St Pancras Parish, Middlesex); we shall see it from the far end later. Opposite it are two houses, **Nos.42&44**, by the architect David Wild. He built No.44 for himself in 1980-85, winning a Civic Trust award for the design in 1986. It shows skilful handling of different planes; set back within the 2-storey portico are glass brick panels, exposed concrete brickwork and glazed screens. A monumental corner column carefully preserves an existing tree. No.42 was also designed by Wild but built in 1986-89 by a general contractor. **Nos.52&54** are old brick buildings with a copper plate inscribed "erected by Philip Wilson 1900". Wilson's, van and wagon builders, occupied this site in that year, and also Nos.70-78, the last buildings on this side of Rochester Place: these were destroyed in WWII and only partially replaced. Hilger & Watts

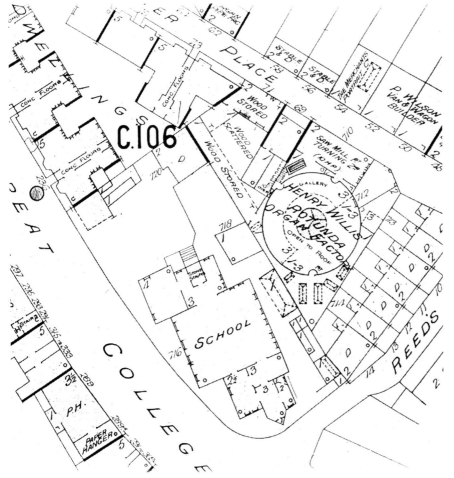

(p 60) had yet another workshop at **Nos.68&70** in the 1960s.

The opposite side is dominated by former school buildings that have recently been renovated. This was the site (**Fig 13**) of The Rotunda, built by George Lever in 1824 on then open land, to house a painting based on Thomas Horner's sketches of London, which the latter had drawn whilst in a box suspended on the exterior of St Paul's Cathedral (then under repair). The Rotunda was subsequently used by Robert Burford for the painting of some of his panoramas – huge affairs, some 80 ft long and 40 ft high – which were exhibited at Leicester Square and at the Diorama at Regent's Park. In 1865 the Rotunda became the Willis Organ Factory, continuing to serve as such until 1905. Its site was then cleared and the school in Royal College Street (p 67) was rebuilt and extended over it.

Farther along we pass on our left the rear of late-Victorian council flats set back behind railings. The view along the road is terminated by St Andrew's Greek Orthodox Cathedral (p 27). Walk towards the church, regaining **ROCHESTER ROAD**. To the right of the church is No.46, **St Andrew's Greek School**, which was the first Greek School in the UK to be built specifically for

13   Goad map (1900) showing Father Willis's Rotunda organ works and College Street Board School

that purpose, opening here in May 1969. The school is under the supervision of priests from the church.

On the corner, left, note an old brick building with two bricked-up archways. This was Rochester Hall, built at the same time as the Victorian flats. It was home to a day school for girls in the 1890s and to the Salvation Army in the next decade. It was built over Rochester Cottage, purchased by the Metropolitan Board of Works as part of their street improvement in this area in the mid-1880s (see below). Walk alongside it and left into Kentish Town Road, keeping left. The roadway becomes **ROYAL COLLEGE STREET**, which continues south-eastwards into Camden Town, eventually passing the eponymous Royal Veterinary College at its southernmost end. Walk past the looming Council flats as far as **No.236** and stop to survey the scene. Built in 1885-87 and once called Kentish Town Residences, these blocks gained an unenviable reputation in the early 1980s, when they were dubbed "Madhouse Mansions" in the local press after squatters had moved in (1979); they were not evicted for five years.

Before the mid-1880s the present stretch of road was known as Monte Video Place. Lying at the north end of Back Lane, otherwise King's Road (from Gray's Inn and the City), this had been one of two entrances into the medieval village of Kentish Town (see front cover). The second entrance to the village was via the road to Westminster (Water Lane, later Kentish Town Road), and the two roads met at the acute-angled junction opposite, as Royal College Street and Kentish Town Road do today. The corner was occupied by the low timber buildings of Cain Place (**Fig 14**), which had frontages on both roads, as did the Nag's Head alongside. Further south along the western side (opposite us) was the Black Horse pub, which had an old horse trough outside it until the 1860s, when an eccentric landlady kept a pig as a companion in her back parlour. Next to this was a large building that was run as a boarding house by a Mrs Neave, before becoming (in 1835) the Norfolk Laundry. Beyond and set back was Pain's Place (sometimes spelt as Payne's Place), three tall houses dating from 1720, and described by Goldsmith as "august buildings of red brick". In 1800 the Vestry rented additional accommodation here for inmates from its overcrowded workhouse. From 1796 to 1808 Edward Burch RA (1730–c.1814), librarian of the Royal

14 Cain Place showing the Nag's Head pub

Academy and once famed for his gem engraving, lived at No.2. He was also a painter of miniatures; both King George III and Mrs Fitzherbert sat for him. In the 1820s Mr Watson, an eminent maker of telescopes and mathematical instruments, was living in Pain's Place, but by 1841 the houses had been subdivided and were in multiple occupation, No.1 with no fewer than 19 people. The run of buildings ended in a terrace called Collumpton Place, developed by the builder Samuel Collard in the mid-1820s.

On the east side, meanwhile, and immediately south of what became Rochester Road, stood Chestnut Row (**Fig 15**), named after two small chestnut trees, said to have been planted by Emma Hamilton, that grew through the pavement here until removed as a nuisance in 1864. South of the Row lay houses numbered as part of Monte Video Place, which continued as far as the National School (see below). Beyond was a small house facing south across fields, which, as King wrote in his *Panorama*, "begins the entrance to Kentish Town".

Monte Video Place and the triangle of houses opposite were in Tottenhall manor and so, unlike the rest of our walk, lay on land not belonging to Lord Camden. The roadway in Monte Video Place was very narrow and in 1873 the Vestry approached the Metropolitan Board of Works to undertake street improvements here. After a decade of prevarication the Board began work in 1883, widening the roadway and pulling down all the buildings on both sides of the road. Most of the buildings we see today date from the late 1880s although the west side (opposite) is now dominated by the interwar **Camden Studios**, which also have a frontage on Kentish Town Road. They were formerly the headquarters of Dunn's, nationally known clothiers and hatters, established here by 1895. This was a central depot from which orders were sent out to over 100 branches. It closed in 1984 and the firm itself ceased trading twelve years later. Farther along is the present **Black Horse** tavern, rebuilt when the road was widened; its name can be seen in the roofline above.

15 Chestnut Row, 1860

The block now ends at the corner with Farrier Street, which was constructed in the mid-1880s to connect the two main roads south of their junction.

Back on the east side of the road, beyond the Council flats, tall chestnut trees stand behind a curving 7-ft brick wall. This encloses former school buildings, recently converted to luxury apartments, visible through the gated entrance that bears an old plaque marked "Boys". King's *Panorama* shows a large 17th-century farmhouse on this site backing on to a 17-acre Hall Field. This, and the 23-acre Upper & Lower Barn Field, which faced it on the west side of the King's Road, were both held by William Francis Esq. in 1801. Most of our present route lies over these two large fields.

The Kentish Town and Camden Town National School, paid for by public subscription by the inhabitants of both places, was opened on the site of the school buildings in August 1815 by Thomas Cartwright Slack, who died in a fire at his house in The Grove (p 52) a few months later. The school continued in use until 1849 when the lease was sold to the builder Charles Crane. He constructed a new building for the school in Islip Street (p 100) and replaced the old school building with a grand home for himself, called Sussex House. The name Sussex was used quite extensively in this vicinity and derived from Augustus Frederick, Duke

of Sussex (1773–1843), Queen Victoria's favourite uncle. The 1851 census shows Crane here with his family and servants; he later moved to Bower Cottage in Leighton Road (p 127). Alongside was a short-lived Sussex House school, run by Mrs Frances Baylis and with half a dozen pupils. Ten years later a laundry was being operated in Sussex House. The buildings were then taken over by the London School Board, who demolished them and built College Street Board School here in 1874. This was rebuilt and enlarged in 1908 as the LCC's Great College Street School. Its handsome 4-storey buildings with stone dressings were considered at the time to be the finest school premises in London. They housed the LCC's Cantelowes Secondary School and Women's Evening Institute until 1958, when St Richard of Chichester RC Secondary School, founded that year, moved in. For three years it shared the building with the Sir William Collins School and an infants establishment. Always desperately short of space, St Richard's eventually acquired a second site in Prince of Wales Road (at the former Camden School for Girls, p 92). The allegedly failing school closed in the late 1990s, and the Royal College Street buildings have been converted to residential use.

The wall curves round to **REED'S PLACE,** full of small stuccoed cottages of the 1860s, built by and named after

William Reed, who lived at No.7 until his death in 1880. George Lever leased the land from Marquis Camden in February 1861. In its early years there was a ragged school here.

Across the road to our right is **College Gardens**. It began as a triangular open space between terraced houses. In 1876 Marquis Camden proposed building on it, but within two years the Vestry had bought the land from him and laid it out as a garden. At its apex is a 7ft-high granite drinking fountain, Listed Grade II, as is the K2 cast-iron telephone box behind it, dating from 1927. The drinking fountain was erected to the memory of Joseph Salter, who died in 1876. He was an insurance office agent, auctioneer, rent collector and later estate agent, with a special line in railway compensation valuations. The firm he founded in 1854, Salter Rex (p 22), is still part of the Kentish Town scene. He was also a Vestryman and Poor Law Commissioner and he had a large family of 12 children.

Beyond the fountain you can see the short **FARRIER STREET,** which cuts through to Kentish Town Road. This was laid out in 1885-86 (following the line of an old field and estate boundary) to connect the two main roads south of their junction. Its construction entailed the demolition of the six houses of Collumpton Place and three in Royal College Street, on the far side of College

Gardens. Treated at first as an extension of Clarence Road (p 73), the new street was lined on both sides by model dwellings known as Clarence Buildings, designed by Samuel Toye and built 1885-89. Inspector Tomkin told Charles Booth in 1898 that Clarence Buildings was mainly occupied by "mechanics" because the house rules were "pretty strict". Massive 5-storey walk-up blocks, they have been successfully updated.

The street was renamed in 1961, supposedly in memory of a horse doctor who had practised in the area before it was laid out. The equine theme was continued in the renaming of Clarence Buildings: the southern blocks became Tattenham House while the northern blocks were renamed **Durdans House**, the home of Lord Rosebery near the Epsom racecourse. The connection with horses was also apposite, as the Victorian ground landlord of this part of Tottenhall manor, Sir Joseph Henry Hawley (1814−1875), "the Purist of the Turf", took a deep personal interest in horse racing, making decisions on where and when his horses should run and backing them, generously rewarding his staff, and upsetting the racing establishment by attempting to change contemporary racing practices. The block containing **Nos.50-54,** Durdans House, covers the site of early-18th-century Pain's Place.

Tattenham House, which faced Durdans House, was demolished in 1979 and its site was used as a garden centre during the 1980s. This was replaced by the 1990s post-modern flats here today: on the far corner with Kentish Town Road, **Atunbi House** (opened 1993, taking its name from a Yoruba word for "reborn"), and the lighter brick flats of **Nos.11&13**, which continue round into Royal College Street as the lower row of three houses (Nos.277-281 Royal College Street) abutting taller Philia House (p 69). These last buildings cover the site of College Terrace, developed by Samuel Collard in the early 1820s. Nos.8-10 were pulled down to construct present-day Farrier Street; No.10 was home in the mid-19th century to the five unmarried Daniels sisters, one of whom, Mary, ran the Norfolk Laundry nearby. The former Nos.1&2 College Terrace were destroyed in WWII; thereafter a petrol station was situated here, known in the 1980s as Gulliver Service Station (its name taken from that of the old local telephone exchange), until Philia House was built over it.

On this side of the gardens, beyond Reed's Place, **ST PANCRAS WAY** begins. This was the former King's Road, the ancient track running down the east bank of the Fleet from Kentish Town to St Pancras Church and beyond towards Gray's Inn. The first terrace dates from the 1830s and has pretty, 4-storey houses stuccoed at basement and ground floor level, and with main doors reached over light-wells protected by railings. It was first called Sussex Terrace, when several of its houses were occupied by artists. In the mid-Victorian period the then No.7 (now **No.120**) housed Miss Jepson's "seminary". Set in the pavement alongside the terrace is a series of interesting iron coal-hole covers, mostly produced by Thomas Sampson Ltd of Euston Road, but a couple by the local firm of Jennings, then at 130 Great College Street.

We soon reach the corner of Wilmot Place. Here note, on the far side of the road, the impressive brick frontage of **Nos.104-106**. These are the former Sussex Cottages, houses of some pretension when built in the 1830s. The Rev. Edward Pett Hannam, author of the tract *The Invalid's help to prayer and meditation*, lived at No.2; from 1836 he was the minister of the new Camden Chapel (now All Saints Greek Orthodox Cathedral) in Camden Street, Camden Town. Soon after Sussex Cottages were built they faced Roseman Cottages, a semi-detached pair, still standing as **Nos.189&191** opposite. After WWI Sussex Cottages were incorporated into a large block which served for many years as a Labour Exchange, latterly a Job Centre. Beyond is the post-war **No.102**, HQ of Camden's Community Meals Service. This was the site of detached No.1 Camden Cottages built in the 1820s and home of the artist Albert Ludovici (1852−1932), a genre and landscape artist influenced by Whistler, whose cause he championed.

Cross over to a row of three houses facing the gardens, which was built as Sussex Place by George Lever in the early 1840s. The roadway is now a continuation of Wilmot Place although the two end houses are numbered as part of St Pancras Way and Royal College Street respectively. The building in the middle has always been a pub, first known as the Sussex Arms until it became the Falcon in the 1860s. It is now the down-at-heel **Camden Falcon**, at present closed. The 'Camden' prefix was attached only recently, but the pub has been a rock venue since the 1970s and has given many up-and-coming bands, e.g. Blur, their first breaks.

Crossing over Royal College Street we enter **JEFFREY'S STREET**. This was named after Elizabeth Jeffreys, who married Charles Pratt, 1st Earl Camden. Laid out just before 1800 and developed over the next 20 years, the street is lined, on either side, mostly by terraces of Georgian houses, apart from post-modern **Philia House** extending from the corner of Royal College Street as far as No.35. Their survival is due in part to the failure to construct the Motorway Box, a scheme for a motorway to encircle inner London originating in Abercrombie's 1943 County of London Plan which the GLC resurrected in the 1960s. At Camden Town there would have been an enormous

three-level interchange at a roundabout linked to a Camden Town bypass, which would have cut a swathe through Jeffrey's Street and the streets to the south. The scheme was not abandoned until the mid-1970s, so there was a period of planning blight in this area, during which nothing was done to the houses.

Nos.11-33 are original, 'third-rate' houses, some with fanlights and all with iron balconies, **No.23** having a fine example. In the back gardens a well, probably predating the houses, was recently uncovered by the residents. **Nos.3-9** beyond are two storeys high and their entrances are set back so that they look like two semi-detached pairs. These are the earliest houses in the street, initially numbered part of Molesworth Place that also fronted Kentish Town Road (Frances Molesworth married the 1st Marquis Camden). On the street's south side, John G Howe, an artist in stained glass, as was his brother Benjamin, lived at **No.22** in the 1860s; John designed windows in a number of Buckinghamshire churches. The comedic actor Rowan Atkinson lived in the street in 1981.

The quiet charm of Jeffrey's Street is enhanced by the lack of vehicular access from Kentish Town Road, which we reach at the far end. This is also the junction with **CAMDEN STREET**, left. Look along the houses here (perhaps best viewed by crossing over Kentish Town Road).

They were built as Camden Terrace, but renumbered as part of Camden Street in November 1863. Plots at Nos.1&2 (on the site of **Nos.174&176**) on the corner were let by Lord Camden to George Lever for building in 1816, and Nos.3-13 were developed by the mid-1820s. No.174 was home in the 1840s to John Seguier (1785–1856), whose brother William was the first Keeper of the National Gallery. John worked there as a picture restorer after his brother's death. Camden House School, owned by Frederick Cheshire and listed in the 1864 street directory, was at No.160 (previously No.8 Camden Terrace). The mathematician and physicist Oliver Heaviside (1850–1925) attended the school in his youth. The house was pulled down when the railway line was widened in 1869-70, and Cheshire moved to **No.168**, where he erected new school buildings in his garden. These were listed in 1874 as the Camden Lecture Hall and subsequently as an "academy". The Camden High School for Boys was here by 1883, and until the close of the Victorian period; soon after that the buildings were being used for cap making, which continued here into the 1970s. From c.1870 space in "the High School" had been rented by a peripatetic Baptist congregation with its origins in the Beulah Chapel, Somers Town; this was its fourth and last base, used until c.1903, when the congregation "expired". **No.164** has remarkable ironwork, said to be the finest in the borough, although now rather neglected. Note the splendid covered balcony and the canopies to the ground floor windows. **Nos.162-168** are Grade-II-Listed.

Turning round, walk back into Jeffrey's Street and shortly turn right into cobbled **PROWSE PLACE**. The road is early, shown on Greenwood's 1827 map as running behind the gardens of Camden Terrace, but with no buildings along it. By 1849 it was called Priory Mews and from May 1882 Priory Place. It was renamed in July 1938 after Captain William Prowse, one of Nelson's fighting captains, who commanded the *Sirius* at Trafalgar and who died a rear admiral in 1826; he had lived in the parish of St Pancras on the New (now Euston) Road. An original entrance to **Nos.19-23** is bricked up; this was the back of the Camden High School.

Look left along cobbled **JEFFREY'S PLACE**. On its north side **Nos.12-20** are 3-storey flats, built in the 1970s using old bricks. They replaced the former Priory Works, Nos.16-18, used after WWII by Hilger & Watts. On the south side are small industrial buildings and workshops. Note the hoists on two buildings at the far end. The film company Key Productions is at **No.8**, which was previously used by the briar pipe makers Barling Bros.

Continue along Prowse Place. On the right-hand side are late-19th-century workmen's cottages built right onto the pavement, each with a cast-iron foot scraper. Beyond them is the magnificent brick arch of the railway line. We, however, turn left into **IVOR STREET**, past a cast-iron St Pancras Parish bollard. Ivor Street was originally known as Priory Street, after Brecknock Priory, the Welsh home of Elizabeth Jeffreys. In 1890, Mrs Phoebe Hogg and her infant child were murdered by Mary Pearcy, who lived in the street and who was Mr Hogg's lover. Pearcy was hanged after a trial which attracted a great deal of press attention, particularly for the image of a blood-stained and empty perambulator (used to convey the body of Mrs Hogg from the scene of the crime). Priory Street gained a certain notoriety, which may well explain why it was renamed in 1937 by the London County Council; the significance of Ivor is unclear. This short, quiet street has some delightful trees and retains its York stone pavement. The road was first laid out in the late 1820s after Richard Dent had leased the land here, although the first houses along it – at the far end – date from 1831. On the north side, stuccoed **Nos.8-10** are Listed Grade II. They date from 1837 and all have central doors. **No.** 7 follows the same pattern but is mid-Victorian and displays 'constructional polychromy'. The 3-storey terraced houses on the south side back onto the railway viaduct, and the arches of the latter at this end are numbered **Nos.11-14**. These were long the base for a taxi firm and garage; the forecourt is now disused, but the arches are now occupied by wood machinists. The writer Deborah Moggach (b.1948) lived in Ivor Street in the 1980s.

Regain **ROYAL COLLEGE STREET**. The **Old Eagle** is at No.251 on the corner, part of an 1830s terrace. The 'Old' prefix was presumably added to distinguish the pub from the better-known Eagle (now Mac Bar) only yards to the south at No.217, although the two establishments were built at much the same time. We turn right and cross the road (with care) to reach 1960s **Foster Court**, a tile-hung council block, being renovated at time of writing, shaded by huge mature plane trees on the pavement. This replaced Broadway Terrace, developed by William Dunsmore in the early 1850s and renumbered as part of Great College Street in 1866. An early occupant of No.6 Broadway Terrace was John Gilfoy, an artist in coach building, some of whose paintings are held by the Science Museum. When Foster Court was constructed, four Victorian houses beyond it were demolished. In one of these, No.222, lived William Hardy, a Victorian wood engraver. The last building before the corner with Wilmot Place survived until recently. This was No.230, dating from the late 19th century, and first known as College Chapel, a Baptist chapel opened in 1892 by Rev. G Cousins, who moved from a chapel in Grange Road (Chalk Farm). After 1904 the chapel was "leased to another body". It was later renamed the College Street Mission Hall, then from the 1920s simply College Hall, an offshoot of St Thomas's Church in Wrotham Road (demolished in 1955), on the edge of whose parish it lay. It was used for various secular purposes (e.g. dancing and boxing). In the 1980s and 1990s it was home to a Pentecostal Church. The present open space beyond Foster Court is being redeveloped as flats.

Opposite, to either side of the entrance to Ivor Street are terraces of 3-storey houses now mainly used as shops and cafés. Some are rather run down but remain interesting. The block to the south of Ivor Street was built in the 1840s by William Dunsmore. It was called Cornwall Terrace until 1866. The Camden Society for People with Learning Difficulties is based at **No.245**. Note also at **No.229**, Castle's traditional Pie & Mash shop, established here in 1934.

Reach Camden Road (by former Camden Broadway) and turn right to arrive back at the railway station, where this circular walk ends.

The Hawley–Buck estate

Circular walk from Camden Town station
For modern map see back cover

This walk begins and ends at the junction of Kentish Town Road and Hawley Road. To get there from Camden Town Underground station turn left up Kentish Town Road; Hawley Road is the first turning left past the railway bridge. Alternatively, from Camden Road railway station, walk up Royal College Street and turn left along Jeffrey's Street; Hawley Road then lies opposite across Kentish Town Road.

The walk traverses the Hawley-Buck estate, once part of the manor of Tottenhall. The estate extended from just north of the site of Camden Town Tube station to present-day Prince of Wales Road, bounded on the west by the then Hampstead Road and on the east by Kentish Town Road. The 40 acres of meadowland, watered by tributaries of the River Fleet, were held in 1761 by Dr James Hawley of Leybourne Grange, Kent. His son, Sir Henry Hawley, went into partnership with Lewis William Buck MP (1794–1858) of Hartland Abbey, Devon, and together they laid out part of the land in 1815 as picturesque gardens. The latter and his son George Stucley Buck (later known as Sir George Stucley Stucley, Bt) and Sir Joseph Henry Hawley Bt decided to lease the land for building from 1835. Our walk lies over land that was before the 1840s mainly pasture, which was leased to Richard Mortimer of Green Street (Highgate Road).

Few of the houses built on the estate were likely to attract high-class residents. Proximity to the large railway yards at Chalk Farm did not help, and the houses deteriorated in status after railways cut across the estate in the mid-19th century. A largely working class area from that time, it suffered badly from bombing during WWII.

Turn along **HAWLEY ROAD**, now a one-way street carrying busy traffic. It was built near the village cricket ground in the late 1830s and was one of the estate's first streets, planned as a residential road with generous proportions. Remnants of its anticipated high standing can be seen in the original detached and semi-detached houses remaining on its south side, several listed as occupied by "gentlemen" on the 1851 census. Note in particular detached **No.1**, dating from 1837, with a central door, columned portico and pilasters, now in a sorry state despite being Listed Grade II. The house was built by Francis Holdsworth, who was living here with his family and two servants in 1841. The low brick addition alongside, now a garage, contained in the early 20th century the mission room of the Plymouth Brethren, a non-denominational Christian sect first established in the 1820s. **Nos.3-7**, built in the late 1830s by the busy local builder James Taylor, are better maintained, their stucco brightly painted.

Pause at the corner of Torbay Street (see below). **Bradfield Court**, the block of flats opposite us to the right, lies over the site of St Paul's Chapel. Edward Oughton took out the lease of the land in 1842 and the Chapel's first proprietor was Rev. Samuel Smith (d.1850). In 1852 Edward White hired St Paul's and organised a Baptist Union church. He bought the premises in 1865, and a lecture hall and school room were added in 1868. By the mid-1870s the chapel meetings had become Congregational and in 1918 the chapel was united with the Congregational Church in Kelly Street. The building passed to the Church of England's Holy Trinity Church, and became known as Memorial Hall, but was pulled down after WWII. Alongside the Chapel was a row of three houses, including No.4, which was home in 1861 to Frederick Lawrence, who described himself as a dramatic author; he had written a *Life of Henry Fielding* in 1855.

TORBAY STREET, a short rump of which survives to your left, once continued north of Hawley Road, forming the spine of a grid of streets developed in the 1840s, primarily by the builder Edward Oughton, who lived in Moreton Terrace, Kentish Town Road. From 1836 onwards

he took out building leases on most of the central portion of the Hawley–Buck lands north of the Regent's Canal. The streets he developed were largely replaced when the **Clarence Way Estate** was built after WWII. Tall and well planned, and originally designed by the architects Hamilton and Chambers, the Estate was begun in 1947 but added to until the 1980s. From where you stand there is a good view of the Estate's centrepiece, **Torbay Court**.

The original Torbay Street, known as Exeter Street until renamed in 1879, extended northwards to the site of Torbay Court, the houses along it there called Melverne Cottages, and all now gone. In one of these in the 1890s, at what was by then No.12 Torbay Street, lived the watercolour and genre painter William Harris Weatherhead (1843–c.1903), who exhibited at the Royal Academy and was a member of the Royal Institute of Painters in Watercolour.

Only a few of the original houses remain (on your left) in the street's short surviving south end, which was badly affected by the construction of two railway lines: in the late 1840s by the North London line (then known as the East and West India Docks and Birmingham Junction Railway) and in the next decade by the Hampstead Junction Railway. James King in his *Kentish Town Panorama* notes that the railway company pulled down the

houses which had been built over the Fleet Ditch but did not secure the foundations of the railway arches, which gave way one morning and had to be rebuilt at great expense. Newspaper reports in November 1849 confirm that seven arches to the west of Kentish Town Road did indeed collapse, although the arch over the main roadway survived. Alongside the railway line a goods depot was opened in 1851, known as Camden Road or Locket's Coal Depot, after Locket & Judkins, the coal merchants established in 1737, who were then based at No.49 Kentish Town Road. The firm was taken over by Charrington's in 1922 and the depot was closed in 1940. Now half a dozen businesses, mainly connected to the motor trade, operate from the yard. The builders' yards on either side of Torbay Street have been here since the late 19th century and their current occupant, Phelps, the builders' and plumbers' merchant, has been here for more than 50 years.

Continue along **HAWLEY ROAD** past some pleasant, original terraced houses and detached **No.17**. In **No.13** the figure and still-life painter William Frederick D'Almaine was living in the late 19th century. Beneath these houses was the main confluence of the Hampstead and Highgate arms of the River Fleet, at least until the 1830s when it seems that the former was diverted to meet the latter farther north (see p 13), thus enabling this area to be developed. Opposite lies **Welford Court**, built over an 1840s terrace that was damaged in WWII. In 1847 the house on the corner of the terrace, then numbered No.15, was home to Harriet and Rose Acton, who published a volume of poems that year.

Hawley Road continues under the railway bridge but is now cut in two; the main roadway bends to the left just before the bridge to become **CASTLEHAVEN ROAD**. This road comprises three sections that once had different names, but which were united in 1938 by a name chosen randomly from a gravestone at St Pancras Old Church, that of Elizabeth, Countess of Castlehaven, buried there in 1743. This first section of the road that starts by Camden Market − outside our area − was originally Grange Road. At the bend by the bridge are **Nos.20-22**, a 4-storey block of flats built in buff-coloured brick in a post-modern style, with a parking area entered under an arch. It replaces houses built in 1845 by James Taylor. Alongside, abutting the railway arches, is the entrance to **Scar Studios**. Its fancy ironwork sign reveals that this is a workshop for wrought iron (it has been that, under different names, for many years); it has a rehearsal space for aspiring bands above.

We turn right (avoiding traffic from your left) into the two northern sections of Castlehaven Road. The next section was initially Moreton Street (the Buck family

owned Moreton House, Bideford), until its name was subsumed into that of the northernmost section, Victoria Road, in 1864. At No.5 Moreton Street in 1853-56 lived Charles Thomas Dixon, a landscape artist who exhibited scenes of Hampstead at the Royal Academy. There are 4-storey red-brick Council blocks (Welford Court and **Donnington Court**) along the right (east) side of the road, built around courtyards for parking. Some of these flats have balconies. They cover the site of a row of 1840s semis which once bore the delightful name of Arcadian Cottages. By 1898 Booth called these "shabby-looking".

The west side is a recreational area known as the **Hawley Road Open Space**. Houses along the road were bombed in WWII and the site lay derelict for many years. In the 1980s it was home to travellers before they and their caravans were moved on after a High Court case in 1989. The Open Space was created thanks mainly to Lord Stallard, formerly Jock Stallard MP for North St Pancras, who fought for many years on Camden Council to have the large area of bomb damage in this vicinity turned into a recreational space. The central sports pitch was surrounded by a wall laden with graffiti and often used for weekend parking until the Open Space was improved in 2003 with help from the central government 'Liveability Fund' and a Sport England Lottery grant. It was extended to its

present size over the site of a factory that adjoined the railway in Hawley Road, and fenced all round.

At the far end of the playground turn left into **CLARENCE WAY**. Known as Clarence Road until 1937, it had been laid out exactly 100 years before that. It appears to have taken its name from the Clarence pub (p 26) in Providence Place, Kentish Town Road; William IV, who was Duke of Clarence before he became king, died in 1837. Before the post-war Clarence Way Estate was created, the road continued eastwards into Kentish Town Road. The eastern section is now a cul-de-sac, serving as an entrance to the car parks for the blocks of flats on Castlehaven Road. At its corner is an original 1840s building, **No.41**, the former Victory pub, recently converted into a restaurant. In the late 19th century the Victory had a reputation of being rather rough; in 1880 a barmaid was murdered here.

From this corner, there is a clear view of the railway viaduct of what was once the Hampstead Junction Railway. It opened from the Camden Road Junction (with the North London line) to Willesden Junction in January 1860, after several years of legal wrangling with the landowners Lewis William Buck, George Stucley Buck and Sir Joseph Henry Hawley. In 1853 they had petitioned unsuccessfully against the parliamentary Bill authorising the railway on the (not unreasonable) grounds that its

30-ft-high embankment would injure their property. At first run by an independent company, the railway was taken over by the LNWR in 1867, and the line was electrified in 1916. Construction of the railway through Kentish Town involved relatively small-scale demolition of the houses so recently constructed, but in marching across the area at roof-top level the railway inevitably contributed to the social decline of the locality.

This part of Clarence Way now has no buildings save for Holy Trinity Church on the north side. The Open Space which faces it was laid out not only over houses in Clarence Way but also over the site of former Hartland Grove behind. Hartland Grove was a narrow street lined with just four pairs of semi-detached houses, built in 1849 by James Taylor, which faced the back gardens of the houses in Clarence Road. Charles Booth in 1898 called it "respectable".

The church of **Holy Trinity** arose mainly through the efforts of Rev. David Laing, who in 1847 persuaded the Vicar of St Pancras, Thomas Dale, to form a new district in the parish – Holy Trinity, Haverstock Hill – which then had 9,000 inhabitants and no church. A church school was built in Hartland Road (see below) and from July 1848 services were held there while the church itself was built. The latter was designed by the prolific church builders Thomas

Henry Wyatt (1820–1877) and David Brandon (1813–1897), although it is their only church in London. Built of Kentish ragstone in a 14th-century style, its battlemented west tower originally had a spire, destroyed in WWII, after which the northern aisle was converted into a church hall. The interior has a fine east window, with stained glass depicting the Crucifixion, designed by Arthur Edward Buss (1905–1999) and installed in 1951. The church was consecrated on 13 October 1850 and 856 of the 1426 seats were free. Laing committed so much of his own money (£5000 or a third of the cost) that he felt compelled to resign in 1857, becoming rector of the "valuable preferment" of St Olave, Hart Street in the City. (He had also been a great supporter of the Governesses' Benevolent Institution, see p 91.) One of Laing's successors as curate, in the 1860s, was Septimus Buss, brother of Frances Mary Buss, the founder of the Camden School for Girls (p 123). He was married here in 1860 and named his second son David Laing Buss.

Turn the corner into **HARTLAND ROAD** (Hartland Abbey in North Devon was a Buck family home) and walk to the right. This stretch of the road was known until 1871 as Upper Hartland Road. To the left, up against the railway viaduct, is the **Royal Exchange** pub, with 1930s Tudor beam work and painted a flaming orange and blue; it is currently closed for

renovation. The present building replaced the original 1850 pub of the same name.

Facing it is **Holy Trinity & St Silas Church of England School**, which was built in 1848 and used temporarily as a church before Holy Trinity opened two years later. It is now a voluntary aided day school for infants and juniors. Behind it is a very pleasant playground, extended to its present size over the site of four bomb-damaged houses in the terrace beyond.

The existing **Nos.69–81** were developed by Edward Oughton in the 1850s when they backed on to the large brickfield owned by the Bassett family, agents and surveyors to the Southampton Estate who were developing much of West Kentish Town at the time. Over the years the houses were not well maintained and in June 1975 the tenants took the owner, the Greater London Council, to court for failure to repair; they look much smarter now. On this side we walk along the back of the red-brick flats called **Tiptree**, part of an extension to the Clarence Way Estate built in 1970 (when the new blocks were given Essex place names). Shortly before Tiptree was built the GLC had been renting out a number of mobile homes on its site, which had been badly damaged during WWII.

Stop at the corner of **LEWIS STREET**, named after Lewis William Buck. To our right, it is now just a footpath between more Estate blocks – the back gardens of small **Barling** and the lock-ups behind **Roxwell** – that emerges in Castlehaven Road between **Havering** (with its integral garages) and Widford. East of Castlehaven Road, a wider part of Lewis Street now gives access to the car park of the Clarence Way Estate; the street used to end where it met the northern arm of Torbay Street. At that end, at former No.9, the Camden Town branch of the Mormon Church met during the first half of 1854, when the sect was inviting people to emigrate to America and live as farmers near Salt Lake City. Opposite us here, at former No.26, the architect George Grayson (1831–1912) was living in 1861; he later did some work in Liverpool. In 1898 Booth records that Inspector Tomkin called this a street of mechanics, some "not as clean as they might be". Before WWI a turning off Lewis Street running south (across the site of Barling) led behind the houses in Hartland Road to the works of the piano makers Hemingway & Thomas, here from the mid-1870s to about 1907. For a few years this was the base of the piano making firm of Keith, Prowse & Co; it then housed the St Pancras Reform Club, which moved here in 1912 from premises in Prince of Wales Road (p 77) and remained until 1970 when the surrounding blocks were built.

Turn left, into a quiet section of Lewis Street with just two Victorian houses, dwarfed on the opposite side by an 8-storey red-brick block of flats known as **Heybridge**. In 2004 the tenants of the block fought a campaign to prevent the playground and car park being redeveloped for extra housing. The car park was built on the site of bomb-damaged houses which used to line **HADLEY STREET**, which we now join.

Hadley Street was laid out on Messrs Bassett's brickfield in 1859, although the houses took some years to be completed. The derivation of the street's name is unknown. To our left the road ends in a cul-de-sac with 1860s houses painted in cheerful, pastel colours. The terrace on the west side, **Nos.32-50**, facing the back of Heybridge, was built in the mid-1990s and sympathetically designed to fit in with the older terrace alongside. The houses are overlooked by the railway, as were their predecessors, which were cleared in the 1970s. They were, one hopes, shielded by it from the smell that must have emanated from the yard behind, where before WWI several forage dealers or "manure merchants" were based. On part of the cleared site a youth club existed before the present houses were built. The modern terrace abuts the **Tavern Inn The Town** on the corner with Castle Road. In the 1980s the pub was known briefly as the Fuzzock & Firkin, but for more than a century before that had been the Trafalgar. Hadley Street continues northwards. On each side of the street are original 2-storey terraced houses, with small front yards protected by low brick walls and gates. The gardens of the houses on the west side back on to the elevated railway. There is some delicate ironwork on windowsills, and some houses retain their iron fences, having evaded the war-time salvage operation.

Continue to **PRINCE OF WALES ROAD**, renumbered in 1863 when its terrace block names were abolished. It took its name from the title of Prince Albert Edward (the future Edward VII), born in 1841 when the road was being formed. On the left, **Nos.53-55** are partly original buildings at first associated with Kentish Town West station (opposite), which opened in June 1867. They are now part of Buttle's, the timber merchants, a firm established in 1919 in Castle Mews behind the railway line (just outside our area).

Cross to the entrance to the station and turn right, walking along this northern side (described in Route 6) to view the fine houses opposite. The impressive stretch of six very large terraced houses (**Nos.35-45**), with a pediment over the central pair, was built in the 1850s as Victoria Terrace. Its early inhabitants were well-to-do: in 1861 at No.4 the household of Edward Paterson, attorney and solicitor, had 4 servants while at No.5 lived Patrick Campbell Auld, a landscape painter of Scottish scenes; the curate of Holy Trinity church, Frederick Russell, lived at No.6.

Look down **HEALEY STREET**, now blocked off from Prince of Wales Road. The street was shoehorned into the space between Hadley Street and Grafton Crescent (ahead) in 1860 and was until 1865 known as Arthur Street (possibly after Prince Arthur, Duke of Connaught, born in 1850). It takes its current name from Francis Healey JP of Euston Grove, who represented this district on the Vestry and the Metropolitan Board of Works. Look along its 3-storey Victorian houses, stuccoed at ground floor level and screened by trees. The taller houses on the left were built in the 1850s before the street was laid out. The Beckford Society, which promotes interest in the life and works of William Beckford (1760–1844), is at **No.15**.

The next houses opposite in **PRINCE OF WALES ROAD** were built in the 1850s as Grafton Villas. **Nos.21-33** appear as large, tall semis although they are linked by set-back wings. The genre painter Frederick Johnston lived at No.23 in the 1860s. A row of shops follows to the corner of Castlehaven Road.

Cross Grafton Road (p 91) past the imposing terracotta façade of the former Baths (p 91) and return to the south side by way of the traffic lights. Here is the last and oldest section of Prince of Wales Road, begun in the early 19th century as a turning from Kentish Town Road called Grafton Place, and known as such until 1863. The name Grafton derived from the ducal title of the Fitzroy family who owned Tottenhall manor. A drawing dated November 1837 by A Crosby (in the Guildhall Library) shows the River Fleet running behind the houses on the south side, crossed by a little gated bridge and lined by old willow trees.

We are now in front of **Hope Chapel**. It dates from 1870 (although the inscription states 1871) but the church itself began in Hatton Garden in 1837. When the Chapel opened its members were described "simply as Christians". The Church of Christ continues to meet here every Sunday, "pleading for a return to New Testament Christianity" as the board outside announces, and a monthly newsletter, *Christian Worker*, is published from here. Beyond to the corner of Kentish Town Road is a large building, **No.1**, which has "Women's Entrance" inscribed on its west side, facing the chapel and the old K2 telephone kiosk. No.1 was the North Western Polytechnic, designed by W E Riley. A scheme was approved for a Polytechnic in St Pancras in 1892, and a governing body was set up. Land was found on this corner site, although the leases did not expire until 1910 and the project was held up during and after WWI. The final impetus was largely due to Sir William Job Collins, a well-known eye surgeon and latterly MP for West St Pancras, who served on the governing body from 1893 to 1946. At his express wish, it was opened by the Prince of Wales, in October 1929, in the presence of one of the largest crowds ever seen in Kentish Town; "a moment of glory indeed".

Regulations forbade intoxicating liquors, smoking, gambling and profane or indecent language on the premises. A girls' day trade school and a women's department were housed on the top floor, accessed from the separate Women's Entrance. The main entrance was hit by a bomb in 1940. During the 1950s higher-level and professional courses were gradually introduced, and from 1958 external degree courses were set up. The number of students multiplied and branch buildings were opened in Camden and outside the borough. It had become the largest polytechnic in London by 1967, when a Teacher Training Department was established.

The Polytechnic made the headlines in the 1970s when the students demonstrated against its Director, Terence Miller. Upon merger with the Northern Polytechnic it was known as the Polytechnic of North London, and external London degrees were replaced by courses devised by academic staff and independently validated until 1992, when it became the University of North London. Four years later, the University moved away from Kentish Town and the building was left empty. Local people wanted it retained for educational purposes but their campaign was unsuccessful and it was turned into luxury apartments designed by Allies & Morrison. The building now encompasses a restaurant at the corner with Kentish Town Road, two communal internal courtyards and underground parking, and is Listed Grade II.

The Polytechnic had been built over the site of a large detached house, once called Grafton Lodge, which in 1841 housed a dame school run by Eliza King, with 16 female pupils. At the end of 19th century the St Pancras Reform Club met here. Booth in 1898 called it "a neglected looking place; not much doing, carried on very quietly". The house had large gardens laid out alongside the road, in which Ernest Mansell started an open-air cinema in 1911. Perhaps not surprisingly, this 'Garden Cinema' operated only in the summer, and it closed in 1913 when the indoor Palace Cinema (p 24) opened opposite. The whole site was then cleared before the Polytechnic building was erected several years later.

Go back to Castlehaven Road and turn into it. On the left is a modern terrace (**Nos.116-122**) by the designers of the flats at No.1 Prince of Wales Road and developed at the same time. Cross the road and walk down curving, tree-lined **GRAFTON CRESCENT**, its name deriving from nearby former Grafton Place. It was laid out in the 1850s on an old field boundary alongside the Bassetts' brickfield. Each side has 3-storey Victorian terraced houses, stuccoed at ground floor level and with small front yards protected either by low brick walls or by wrought iron railings. The left-hand side was developed first and initially called Grafton Crescent, but when the opposite side was completed a few years later the road was called Junction Street, a name it retained until 1872. On the right, in a space created by WWII bomb damage, is the interesting town house recently built at **No.2**. Beyond is **No.3**, a three-storey 1960s block, until the 1990s Water Board offices. The Conference of Drama Schools, the representative body for leading drama schools in the UK, is based at **No.11**. In the early 1970s the writer of children's books, Eve Barwell, lived in the street.

Grafton Crescent ends in **CASTLE ROAD**, into which we turn, left. The road was projected in the late 1830s and laid out in the next decade across the two-acre grounds of the ancient Castle Inn that ended by the brickfield. It was first called New Hampstead Road, and the houses in this stretch (then a cul-de-sac) were built in the 1850s and called Nelson Terrace; they faced the Nelson pub on the corner of Victoria Road (now Castlehaven Road), which had been constructed in late 1848. New Hampstead Road and its terraces became Castle Road in 1864. All the original houses, many long used as shops, have gone, to be replaced on this north side by an early-1980s interpretation of a Victorian terrace, designed by David Webb of Camden Architects Department. Opposite is the taller 1970 block called **Widford**, which covers the site of the pub, closed in the late 1960s.

Pause at the corner of **CASTLEHAVEN ROAD**. This northernmost section (north of Lewis Street) was first built as Victoria Road. No.32 Victoria Road (now **No.51**) on the corner was a dairy in 1861, when the Barbadian artist Haynes King (1831−1904), a genre and landscape painter, took rooms above the shop shortly after coming to London. In 1864 Victoria Road was extended south to Hawley Road (subsuming Moreton Street) and all the houses were renumbered. At No.39, the Victorian watercolour artist, James H Lowes, who painted scenes of moonlit Camden streets and views of Hampstead Heath, was registered on the 1881 census as a lithographic artist. The site is now covered by Widford, across Castle Road to our right. We now turn left up Castlehaven Road, which is here lined with a terrace of elegant 1850s 3-storey houses, built of London stock brick with incised stucco ground floors, stucco window and door surrounds and other enrichments, including wrought-iron balconies on the first floor. Some of the terraced houses opposite have round-arched windows with stucco surrounds.

Cross over to the long front garden of **No.98**, on the corner with Kelly Street, here blocked off from Castlehaven Road. This is one of a pair of rather grand semi-detached houses first known as Victoria and Albert Villas. They are Listed Grade II and have doorcases of Corinthian columns. Here turn right into **KELLY STREET**, which was called Church Street until 1870. The eponymous John Kelly was a local builder who built many houses along Kentish Town Road and on the fields behind during the 1840s and 1850s. He and his partner, John Eeles Lawford, had leased most of the Hawley−Buck estate north of Lewis Street for building. Kelly Street is now a charming, leafy cul-de-sac of quaint, 2-storey, Grade-II-Listed houses dating from the late 1840s, with ornamental ironwork on the ground floor and arched first floor windows. It was designated a Conservation Area in 1975. All the houses are stuccoed, most are painted in pastel colours, and the ornamental Victorian street lamps have survived, interspersed with whitebeam trees. It seems today a far cry from its image in 1898, when Booth visited it in the company of the local police inspector and recorded that it was "the worst street for immorality" in Kentish Town. Certain houses (No.48 and No.51) were suspected brothels.

Nos.36-42 form a row of modern terraced houses by Allies and Morrison designed to echo the scale and arched first-floor window detailing of the historic properties in the street. They were built on the site of the old Congregational Church. A small turning left beyond them leads to the modern brick building of **Kentish Town Congregational Church**, looking like a private house. The church moved here in 1848 after it had outgrown its old building on Kentish Town Road (p 28). The first pastor in Kelly Street was Rev. William Forster (d.1871), who resigned in 1853 when he changed his theological views and became a Unitarian. The church building is the third on the site, the first one designed in 16th-century Gothic style by Hodge and Butler (**Fig 16**) having been demolished in 1955 after wartime damage and falling attendance, to be replaced by a prefabricated hall built using the Reema System. This was pulled down in 1990 and the site was redeveloped in co-operation with a local housing association. The church was re-opened in the current premises the following year.

Behind the church lies the former Congregational Church Avenue, a turning off Kentish Town Road. This was the main entrance to the church in the 19th century and was flanked by trees and lawns. Its construction involved the removal in 1849 of the St Pancras parish pound, which lay immediately behind the church (as Hawley−Buck estate papers reveal) and on whose site the church was at the time planning to build a vestry room. The pound had moved here from its ancient site next to the second St Pancras workhouse (now Camden Town Tube station) after the Vestry opened a new workhouse in the King's Road (St Pancras Way) in 1809. The road was much changed in the early 20th century when the Post Office was extended, a telephone exchange was formed and the back of the North Western Polytechnic was built right up against it. It is now a private, gated road called Church Avenue (p 25), leading to the concrete-faced British Telecom offices and telephone exchange that tower above the church.

Continuing along Kelly Street we pass the British Telecom yard, the site of the relocated parish pound. After a wild ox kept here had to be put down, Lord Southampton instructed his agent to keep the pound locked up. Not very securely, it seems, as by the 1870s residents of Kelly Street were complaining to the Vestry that the pound was "the resort of noisy youths and used by tramps and for indecent purposes". The Vestry's Sanitary Committee took action to clear the site. In the 1890s the Antelope Cycle Works was based here.

Nos.8-24 were designed and erected as a group, the centre of the terraces being made more prominent as these were the most valued properties. Hence **Nos.14-18**

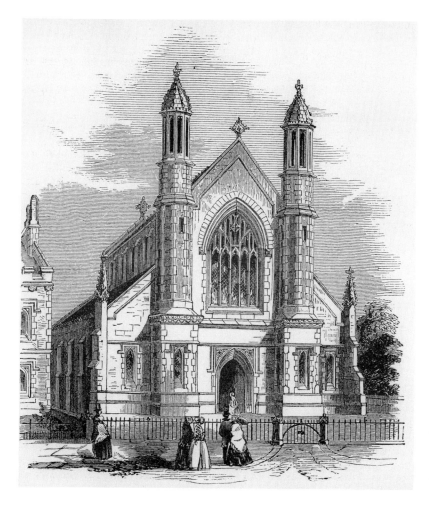

project forward slightly and are emphasised by a shallow pedimented parapet. They also have original 6-pane timber doors. Further along, the tiny building at **No.6** now houses Mario's Cafe.

Turn right into Kentish Town Road across from St Andrew's Greek Orthodox Cathedral (p 27) and shortly right again into **CASTLE ROAD**, at the entrance to which is No.147 (now the Bullet bar), until 2002 the Castle pub. This is the Victorian building (p 25), but the original Castle Inn was sited in the middle of the present-day roadway, roughly opposite **Nos.3&5** on the south side. These were built in 1849 at the same time as the new pub by the builder John Eeles Lawford. No.5, where we pause, now houses the Piccadilly Press, publishers of children's and teenage books. Further down the road an 8-storey red-brick block, **Castle Court**, numbered as part of Castlehaven Road, dominates the south side, which was lined by the 1850s Castle Terrace, whose houses survived until the 1960s. On the north side note the old building of **No.2**, set obliquely to the roadway and with a curious arched doorway, now part of Leverton & Sons, the funeral directors, in Kentish Town Road. The house was built in the late 1830s by John T Clark, then lessee of the original Castle Inn next door, and became the first house along the new road.

16 Kentish Town Congregational Church, 1848

Past the tattoo parlour is a terrace of modern houses dating from the early 1980s, with distinctive iron railings and gates. It replaced the original 1850s terrace that included No.12, in which Edwin Cosser, a local bookbinder lived for many years until WWI; and No.34, home soon after WWII to the song composer Henri Kimbre Jones.

The grounds of the Castle Inn stretched west to the River Fleet, and north to what is now Kelly Street. The inn (**Fig 17**) was ancient – there was a tradition in the late 19th century that it dated from the time of King John, but this was then a relatively common claim for many an old pub near London. It certainly dated back to at least the 17th century as there is a record of the sale of the property for £1,000 in 1651, and it had a Tudor-style stone chimney piece. It may have originated as a hunting lodge in the 16th century, when hunting was very popular in the area. The inn catered for the needs of passing travellers, and in the 18th century its trap ball and skittle grounds and tea gardens attracted day trippers from London. Visitors might also arrive across the fields from the Hampstead Road, entering the gardens across the little footbridge over the River Fleet.

Early in the next century the inn's tea room was converted each year into a theatre for itinerant comedians. In the 1830s hourly omnibuses ran from the inn to the City via Tottenham Court Road and Holborn, and in November 1835 the first general meeting of the short-lived Camden Literary and Scientific Institution was held here in its upper rooms, which had long been used for concerts and meetings. A contemporary description in the Heal Collection gives the inn a Pickwickian air,

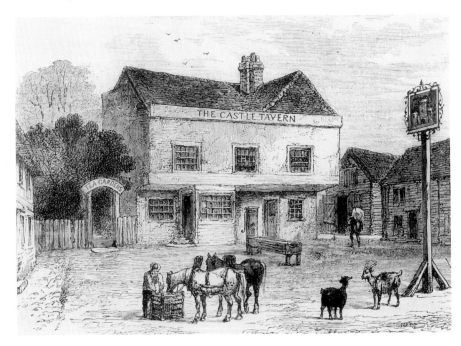

with a smoke-filled back parlour; it states that its "bowling green has boxes round it, as in olden times". The old inn was sold to the builders Kelly and Lawford in 1848 and pulled down the same year.

Turn left into **CASTLE PLACE**, which was built over a 'cow lair' next to the inn let in 1802 to Thomas King (father of James King, author of the *Panorama*). He converted it into a beautiful lawn for his

17   The Castle Inn, c.1800

house, which his son wrote was "set back a pleasant distance from the [Kentish Town] road". The house formerly belonged to William Suckling (d.1798), uncle of Lord Nelson (**Fig 18**), who as a boy often visited him there; Suckling may also have owned a house in The Grove (p 48). There is a newspaper cutting in the Heal Collection which reports that 'Nelson's Tree', a sycamore the Admiral planted as a boy, stood at the southern wall of the Castle Inn and was about to be felled so that this street could be formed. There is a tradition that after Nelson's death, Emma Hamilton came to live in a house with a beautiful garden near The Castle, and this might have been the King residence, although it is strange that James King himself does not refer to this. An alternative is suggested in Route 1 (p 25). The wide paved passage was developed in 1847 by the builders Kelly & Lawford and Robert Wills and was originally lined on both sides with small houses. Nos.12-14 on the east (left) side were taken down during the construction of South Kentish Town station (p 25) and the rest followed after bomb damage in WWII.

Halfway along the passage go down steps right (roughly on the site of Thomas King's house) and bear left past a 1960s terrace of tile-hung houses, now numbered 1-4 Castle Place but part of the large Clarence Way Estate, towards a high-fenced playground.

Before we reach it we cross Lewis Street (whose detached western end we visited earlier) and over the site of Orchard Place, a row of six small cottages facing a narrow footpath built in the 1850s and later numbered as part of Clarence Grove (see below). By the side of the playground a footpath leads alongside tall **Lorraine Court**, completed in 1952, when it included the 1000th flat to be built by St Pancras Council since WWII. Several block names here have Shavian connections, George Bernard Shaw having served on the St Pancras Vestry; St Joan was from Lorraine. (Shaw didn't have a high opinion of Kentish Town, or at least of the local accent: he makes Henry Higgins declare in Act I of *Pygmalion*: "This is an age of upstarts. Men begin in Kentish Town with 80 pounds a year, and end in Park Lane with a hundred thousand. They want to drop Kentish Town; but they give themselves away every time they open their mouths.")

Lorraine Court was built over Clarence Grove, one of the earliest roads on the Hawley–Buck estate, let to Edward Oughton in 1836. It was developed as a cul-de-sac of six small semis, at first with wide views across fields alongside the then open River Fleet, but within a few years facing back gardens. By 1889 Charles Booth considered it the poorest street on our walk, marking it blue or "poor" on his poverty map, although nine years later he said it was full of pianoforte workers. St Pancras Council used compulsory powers to purchase Clarence Grove shortly after WWII, during which most of the houses had been destroyed, although No.11 was not pulled down until 1951.

Clarence Grove overlooked the back of Orchard Street (the great-grandfather

18 Young Nelson "as a captain", painting by J F Rigaud

of Lewis William Buck, Paul Orchard, acquired the family home of Hartland Abbey). During the 1850s Mrs Lavinia Ryves, the divorced wife of the portrait painter Anthony Ryves and eldest daughter of Olivia Serres (p 28), was living at No.4. She upheld her late mother's claims to be related to the Royal Family and styled herself Princess Lavinia of Cumberland. In 1866 she took her case to court, producing all the documents on which her mother had relied, but the jury, without waiting to hear the conclusion of the reply for the Crown, unanimously declared the signatures to be forgeries. The trial was remarkable for the claims made by her barrister that George III had privately married a Quaker, Hannah Lightfoot, and had children by her, and hence neither George IV nor Queen Victoria had any right to the throne. Lavinia continued to write pamphlets in support of her claims, and her case was reheard by the House of Lords. She died in 1871, her claims unrecognised.

After 1879 Orchard Street became the northern end of Torbay Street. Houses on both sides of the latter were destroyed in bombing during WWII and a large green space (with playgrounds) now borders **Candida Court**, opposite. This large block (its name taken from another play by Shaw) has wings to the north and south called **Ivybridge Court** and **Kingsbridge Court** respectively, South Devon place names to accompany 'Torbay'. The River Fleet flows underneath the centre of the green on its way towards Hawley Road and the Thames.

We reach **Torbay Court**, the tall centrepiece of the estate, which lies alongside what was once Clarence Road (later Clarence Way). Facing the site of the block in 1846 was the semi-detached No.14, then home to Robert William Buss (1804–1875), artist, illustrator of *The Pickwick Papers* and editor of *The Fine Art Almanack*. It was at No.14 that the redoubtable Frances Mary Buss, Robert's daughter, embarked on her career in education for women, when, aged 18, she opened with her mother a preparatory school for young children here, using a system of education based on J H Pestalozzi's method "which renders the important duty of Instruction interesting to the teacher and attractive to the pupils". In 1849 the Clarence Road school moved to larger premises in Holmes Terrace, where her father and her two brothers – Alfred J Buss and Septimus Buss – assisted with the teaching until the school was given up. The family moved in 1850 to Camden Street, where the North London Collegiate School for Girls (p 122) was established (see also p 92).

Turn right. The small block on our left is **Ellen Terry Court** (after the actress closely associated with Shaw). We are now in **FARRIER STREET**, as the rump of Clarence Way here was renamed in 1961. The rather forlorn house to our right **No.1,** standing alone, dates from the 1840s, when it was called Hope Cottage. Take the path beside it to reach **Clarence Hall**. This houses a number of young people's clubs, including Le Club Français, an after-school French club for children aged 5–11. The Hopeful Monsters drama club for youngsters, which meets in the Castlehaven Community Centre (just outside our area), performs here three times a year.

Clarence Hall is on the site of the Free Christian Church, which was likewise reached from Clarence Road, past a Sunday school, whose building was taken down after WWII and not replaced. The church (**Fig 19**) was founded in 1855 by Rev. William Forster (d.1871), formerly pastor of Kelly Street Congregational Church, who had become a Unitarian. Forster obtained funds to build the church from collections after sermons he gave throughout Britain. The church was open to all: "no doctrinal test whatsoever can be imposed, either on membership or on participation in the communal service", as terms of membership in 1879 made clear. In the 1870s there was a branch of the church in Agar Grove, Camden Town. The Kentish Town building, which has a capacity of 300, was pulled down after WWII and the present early 1950s structure erected.

Continue past the back of Bradfield Court (p 72) and regain Hawley Road by Quinn's pub, turning left to reach our starting point in Kentish Town Road, thence to return to either Camden Town Underground station or the Silverlink Metro at Camden Road.

19 Free Christian (Forster's Unitarian) Church, sketched in 1855

Route 6

The 'Crimean' area and Holmes estate

Circular walk from Kentish Town station
For modern map see back cover

Covering an area west of the 'High Street', this is a walk of two halves. First we delve into a fairly homogeneous, mostly residential neighbourhood built up soon after the end of the Crimean War, with appropriately named streets. Then we explore a more mixed, industrialised area bordering the two railway lines (Midland and North London) that form the northern and western boundaries of this route. Bisecting the district, underground, is the 'lost' River Fleet, which once flowed here through fields and orchards on its way to the Thames, and which, with its associated springs, contributed to the area's early industrial development.

Leaving Kentish Town station, turn left down Kentish Town Road and, crossing over at the traffic lights, turn right past McDonalds into **HOLMES ROAD**. 'Le Petit Prince' at **No.5** is a popular small restaurant. It has a delightfully painted upper façade based on the French cartoons of the tales by Saint-Exupéry. Among the earliest developments in the area, Holmes Road lay on the estate of farmer Richard Holmes (p 21). It was already in place by

1795, striking west across Spring Fields towards a small industrial community at its far end, near the river. It was then known as Mansfield Place, probably in honour of Lord Mansfield (d.1793), Lord Chief Justice and local grandee, whose Kenwood estate was, however, considerably farther north. By 1801 Mansfield Place was well developed, with substantial houses along most of its length, and three short tributaries off the south side. The first of these was Vicarage Place, a row of cottages behind the gardens of houses on the main road, set at right angles to the later bay-windowed terrace at **Nos.7-23**. Opposite is the Kentish Town **Snooker & Pool Club**, a successor to the billiards hall that the Electric Alhambra (p 21) became after closure in 1918.

Beyond stands the blue-lamped Kentish Town **Police Station**, relocated here from near the Assembly House and opened in 1896 as headquarters of the Y (or 'Highgate') Division of the Metropolitan Police. Built in yellow stock brick, it was designed by Richard Norman Shaw, architect of the original New Scotland Yard. The station was renovated in 1984. The fine arch on the right that was once the entrance for horse-drawn Black Marias is now bricked up, and a hi-tech control centre has been installed behind. To the right of the police station, and set back from the road, is its 1960s **Section House**, a 9-storey concrete slab.

ROUTE **6**

To the left, and now also part of the police complex, gable-fronted and stuccoed **No.14** previously housed the Camden Cardboard Box Company and was before that, from late-Victorian times, a factory of the London Piano Company.

Take the next turning left into **RAGLAN STREET**. This northern end began as Spring Row, a cul-de-sac of houses off early Mansfield Place, becoming part of Raglan Street in 1937. Lord Raglan was British commander-in-chief in the Crimea whose notoriously ambiguous order prompted Cardigan's ill-fated Charge of the Light Brigade, and who died soon after the failure in June 1855 of the assault on Sebastopol. Houses on the west side have given way to the grounds and caretaker's house of St Patrick's School which, with the remainder of Holmes Road, we describe later (p 97). You are entering a residential area built up after 1852, and mostly from about 1855 in the wake of the Crimean War, which is commemorated in most of the street names in this vicinity. Ahead of you is **Monmouth House**, a modest 13-storey tower block of the later 1960s, presumably named after Lord Raglan's home county. On your left, garages cover the site of the Redan beershop, which closed in 1959. A redan was a military fieldwork to protect artillery, much used in the Crimea.

The pub stood on the northwest corner of Crown Place (p 22), which intersected here from the east, running through from the 'High Street' until truncated after WWII. Off the north side of Victorian Crown Place was a short, even smaller street called Eden Place, home to a mission hall in 1900. Off the south side, another short impasse served the works of the British Pianoforte Manufacturing Co., which survived until the 1930s. In November 1898, Charles Booth walked the area with Inspector Tomkin of Y Division, collecting data for an update to his poverty map. In Crown Place he found "2 or 3 of the outhouses fitted up as queer little one-room domiciles". A few years later, at No.19, one J M Boekbinder was making 'carton pierre', a form of papier mâché imitating stone, which originated in mid-16th-century France.

Follow Raglan Street round as it veers right along a short stretch of road once known as Raglan Place. Houses that stood to your right were demolished and their site left derelict for decades until local pressure led to the creation of a landscaped area, which struggles to be a thing of beauty. Continue left down what was the original Raglan Street, which made its first ratebook appearance only in 1857, a couple of years after Raglan Place. **Nos.34-42**, at the top, are modern replacements of houses bomb-damaged in WWII. Beyond these, this side is lined mostly with the 2-storey cottages typical of the area, in London yellow stock brick and with a stuccoed parapet concealing the roofline. Houses built here were generally modest. The Crimean area was quickly populated by the respectable working class – dressmakers, wood engravers, piano makers and railway workers. For a century or so, this was a shabby-genteel locality, with some pockets of real poverty, until gentrification in the later 20th century transformed it into the desirable, expensive area it is today.

Behind the terrace that constituted the east side before WWII was an industrial site that included, in late-Victorian times, the blacking factory of Carr & Sons (later Carr Bros), accessed from Crown Place. This was later superseded by a works and depository of the furniture firm Maple's. In 1927 the 4-storey building was acquired by St Dunstan's to serve as its works, stores and sales department. The charity was founded in 1915 to help soldiers and sailors blinded in WWI, training them in the skills needed to lead useful, independent lives. Trainees went into such fulfilling occupations as joinery, telephone switchboard operating, boot repair, massage and poultry rearing. Raglan Street purchased the raw materials required for the making of baskets, coconut-fibre mats, articles of joinery, netting and wool rugs, or for boot repairing. Materials were supplied to over 1000 men throughout the British Isles. Some St Dunstan's war-blind craftsmen sold their products locally, but most were sent to Raglan Street for sale after inspecting the work and applying any necessary finishing processes (**Fig 20**). Some quarter of a million articles were received and sold in an average year. A fire broke out in the stores on 26 December 1944, and as a result some departments were temporarily moved to adjacent

20 A St Dunstaner attaching metal fittings to nursery furniture at the Raglan Street works, late 1920s (courtesy of St Dunstan's Archive)

premises off Crown Place. St Dunstan's finally left Raglan Street at the end of 1961.

Later in the decade all the land to your left was cleared by Camden Council, who erected there the **Raglan Estate**, comprising Monmouth House and the two low-rise blocks of flats named **Alpha Court**. At the end of 1-14 Alpha Court look left across the grass to the sculpture set in cobblestones, comprising 10 concrete slabs carved with abstract designs.

Ahead lies Anglers Lane, one of Kentish Town's most historic by-ways, off which was built (by 1835) a short row of very basic cottages called Alpha Place, much later absorbed into Raglan Street. On their site stands the very active and much appreciated **Raglan Day Centre**, also known as Raglan House. Built partly on the site of a Victorian 'parish depot' (facing Anglers Lane), this originated as a St Pancras Maternity & Child Welfare Centre, and later served, until 1965, as an LCC Welfare Centre. Re-launched in c.1973 as a 'Psycho-Geriatric Day Centre', it now provides day-care facilities for elderly people suffering from dementia.

In former times there was a gateway leading from Anglers Lane into a field called Upper Spring Garden (see Thompson's 1801 map opposite the title page), which together with Spring Garden further west served in 1835 as Baker's Nursery. The presence of springs may have made the land locally rather damp,

deterring developers from building houses any earlier.

First turn left along part of **ANGLERS LANE**. Not quite opposite is a curious building at **No.1A**. When the tiny pet shop here closed, the new owner/architect ingeniously squeezed into the minute, apparently useless, triangular site a stylish stone-faced home. The intriguing balcony 'railings' have been described as 'Gaudí-esque'. On the other side of the Lane is a modest low building, built on the site of long-lost public urinals, now occupied by a Chinese herbalist. The last bollard beyond on the left (by the entrance to Kentish Town Road) is a stray from another part of Camden, bearing the initials of the St Giles District Board of Works. The junction with Kentish Town Road was, surprisingly, opened up only in 1881, Anglers Lane having previously been accessed through a narrow covered entry. On the right-hand corner is **Nando's** Portuguese chicken restaurant, formerly the Jolly Anglers pub (p 23), which was recently the shabbiest and least jolly hostelry in the whole of Kentish Town. Painted on a side wall is a well-meant imitation 'blue plaque', inaccurately stating that the River Fleet "ran here till 1766", whereas it actually passed under the Lane near its far end (to be visited later). Below the plaque is reproduced a charming quotation about the Fleet that we shall save until we reach a more appropriate spot (p 90).

Now walk back along Anglers Lane, passing on your right **Nos.21-24**, formerly Raglan Cottages, some of which are known from census records to have once housed workers from the factory opposite (see below). The first, **No.24**, on the corner of Raglan Street, has rebuilt upper parts. A plaque on the front informs us that "Boris the Cat lived here 1986-96". Boris was a feral tomcat, the terror of the neighbourhood. Taken in by residents and 'seen to', he became a permanent fixture, sitting on the wall passing the time of day with passers-by until, after 10 years, he atypically wandered into the road and was killed. Just ahead of the next junction, observe to the right **Alma Cottage**, a tiny one-bedroom cottage slipped into the gardens of houses in Alma Street.

Now dominating the southeast side of Anglers Lane is the long, solid, somewhat dishevelled factory building at **Nos.5-6A**. Marred by an ugly timber lean-to addition in front, it is nevertheless essentially a handsome example of Victorian industrial architecture, with a polychromatic gabled façade in red brick with terracotta bands, and sculptural decoration beneath the eaves. It was the factory of Claudius Ash & Co. for the making of false teeth. Claudius Ash was a West End silversmith who made false teeth for the wealthy from precious metals, at a time when the only alternative was using the teeth of corpses or skeletons. By 1840 Ash had become a manufacturer

of 'mineral teeth', made from substances such as feldspar and rock crystal, crushed into a perfectly gritless white cream, then moulded into the required shape and fired. The business thrived, moving in 1864 to Anglers Lane, and into what became the largest false-teeth factory in Europe (**Fig 21**). By 1915 the company was a huge international concern with a presence in 24 cities across the world, and its female staff (who had to be unmarried) considered it a prestigious place in which to work. It merged with a rival in 1924 to form the Amalgamated Dental Co., which moved away from Kentish Town only in 1965. The factory became an electrical works, and the kiln and chimney behind it – which long dominated the Kentish Town skyline – were demolished. The building has since served various light industrial purposes, and is now used increasingly as offices of charities – such as War Child, founded in 1998 to alleviate the suffering of children in war zones – and as studios. At **No.6** are Brook Lapping Productions, described by the *Wall Street Journal* as "the Rolls-Royce of documentary makers", and whose directors, Anne and Brian Lapping, were awarded CBEs in the 2005 New Year's Honours for their services to broadcasting. Similarly honoured was Simon McBurney, the artistic director of Théâtre de Complicité, an experimental drama company noted for its National Theatre productions, and until recently based

at **No.14**, further down on the right.

From the side of the factory there is a good view of the ornate lead-clad cupola that crowns the Prince of Wales Road Baths (p 91). If you have strayed past the Alma Street junction, return to it and turn up **ALMA STREET**. Its name commemorates the Battle of the River Alma on 20 September 1854, the first engagement of the Crimean War and an indecisive victory for the Allies. This is a homogeneous street of small 2-storey terraced houses with or without a semi-basement. **Nos.1-4**, the first four houses on the left, were originally numbered as Nos.1-4 Alma *Road* and were first occupied slightly later than the rest of the street, which dates from c.1856. Within two years, Alma Road was absorbed into Alma Street, and the numbering was adjusted to accommodate the change. Booth (in 1898) considered Alma Street better than Raglan Street, "very decent indeed; 2 families to a house generally. Remains pink [fairly comfortable]". Today it is particularly well treed, the result of pressure from one local gardener who also maintains small gardens at the base of the trees and the gardens of less able-bodied neighbours. **No.7**, on the left, was home in the 1940s-50s to the composer Phyllis Tate (1911-87), whose opera *The Lodger* was

21   Claudius Ash false-teeth factory, 1871. The rural background is a fiction.

based on the Jack the Ripper story. **No.34**, well beyond on the right, housed a mid-Victorian 'Alma Press', run by a printer, Nicholas Creswick. Living at **No.30** in the late 1960s and until 1971 were the publisher James MacGibbon and his wife Jean. Jean was the biographer of Adrian Stephen (brother of Virginia Woolf). James was co-founder of MacGibbon & Kee, publishers of such diverse authors as Cecil Day Lewis and Solzhenitsyn and he edited the poems of Stevie Smith. A communist, during WWII he passed to Russia secret information that he felt the Churchill government should have shared with its ally. The Hungarian uprising of 1956 changed his political views and he subsequently joined the Labour Party, becoming a Camden Alderman.

Alma Street leads to **INKERMAN ROAD**, named after the Battle of Inkermann on 5 November 1854, one of the bloodiest engagements of the Crimean War, in which 17,500 (mostly Russian) soldiers were killed. Dubbed the 'Soldier's Battle' (because there was little leadership), it raged all day, fought in thick fog and heavy undergrowth. The street, in turn, lent its name to both the local Environmental Area of the early 1970s and to the Conservation Area established in 2001. Booth (in 1898) described Inkerman Road as comprising "2 and 2½ storey houses, roughish some of them. 2 or 3 prostitutes living in the basements of 2

houses, on the N side SW of Cathcart St but no brothels: the women widows, with families, who ply their trade away to eke out earnings. The street as a whole decent and remains pink". On the opposite corner, at No.36, is a 3-storey building that was for over 140 years the Crimea public house, a favourite haunt of police from the Holmes Road station and section house. Quite recently closed as a pub and converted into flats, the building retains its inn-sign, with a fading image of a cavalry charge. Turning right along Inkerman Road, walk 100 yards before reaching a dead end at the back of St Patrick's School. There on the left, at **Nos.20-21**, is a pair of semi-detached houses that appear to have escaped from the suburbs. They were built on a bomb-damaged site in the 1950s.

Returning to the former pub, turn right up still cobbled **CATHCART STREET**. Named in honour of General George Cathcart, who lost his life in the Battle of Inkermann, this was always the least affluent of the Crimean streets, coloured "all purple" (mixed) by Booth. To your left is a terrace of small cottages typical of the area. On the right, near the top of the street and shaded by trees, is a quite attractive Housing Association development called **Azania Mews**, edged with cornices. (The Pan-African Congress used the name Azania for South Africa, but it never really took off.) This was built in the 1990s on the site of a bus depot.

We shall visit it again later.

On the same side, the large white-framed entrance (labelled "Better Sound") is the only tangible reminder of Cathcart Street's former domination by the bus industry. This east side was initially left undeveloped, and the OS map of 1870 shows an avenue of trees there. Behind the houses eventually built were two bus depots. One belonged to Birch Brothers, a staunchly independent operator. In 1847 Mrs Birch, a cabman's widow launched (with others) a horse-bus service from Pimlico to the City. In 1878 one of her sons, John Manley Birch, joined the Camden Town Omnibus Association, operating a route between Charing Cross and the Adelaide Tavern at Chalk Farm. As a base he bought freehold premises at No.20 Cathcart Street, adjoining the pre-existing stables of the London General Omnibus Company. John Manley, with his son, formed the firm Birch & Son in 1885. Two years later it secured a contract to carry night mail and parcels between London and Brighton. Thenceforth the Cathcart Street depot was always known as Royal Mail Yard. In 1899 John Manley's brother William joined the firm, which thus became Birch Bros Ltd. Among the pioneers of motorbuses in 1904, Birch ran bus services in many parts of London (including Hampstead) and a fleet of taxis too. Royal Mail Yard was reconstructed in 1924 as a modern bus garage, absorbing the former LGOC depot further down the street, which in the meantime had been occupied by the Associated Omnibus Co. Birch's bus routes in the capital were lost in 1934 to the London Passenger Transport Board, and the company then concentrated instead on coach services and excursions, and on establishing a network of bus routes in rural Herts., Beds. and Northants. Birch's long-established long-distance bus service from King's Cross to Rushden was finally surrendered to another operator in 1969, and the remaining coaches were taken over by Grey-Green.

Running directly below Cathcart Street is the River Fleet. Small metal gratings in the middle of the road near the "Better Sound" entrance allow you to trace its course, and through larger access hatches the noise of it is clearly audible after heavy rain, when it is sometimes rather smelly. It still has the potential to flood, having done so as recently as 2002.

Return to Inkerman Road and turn right. The river does likewise, bending briefly westward before continuing south under **WILLES ROAD**. The latter is named after Lieutenant-General James Willes, commander of the marines in the Crimea. Occasionally spelt 'Willis' in early directories, the name is still pronounced accordingly by many locals. Approaching from the left, Willes Road does a dog-leg as it crosses Inkerman Road, continuing

north on a more westerly alignment. In the kink is southeast-facing **No.38**, with its Corinthian portico, home in the 1970s and '80s to Nick Ross, the journalist, broadcaster and presenter of BBC television's *Crimewatch UK*. Wander up the road's northern section to your right, known briefly as Willes Road North when first built in c.1855, and lined by 3-storey terraced houses of relatively simple design. Charles Booth described this part of Willes Road as "mixed" in 1889; nine years later he found "3-storey houses; many done up, and tenants of a better class have come in as far as the bend in the road … Up to this point, from purple to pink." By the 1980s **No.53** (on the left) was home to Patricia Hewitt MP, previously Secretary of the National Council for Civil Liberties, then serving as personal press officer to the Labour Party leader Neil Kinnock; at the time of writing she is Secretary of State for Health. In the gap ahead on the right stood No.72, one of eight Willes Road buildings demolished to create a playground for the infants at the adjacent Board School (p 97). Here, accessed through a covered entrance, were the workshops of glass stainers William James & Co., who made ornamental glass for pubs. The road's northernmost extremity, beyond a slight bend ahead, we shall visit later (p 96).

Turn round and, re-crossing the staggered junction with Inkerman Road, walk down the southern half of Willes

Road, originally Willes Road South. Broad and especially leafy at the far end, this is lined mostly by elegant 2-storey semi-detached houses behind front gardens well stocked with bushes and shrubs. The building style is early/mid-Victorian, with classical features and stucco ornament. Some houses have decorative iron balconies, particularly impressive on **Nos.17-21** on your right and **No.22** opposite, while others boast porticoes with Corinthian columns and studded doors. The individuality of each house is emphasised by vertical stuccoed chamfered quoins. The 1960s terrace at **Nos.16-20** replaced houses damaged beyond repair during WWII. **No.14** was home in the 1970s-80s to Victor Sassie, proprietor of the celebrated Gay Hussar restaurant in Soho. This was the only section of a 'Crimean' street to be coloured a "well-to-do" red by Charles Booth on his original map. On his walk in 1898 he spotted 'Apartment' notices in some windows and decided to downgrade the coding to "pink barred". In the same year houses at the south end of the road were demolished to make land available for the St Pancras Public Baths (right).

Ahead of you lies Prince of Wales Road, while **ANGLERS LANE** (see also p 85) approaches diagonally from the left. The squat octagonal cast-iron bollard on the near corner is Grade-II Listed. Some other, more functional, specimens nearby bear the initials "SPPM", for St Pancras Parish, Middlesex. A short distance up Anglers Lane, the Fleet passed beneath it, having swung briefly eastward before turning south again though the gardens of the Castle (p 80). Though it is hard to imagine now, you are near the spot, once a favourite haunt of fishermen, which gave Anglers Lane its name. An elderly man, writing to the local press in 1909, recalled:

"When I knew it as a boy it was one of the loveliest spots imaginable – so deserted in the early hours of the morning that, when the anglers were not there, some of the youngsters from the cottages around, and some who were not youngsters, used to bathe in the river. I passed through Anglers Lane some time ago, an aged man in a bathchair, and I found it hard to realise that my wheels were rolling their way over the River Fleet."

Cross over to the corner of Anglers Lane with **PRINCE OF WALES ROAD**, turn left and walk to the gated entrance of **Una House**. Consider now the complex story of the site east of Anglers Lane and facing Prince of Wales Road. A map of 1842 shows that the latter had been laid out throughout its length by then but was still undeveloped, apart from a few villas here at its east end, initially known as Grafton Place, which had begun as a turning out of the 'High Street' in the first years of the century. Three pairs of semi-detached villas lined the north side east

of where you stand. Living there at No.6 Grafton Place towards the end of his short life was the naturalist Samuel Pickworth Woodward FGS (1821-65), an expert on invertebrate fossils, most noted for his 3-volume *Manual of the Mollusca*. The near acute-angled corner was later filled by what the 1870 OS map shows as a "temporary" church. This was first occupied by one of five London branches of the Catholic Apostolic (Irvingite) Church, founded in 1833 by the charismatic defrocked Presbyterian, Rev. Edward Irving. The local minister, Rev. Albert E Whish, lived in Oseney Crescent (p 104). In 1880, the church became a mission hall, and later parish room of the newly created Anglican parish of St Barnabas (see p 27); its incumbent, the Rev. Charles J Priddle, lived next door in the villa that had become No.12 Prince of Wales Road.

In 1905 the whole block was acquired by the Progressive-controlled St Pancras Council, as part of an arrangement with Andrew Carnegie to build here a central library for the borough (as well as four branch libraries). The purchase, for £15,000, was controversial, as the owner of the land was Horace Regnart, a Progressive alderman, who lived in Camden Road (p 120). No sooner had the site been cleared than there was a change of party control, and the new Conservative/Ratepayers alliance abandoned the central library scheme. The site lay vacant for

many years until the building of Una House, opened by the Mayor, T W McCormack, in 1922. Its name, as the *St Pancras Gazette* reported, had been proposed by Councillor Frank Combes, and was borrowed from Una, "the embodiment of truth and honour" in Spenser's *Faerie Queen*. Combes' object in suggesting the name was "to make the children think", and "he considered it would have an educational value". Walk east past the front to observe how, to fit the site, the flats were arranged in three blocks built around a triangular inner courtyard. They were rehabilitated in 2003.

Beyond Una House lies **GRAFTON YARD**, known as Grafton Mews till 1937, and once L-shaped, extending through to Anglers Lane. The Mews was home in the 1880s to a wheelwright, an organ machinist, bicycle makers Sargent & Petts, and a piano manufacturer, Charles McVay. The piano-string makers Charles Atto Dettmer & Sons later had a factory in the Mews, in company with John Smith Tozer, a coverer of piano hammers. By WWI the sole directory-listed business was the amusingly named Bi-Gum Adhesives. From Grafton Yard one gains a good view of the white-painted rear face of the Ash false-teeth factory (p 86), across the site of its demolished chimney and kiln. No.2 Prince of Wales Road, beyond, houses the **Camden Community Law Centre**, established here in 1973 and offering free legal advice and representation for Camden residents. The centre occupies part of the former Palace cinema (p 24).

Backtrack now along **PRINCE OF WALES ROAD**, past Una House, ignoring the road's opposite (south) side, for which see Route 5. Re-cross the Anglers Lane junction to the **Kentish Town Sports Centre**, better known as Prince of Wales Road Baths. The St Pancras authorities were keener on baths than books. No expense was spared on the borough's third public baths, which was opened in 1901 for the newly formed Borough Council by the furniture magnate Sir Blundell Maple. Designed in an exuberantly free Tudor/François Premier style by Thomas W Aldwinckle, it is built in red brick with generous applications of Doulton terracotta. On the Prince of Wales frontage, inspect the triple arcade of entrances, each surmounted by a cartouche with Art Nouveau lettering. High above the first, the old entrance to the "Public Hall" (*alias* Grafton Hall), are statues of St Pancras and St George. The other two are entrances to the public baths. Note the Art Nouveau cartouches inscribed "1st" and "2nd class", and the four leering devils. Over the pedimented entry to the "Men's First Class" swimming pool, bearded river gods recline in front of a bas-relief (top left) depicting Tower Bridge. Second-class men were greeted by female figures labelled AQUA and PURA, and did not get a towel and soap, unlike those using the first-class facilities.

Turn right along **GRAFTON ROAD** by the side of the Baths, past the tiled entrance to the Sports Centre, to a building in Flemish style with a terracotta plaque announcing that it was built in 1900. At the end are the old entrances to the "Ladies Bath" and the "Public Washhouse", still functioning today as a laundrette. Other facilities originally provided included 129 slipper baths (individual baths in cubicles) and a gymnasium, added in 1905. Grafton Road was built on the line of a western arm of Anglers Lane. Having bridged the Fleet (see above), it turned briefly west in front of the present baths, and then struck northwards. Land to the west of here (and a small pocket to the east, on which Grafton Place was built) lay on the Southampton estate. Lord Southampton was a member of the Fitzroy family of which the Duke of Grafton is the head. The road, lined by plain 3-storey terraces of the early 1850s, runs north to where we rejoin it later.

Meanwhile, return to Prince of Wales Road and the **Grafton Arms** on the right-hand corner. The early-Victorian pub, with a later decorative ground floor projecting beyond the main elevation, is now painted all over in a bold blue. The pub once hosted meetings of the Grafton Cricket Club, whose first match was played in June 1869. Continue west along **PRINCE OF WALES ROAD**, past houses that were at first individually named. No.22, for example, was Claremont House. The Beardsmore Gallery now occupies a front extension at **Nos.22-24**. Formerly the London Youth Advisory Centre, the Brandon Centre at **No.26** offers psychotherapy and counselling to young people. For much of the 20th century the building housed the St Pancras Schools [medical] Treatment Centre. Cross Ryland Road (p 93). Ahead, on the western boundary of our survey area, are the brick arches carrying the railway across Prince of Wales Road. Opened in 1860, from Camden Road to Willesden, as the Hampstead Junction Railway, this now forms part of Silverlink Metro's North London Line. The adjacent Kentish Town West station was opened seven years later as 'Kentish Town'. Short of the bridge are six surviving houses, once part of Claremont Terrace, which was bisected by the railway.

On your immediate right is a handsome, gabled, Tudor-style building. Designed by Thomas Henry Wyatt and David Brandon, and built in ragstone with a slate roof, it opened in 1849 as the Asylum for Aged Governesses. The Governesses' Benevolent Institution was promoted by Rev. David Laing of nearby Holy Trinity (p 74), and it created the 'Asylum' as a sanctuary or retirement home for governesses who had fallen on hard times in later life (**Fig 22**). The Asylum, when first built, was set amid open fields. Its creators did not anticipate the imminent arrival of the railway. Within a few years a report says "The increasing encroachment of the railways, disturbing this once peaceful home with shrill shrieks at all hours of the day and often of the night, besides shutting out the access of the sweet air that used to come from Hampstead and Highgate, has caused the removal of the old ladies to be seriously contemplated". They did move, to Chislehurst in Kent, in 1872.

The premises were then used by a succession of schools. The Camden School for Girls (CSG) acquired it, with financial help from the Clothworkers' Company, and moved here from Camden Street on 7 May 1878. The school at that time was usually listed as "Frances Mary Buss's School for Girls". The building's diminutive spire is topped by a sailing-craft, a Buss family motif (a 'buss' was a 2-masted Dutch vessel used for catching herrings and mackerel). Evacuated to Lincolnshire during WWII, the CSG girls returned to Prince of Wales Road in 1943 before their final move to Sandall Road (p 123) in 1956. The Ryland Secondary School for Girls subsequently moved into the building, which in the late 1970s became an annexe of the St Richard of Chichester Catholic Secondary School (see p 67). Branded by inspectors as a failing school (unfairly, many believed), this closed two decades later. The building was used until 1999 as a training centre for hotel workers. Developers then moved in, converting it into luxury flats.

Particularly notable are the wrought-iron railings and gates, which (like the building behind) are Grade-II Listed. The imported gates, in an early-18th-century style, are said to have influenced the design of the railings. Included in the elaborate ironwork are the initials "GI" (Governesses' Institution). Built as 'The Gates', the flats are known officially – and pretentiously – as **Hampstead Gates**, although the only connection with Hampstead would seem to be the nearby former Hampstead Junction Railway.

The departure of the old ladies in 1872 opened the way for housing development

22   Drawing Room of the Governesses' Asylum in Prince of Wales Road, 1849

over what had been their extensive garden to the east of the Asylum buildings.

RYLAND ROAD was the result, named in 1873, probably after a local builder. Turn north along it, passing on the left extensions to the asylum buildings erected in 1877-9 for the CSG, designed by E C Robins and similarly built in ragstone but with some render for economy. A plaque proclaims this to have been the school's "Ewart Wing", built with a £1000 donation from Miss Mary Anne Ewart, the daughter of the humanitarian Liberal MP, William Ewart. When she died in 1911, she left £30,000 to the Oxbridge female colleges to further the cause of women's higher education. Today, at **No.37**, the Kentish Town Day Nursery occupies part of the old CSG buildings.

Beyond lies **PERREN STREET**, a short turning to the left, named after Richard Perren, a Camden Town 'carpenter' (or builder). In the 1880s the Toledo Steel Co. made bicycles here. Frederick Jones & Co. boasted of being the "sole proprietors and manufacturers of the only Patent British-made Silicate Cotton or Slag-Wool", the latter a fibre made from molten slag and used for boiler insulation. 70 years later the firm was still here (as Jones & Broadbent), and still making slag-wool at their Hercules Works, now (as **No.1A**) white-painted and with barred ground-floor windows. No. 1A lies today in the shadow of a modern tower, part of the Hampstead Gates development,

which has an external staircase spiralling around it leading up to a flat-roofed belvedere open at the sides. Northwards of Perren Street, between the North London viaduct and the back gardens of Ryland Road, runs a narrow industrial corridor once filled with various parts of the Brinsmead piano factory (p 95). The surviving buildings on the north side of Perren Street, labelled "Imperial Works" passed from Brinsmeads to the Imperial Organ & Piano Co., still trading here in the 1965, while British Reeds, on the same site, supplied organ parts. Looking through the archway here, observe the cobbled trackway running north behind the factory. This was once lined by metal rails, used for transporting materials around the constricted Brinsmead site. Perren Street premises have since served a bewildering variety of purposes, for the making or storage of products ranging from buttons and sweets to surgical and scientific instruments, loud speakers and electric lamps, toilet preparations and sanitary equipment.

Return to **RYLAND ROAD** and continue up its north end, which was built on what had been the garden of nurseryman T Ansell, equipped with some 8 or 9 greenhouses according to an 1870 map. The style of the 2-storey terraced housing in Ryland Road, built between 1873 and 1894, is typical of the late-Victorian 'vernacular or domestic revival'.

Hipped slate roofs were the order of the day, with eaves to shed rain and, to comply with various bylaws of the time, party walls projecting above the roof to deter the spread of fire. Bay windows were in vogue; likewise the Venetian tripartite windows espoused by John Ruskin. Gothic columns frame many front doors. Here the houses are charmingly stepped back along the slight bend of the road.

No.32 on the right was the home until 1933 of John Henry Cook, an 1870s music hall artist, billed as the "dancing giant and Continental wonder" and nicknamed 'Black Cookey'. He blacked his face and danced on stilts, and was a champion dancer on "one stilt and a spade". He was, incidentally, a grandson of William Inwood, the co-architect of St Pancras New Church. In the 1980s **No.23**, opposite, was the London pied-à-terre of Fay Weldon, the novelist and sometime advertising copywriter responsible for the slogan "Go to work on an egg". Visible through an entry beyond, just before the road turns right, is the other end of the cobbled way you viewed from Perren Street; look carefully and you may see tiny portions of rusted rail peeping through the adjoining asphalt.

Ahead looms 5-storey, red-brick **Portland House**, today housing Delbanco Meyer & Co, listed previously as bristle makers and trading now in household textiles. This building was part of the main

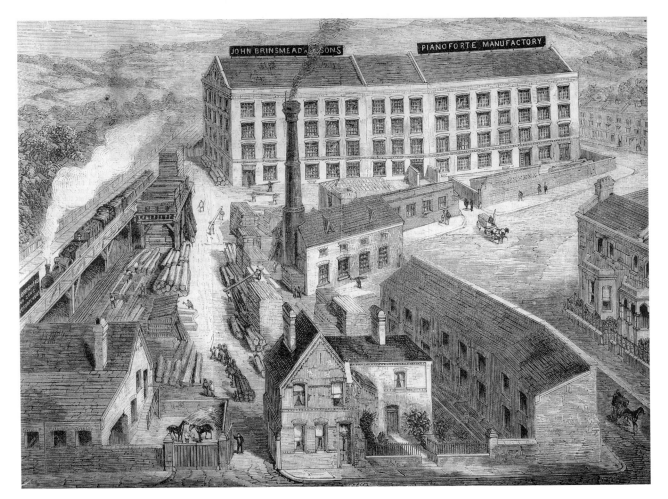

block of the former Brinsmead factory (**Fig 23**). John Brinsmead, a cabinet maker from Devon, began making pianos in 1836, using various workshops in the Fitzrovia area. He was joined in 1861 by his sons John and Edgar, and the firm John Brinsmead & Sons was established in 1870. It moved into its new Grafton Works soon after – and not (as several writers have asserted) in 1841. Brinsmeads "manufactured in a big way", boasting in 1904 of making a piano every hour, or 3000 a year. Prices ranged from 33 to 300 guineas. A Royal Warrant holder in 1893 as "pianoforte makers to TRH the Prince and Princess of Wales", the company also supplied grand pianos to Queen Victoria, various European monarchs and His Holiness the Pope. Crippled by a piano workers' strike in 1919, the firm went into receivership; briefly revived, it was soon taken over by Cramers. The Grafton Works became Dell's Confectionery factory until WWII, when enemy action destroyed its eastern half, where Brinsmeads had made piano cases and performed the finishing processes. **Ryland House**, the undistinguished warehouse that arose in its place, was called Freedex House in the 1960s and occupied by a manufacturer of ladies' handbags. Developers now

23 The Brinsmead piano factory, 1870. Perren Street in the foreground, Hampstead Junction Railway to the left.

want to extend the building upwards and convert it to residential use, but Camden Council and local opinion favour retaining employment in the area.

We regain **GRAFTON ROAD** opposite 3-storey Victorian terraces in various styles: to the left are flat-fronted houses stuccoed in different pastel shades, while **Nos.54-70** are in brick, with round-arched windows and stuccoed ground floors. Turn right down the west side, past **Nos.33-49**, notable for the rusticated keystones surmounting the windows. Living here in 1971, at **No.43B**, was Joseph Sickert (actually Gorman-Sickert), who claimed to be the son of the officially childless painter, Walter Sickert. Stories supposedly told to him by his alleged father before his death in 1942, implicating the Victorian Royal Family in the Whitechapel Murders of 1888, formed the basis of Stephen Knight's book, *Jack the Ripper, the Final Solution* (1976). Joseph was subsequently interviewed by Special Branch.

Turn back north past Ryland House to where Wilkin Street intersects, bridged by the North London Line. Turn briefly left, noting on the near side the stark rear wall of the old Brinsmead works, with barred ground-floor windows. Opposite, and nestling beside the railway viaduct at **No.2 Wilkin Street**, is a small red-brick Gothic building that was once a Methodist Sunday School. Return to Grafton Road, and turn left past **No.55**. This handsome chapel-like

building, labelled East Fleet House, was indeed a place of worship and the chapel to which the Sunday School belonged. It was erected by the Primitive Methodists in 1867, with seating for 450, and used by them until 1923 when they moved to Lamble Street in Gospel Oak. After their departure, the building was converted by St Pancras Council into an electricity substation. Serving more recently as a warehouse of the Abbey National Building Society, and latterly occupied by surveyors and an engineering firm, it was again being refurbished in 2004.

Recently built housing beyond includes the site of No.59, where dairyman James Child was still listed as a "cowkeeper" in 1862. On the east side, meanwhile, **Nos.86-94** form a rather down-at-heel Victorian terrace with a betting shop and some disused old glazed shopfronts, although **Nos.96&98** on the corner beyond are now being renovated. The local sub post office was at No.92. Residential Athlone Street emerges from the left through another railway bridge. **No.61** on the far corner, now Print-in-Time, previously housed lithographic printers the Stanhope Press and before them, after WWII, Scottish Fisheries, who made aquaria. A fourth arched railway bridge crosses Grafton Road ahead. About here the western arm of Anglers Lane (see p 90) came to an end, petering out into a footpath that continued northwest across the fields to the Gospel Oak. In 1937 the later Grafton Road absorbed Carlton Road (beyond the bridge), and today runs north to Oak Village through an area outside the scope of this book.

Turn right, therefore, along a short stretch of road that is the western extremity of Holmes Road (where our walk began). A right turn past the **Cabin Café** on the next corner leads into the north end of **WILLES ROAD** (see also p 89). At **Nos.71-77**, to your right and rounding a slight bend in the road, is a new housing association development that is either characterless or sensitive to the local style, depending on your point of view. It is certainly better than the post-modernist monstrosity that the association originally planned until local protest intervened. The flats replaced the original terrace here, which suffered general blast damage during WWII. Opposite, at No.76, is the **George IV** pub, invitingly bedecked with creepers and flowers, and one of the few traditional pubs still trading locally. A particularly distinctive 3-storey building, it dates from between 1868 and 1874, and combines Italian Renaissance and Classical styles. The seemingly anachronistic name is easily explained: the present pub was a rebuild of a George IV Tavern, which had stood since earlier in the century on the opposite corner (with Spring Place).

Now return to the crossroads. Ahead lies **SPRING PLACE**, well developed by 1801, originally a cul-de-sac at the end of what is now Holmes Road. Local springs, which fed the River Fleet and which gave Spring Place its name, will have been a source of water for a brewery that once stood on the west side. The ratepayer there in 1835 was one Charles Hammond; a decade later it was William Holmes, brewing having been one of the Holmes family's sidelines. Nearby was a 'rope ground', for the making of rope. It was probably to serve this little industrial community that Mansfield Place (now Holmes Road) struck west across the swampy fields so early (see 1801 map on p 2).

The Autograph Sound studio at **No.2** Spring Place occupies part of a site where Winsor & Newton established their first North London Colour Works, probably in a converted house. The world-renowned firm was founded in Rathbone Place [W1] in 1832 by William Winsor, an artist, and Henry C Newton, who provided the scientific expertise. In 1836 they invented Chinese White paint. Appointed artists' colourmen to Queen Victoria in 1841, they moved 3 years later to Spring Place, where colours were ground by hand, then spread out onto stone slabs for partial drying. Winsor & Newton later built a larger, purpose-built, steam-powered works farther along Spring Place, where they stayed until leaving for Wealdstone in 1938. (The building, long multi-occupied, is known as Spring House.) The first factory at No.1 became a warehouse of Walton, Hassell & Port, listed as "Italian warehousemen" in 1874, and 90 years later still running a minor grocery chain with a shop in the 'High Street'.

The J T Coachworks site at **Nos.3-5** has housed road transport enterprises for many years. London Lorries Ltd, "motor body builders", were here before WWII, after which the hauliers General Roadways took over the bomb-damaged site. Charles Pugh, the makers of car windscreens now in Holmes Road (pp 83, 97), moved from Warren Street to erstwhile No.6 Spring Place in the 1930s, when they were listed as simple "glasscutters". Just beyond the (modern) railway bridge, at **Nos.8-9**, the optical works of the Eliott Optical Co. has given way to studios of the Wall to Wall TV company, producers of such historical 'reality dramas' as *The 1900 House*. Here the original Spring Place ended, to be extended later along what became Gillies Street (ahead, out of our survey area).

East of Spring Place lay Brick Field, where the Holmes family had diversified in the late 18th century from farming into the more lucrative business of making bricks. The land was purchased by the Midland Railway to accommodate its Kentish Town Coal Depot, which was fully operational by 1873. A prominent feature on old maps were the 16 raised red-brick arches, aligned east-west, that housed the depot's coal drops. Coal trains approached from the north on a viaduct from the main line; a traverser moved wagons to their final destination above a coal merchant's arch. The fuel was then discharged into the void below through a hopper, for delivery to customers by horse and cart. There were 40 stables and coalmen's offices within the depot site and facing Spring Place and Holmes Road. Coal operations ceased in c.1953, when the site became a British Road Services depot. Demolished in c.1972, this was replaced by the unattractive brick-and-concrete bulk of Camden Council's **Holmes Road Depot**. Some of the 16 arches survived into the 1980s, used finally as workshops and stores. That area now contains the west end of the Kentish Town Business Park, accessed from Regis Road (p 99).

Cross over and follow the depot back around the corner, turning east along **HOLMES ROAD** to its main entrance. As a signboard confirms, the complex, originally built for the then Building Department, now houses a variety of Council services and the LearnDirect centre of Camden Jobtrain, which provides vocational training for young adults.

Turn your attention, with relief, to the fine Grade-II-Listed Arts and Crafts building opposite, crowned by a small spire and weathervane. Built by the School Board for London as the Mansfield Place School, it was designed by E R Robson, the Board's chief architect. Among the

VIPs attending the school's official opening in 1874 was a certain Miss Buss. The central block, with two upper floors of lofty classrooms, is flanked by two lower wings on either side. Bearing an "SBL" plaque, the right-hand (infants') wing was originally single-storey, but was later extended upwards, in defiance of the then common view that infants and stairs did not mix. Built for 1000 children, many from severely deprived homes, the school was enlarged to accommodate half as many again. In 1893 a factory on the east side was acquired and converted into a laundry centre, where girls, often destined for domestic service, were appropriately trained.

A declining population brought about by planned redevelopment of the area led to the school's closure in 1923, after which it turned to adult education as an Evening Institute. The Kentish Town Camera and Weightlifting Clubs met here. In 1927, a Junior Men's Institute was established where less academically gifted boys were taught practical skills. Known as the Kentish Town Men's Institute after WWII, then as the Kentish Town & East Hampstead Institute, the college became part of ILEA's Camden Institute after 1965, and then of Kingsway College, now merged into **Westminster Kingsway College**. Walk along the south side of Holmes Road, passing Cathcart Street (p 88), where eight houses were demolished to provide a

playground for the school.

From here, as we re-cross the Fleet, there is a better view of Azania Mews. This stands on a triangular area on the river's east bank once called Tan Pill Field. Perhaps it was here that William Holmes engaged (in 1805) in another Holmes sideline, the noxious trade of tanning or curing of hides (an old verb 'to pill' meant 'to strip'). It is worthwhile looking inside the modern development, where two rows of terraces face each other across a wide parking area. Each house is topped by an enormous semicircular pediment. Next on the right is the modern **Magnet** kitchen showroom, on a long commercialised site previously housing the Magnet Joinery. The bricked-up arches facing Holmes Road, lofty enough for a double-decker bus, belonged to further premises of the Birch bus company (p 88), on a site earlier occupied by the factory of Richard Jones Allen, a late-Victorian manufacturer of bronze powder.

The slightly curving stretch of road you have just traversed was initially called Mansfield Crescent, but was quickly renamed Lower Mansfield Place. By 1886 the whole route between Kentish Town Road and Spring Place had become Holmes Road. Soon appearing to your left is a short spur of roadway, originally part of Upper Mansfield Place. This initially ran a little farther until it met the River Fleet, beyond which the route westward continued as a field path. On the east bank, off Upper Mansfield Place, was a further brewery, still standing in 1870, when it was among the properties acquired by the Midland Railway. Beer flowed freely hereabouts. On the south side of Holmes Road, just before the bend and boarded up in 2004, No.61 (latterly the neat offices of an electronic instrument maker) was once a beershop, occupied in the early 20th century by Edmund and William Gay, who combined beer retailing there with a bar-fitting business at adjoining No.63. In the 1880s, Charles Gay, presumably their father, lived at erstwhile No.59, with a similar dual role as beer retailer at No.59A and gas fitter at No.61. William Monk, a brewer, had been the occupier at No.59 in 1872, when local directories listed a Malt & Hops "public house" at No.59A, although this was probably only a beer-house. Two doors to the east, at No.53, stood the fully licensed Mansfield Arms, which flourished there in Victorian times.

Nearing completion in 2004 at **Nos.55-57** was a new 4-storey building in concrete and glass, a mixed warehouse, business and residential development. The premises it replaced were always devoted to road transport: bus bodies were made here for a while in the bodyshops of Birch Brothers, whose Royal Mail Yard depot (p 88) they adjoined. W Parkyn & Sons, wheelwrights and makers of carriages and carts, subsequently occupied Nos.55-57,

which later became Beardmore Motors' service station, and after WWII, a taxicab-servicing depot of 'Fifty Taxis'. The last occupants were Charles Pugh (Glass) Ltd, whose car windscreen business has now moved to new modern premises not quite opposite, on a site that previously housed A Richardson's post-WWII waste paper salvage works.

A newcomer next door at **Nos.48-52** is Maison Henry Bertrand, specialising in silk fabrics for theatrical costumes and props. At first mainly residential, the north side of Holmes Road has been progressively commercialised. It was designated an 'industrial zone' in the 1960s, and in 1971 Nos.36-50 were declared a 'clearance area'. 19th-century houses and their front gardens have been whittled away until only one pair remains, at **Nos.20-22**. No.22, however, was long put to commercial use by the Metropolitan Memorial Co., whose monumental masons' yard presumably corresponded to the back premises now named **Studio 22**. Residential use will soon be revived at **Nos.32-34**, where new flats for the Acton (*sic*) Housing Association were under construction in 2004, on the site of a defunct firewood factory. 'Period' fire*places* are for sale at Acquisitions House, the modern block at **Nos.24-26** beyond.

Back on the south side, the driveway at **No.45** (note the weighbridge) corresponds to 19th-century Grape Place: lined by

tiny workers' cottages, this led to a further eight dwellings named Paradise Row, and then to unidentified larger buildings beside the Fleet, shown on the 1801 map as agricultural. The drive now leads to a low post-WWII building occupied by Bird & Davies, suppliers of artists' materials, which previously served as St Pancras (and later Camden) Council's Sheltered Workshops, providing employment for the disabled.

Earlier still this site was part of the hostel premises next door at **Nos.41-43**, where the 2-storey Victorian red-brick building has served the disadvantaged for over a century. The St Pancras Hostel was built by the St Pancras Guardians of the Poor, on land they bought for £7000 in 1895, to replace the workhouse Casual Wards removed from Leighton Road (p 127). Casual Wards offered one night's accommodation to the homeless in cubicles just wide enough to contain a single bed, in return for physical labour. At one time Holmes Road inmates broke rocks to earn their keep. A relic of these grim times is the weighbridge you witnessed, where rocks (whole and smashed) were checked in and out. The hostel was on the 'circuit' described by George Orwell in *Down and Out in London and Paris* (1933), where paupers journeyed around specific London workhouses, seeking shelter. By Orwell's time, hard labour had been replaced by enforced idleness. Daily rations, eaten in silence and sometimes without cutlery, comprised gruel with cheese and 8 oz of bread; tea and butter were provided, if at all, only for over-60s.

After the Poor Law ended in 1930, the Holmes Road Casual Wards became a relatively humane working-men's hostel, administered successively by the LCC, then the GLC, and finally Camden Council. Refurbished to meet modern standards, it now boasts it is among the best of its kind in the country. To the left of the main hostel building is **Bower Cottage**, now rebuilt in a far from cottagey way to provide additional hostel accommodation. This was once the workhouse superintendent's dwelling, its name evidently borrowed from the Casual Wards' earlier site in Leighton Road. Between the Wars, Bower Cottage housed the St Pancras North Relief Station & Dispensary of the LCC, used during the General Strike of 1926 to store essential foodstuffs.

Beyond lies the modern **St Patrick's RC Primary School**, which recently celebrated its bicentenary. It moved here in 1967 from Soho, where it was founded as a charity school in 1803 by a group of Irish merchants to serve the children of immigrant workers from Ireland. It later attracted many Italian pupils, while today there is a very wide ethnic mix. In 1900 a "rag doll store" occupied part of the present school's site, while No.33

was subsequently home to the Excelsior Welding works. At No.39 Holmes Road, where the school's Nursery now stands (to the right), was the 1880s workshop of William Caldercourt, who made cricket bats. The premises were later replaced by a laundry, run for several decades by Harry Andrews and known in 1900 as the Primrose Laundry.

Walk past the police station we saw earlier as far as Kentish Town Road and turn left up its west side. Cobbled **YORK MEWS** (off left) is an L-shaped back lane that once ran as far as the rear of the Bull & Gate (p 31), but was shortened with the coming of the Midland Railway. Stroll as far as the bend, if you will, to observe how surprisingly leafy and rustic it looks today. The artist Barbara Reise (1940–1978) was based in York Mews in the mid-1970s when she was trying to produce an international arts magazine called *ArtstrA*. Continue to the railway bridge carrying Kentish Town Road across the Midland Main Line.

To its left is **REGIS ROAD** – which we shall not traverse – dipping gently down into **Kentish Town Business Park**, and built in the late 20th century on redundant railway land. Here, in a wide cutting, acres of sidings once fanned out south-eastwards towards you from the main line, serving a carriage and wagon repair shed on the south side (adjoining Holmes Road) and, immediately adjacent

to the main line, the Kentish Town Cattle Dock. Here livestock from the country was unloaded and penned, and then either taken to the nearby slaughterhouses established by butchers in local mews – or (until the 1930s) driven on the hoof through the streets of Kentish Town to the Metropolitan Cattle Market off York Way. Beyond lay the extensive coal depot whose site we encountered earlier (p 96). These vital elements of the Victorian distribution system have been replaced by such modern equivalents as Royal Mail's Kentish Town **Delivery Office** at the far western end of the 'Park', and (within view) the glass-fronted, hangar-like warehouse of **United Parcel Services**. The latter was built in 1984, at a cost of £4 million, as a 'super depot' for the brewers Whitbread's.

Well out of sight are such present-day essentials as the Camden **Recycling Centre** and Camden **Car Pound**; the large Howdens Joinery; the offices and workshops of **The Interchange** and **Alpha House** (named after its original occupiers, Alpha Jewels Ltd); and the London base of Fairfax Meadow, "exceptionally fine butchers" and major suppliers of meat to the catering industry. There, too, is the local distribution centre of Asphaltic Ltd, virtual 'sitting tenants' when the 'Park' was developed, having moved onto the Holmes Road coal depot site by the 1960s. Now Britain's largest specialists in roofing material, with 46 branches nationwide, the firm was founded (in Islington) in 1946 and subsequently run by three generations of the Regis family, hence the name given to the new estate's access road.

A short turning off the far end of Regis Road has been dubbed **BROWN'S LANE**. Its name, a purely modern invention, offers a final reminder of the area's agricultural past. Brown's Dairy, famed in Victorian times for its 'Cows' Cathedral' in Camden Town, once grazed its cattle on the meadows of western Kentish Town.

Crossing at the lights to the Assembly House, turn right to regain Kentish Town station for your transport home.

Route 7
'New Kentish Town'
Circular walk from Kentish Town station
For modern map see back cover

Leaving Kentish Town station, turn left and walk south along Kentish Town Road. At the first junction turn left again, into Islip Street, and into the area east of the 'High Street' that is the subject of this walk. Pause beside the Victorian rear extension of the Jorene Celeste bar (p 30) in the 'High Street'; in its earlier days, as the Oxford Vaults, this was the pub's billiards hall.

We are entering the former Christ Church estate, the first and largest of three estates to be encountered on this walk, and until 1955 the property of Christ Church, the cathedral within the Oxford College founded by Cardinal Wolsey in 1525 as Cardinal College and reconstituted 21 years later as Christ Church. The 31-acre field underlying the estate was copyhold land in the manor of Cantelowes, the subject of a bequest by John Morant in 1547 before passing into the possession of Sir William Hewett, a clothworker. In 1689 the property included a barn, a garden, an orchard and a conigree (or rabbit warren). In that year Viscount Hewett of Gowran, a descendant of Sir William, sold the land to a Hackney-born cleric, Rev. Robert South, sometime chaplain to James II (when Duke of York)

and canon of Oxford's Christ Church. On his death in 1716, South bequeathed the Kentish Town property first to his housekeeper and then, on her death, to the Dean and Chapter of Christ Church.

Intersecting from the left is **FRIDESWIDE PLACE**. Frideswide was a Saxon princess who, fleeing from her unwelcome suitor King Algar, took refuge in Oxford. Frideswide founded a convent there that was the forerunner of Christ Church, and she later became Oxford cathedral's patron saint. Frideswide Place is a nondescript cul-de-sac reaching a dead end at the railway (and the estate boundary), originally lined by small terraced houses that were so run down by 1955 that two of their roofs fell in. On the west side now are only lock-up garages, and beyond them the plain-brick rear of the Tube station. On the opposite side is a brick box of 1976 housing the nursery department of the local church school.

Continue along **ISLIP STREET**, which takes its name from the Oxfordshire parish where Dr South served as Rector from 1678. Walk past the unlabelled 1970s **School House**, formerly the caretaker's residence but now divided into flats. On the 1995 OS map, the building was enigmatically marked "Tŷ Ysgol", Welsh for School House, a name presumably assigned to it by a Cambrian resident. The redbrick **Kentish Town Church of England Primary School** had its

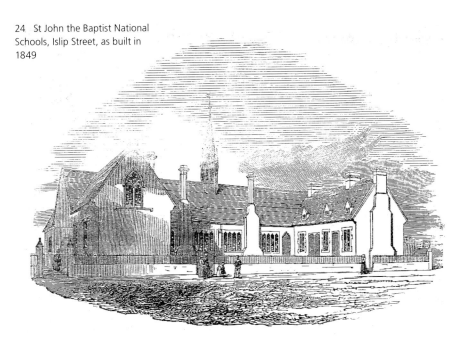

24 St John the Baptist National Schools, Islip Street, as built in 1849

where WWII bombing – aimed, of course, at the railway – took its toll. A terrace of original houses remains intact at **Nos.9-29**. Although of only two storeys (with a semi-basement), they are of some architectural pretension, with rustication and square-cut stuccoed porticoes with Corinthian capitals.

There had been ribbon development along the main-road frontage of the Christ Church estate since the 1830s, but the fields behind remained open land for many more years. When development eventually began in the 1850s, it was intentionally of a different nature from that of nearby areas built earlier. Streets were laid out in a regular pattern. Intended to attract middle-class buyers, the houses had both a generous back garden and a small one at the front. Their design was overseen, on behalf of Christ Church, by Philip Hardwick, the church and railway architect. *Building News*, in 1859, praised the Dean and Chapter for their wisdom: "We have long entertained the opinion that something better was required than the long streets of even roomed dwelling house peculiar to the neighbourhood". The Christ Church development would "tend greatly to improve Kentish Town". For a while, the area covered on this walk was promoted by estate agents as 'New Kentish Town'.

All too soon, the development was disrupted by the advent (1864) of the

origins in the National Schools that were opened in Monte Video Place (p 67) in 1815. When that outgrew the cramped premises there, the vicar of St Pancras appealed to Christ Church to provide an alternative site, and by 1849 the St John the Baptist National Schools (for boys, girls and infants) had opened in what became Islip Street, built by Charles Crane around three sides of a small yard (**Fig 24**). Only a decade later did house

building begin on the Christ Church estate. In 1907 the school was remodelled and its hall was added. In 1980 Madness, a pop group much associated with Camden, shot most of its video for *Baggy Trousers* in and around the Islip Street school, which also inspired the song.

Opposite, at **Nos.1-7**, are maisonettes erected by Camden Council on a war-damaged site. Notice, throughout this walk, the occasional modern infill at addresses

Midland Railway, which sliced diagonally through the estate. Newly built houses were demolished, landlords being compensated by the railway company. Built in a cutting, and invisible from the street, the railway did not form a physical barrier as the North London had done further west; but the estate was nonetheless subjected to its noise and dirt, lowering developers' expectations. By 1898, Inspector Tomkin was informing Charles Booth that Islip Street had "gone down wonderful during the last 7 or 8 years".

Beyond **No.25**, home in 1903 to Francis Grover, the vaccination officer for St Pancras, Hammond Street approaches from the right. This once continued north of Islip Street, bridging the railway. Beyond the railway were small houses, purchased by the railway company but left standing to be colonised by many rail employees, particularly porters. No.18 was listed in 1884 as a "Midland Railway Company's Home". A mission hall was perched above the railway at No.9, occupying the angle of a T-junction with east-running Peckwater Street (see below). These buildings, and indeed the whole north end of Hammond Street with its bridge, were obliterated in 1898, when the railway cutting was widened and the platforms of Kentish Town station were lengthened. A new ingress to Peckwater Street was opened up a little further east.

The railway passed beneath the streets of the Christ Church estate in a shallow tunnel or 'covered way', above which substantial building would be imprudent. Hence, ahead on the right, the pair of unsightly yards dealing today in tyre supply and van hire. The equivalent site on your left, occupied today by the **Boma Garden Centre**, previously housed an Edbrook's Service Station and later a Carmo Garage. Here, until rail nationalisation, stood the Kentish Town Milk Depot of the Midland Railway (later LMS), of which a fragment of redbrick wall on your left is a relic. Churns were unloaded onto a special platform below, reaching the street-level depot by means of a ramp.

Milk was in short supply in this vicinity in the decades before the estate was developed. The last tenant of the 31-acre field was William Morgan, who for some 58 years occupied Morgan's Farm, the Tudor farmhouse off Kentish Town Road (p 30). In 1795 the College's agent noted that Morgan's lease defined the land as a cow-farm and that Morgan was covenanted to "consume hay on the premises and spread dung". The obstreperous farmer had other ideas: he was, he claimed, "too far from London to sell milk to his advantage"; it was more profitable to take his hay to market in the City and return with horse manure. In the 1820s he rented land to an aptly named Giles Silverside, a carcass (or wholesale) butcher, to rear

beef cattle for market. Morgan gave up farming completely in 1831, declaring that he would otherwise end up either in the workhouse or in gaol.

Next on the left is what remains of **PECKWATER STREET**, named after the Peckwater Quadrangle at Christ Church. Modern Peckwater Street corresponds to the new ingress created in 1898 (see above) to link Islip Street with its original east-west section. Development on the Christ Church estate was mixed, mostly comprising middle-class streets, but with lowlier housing at this northern end, let in 1865 to "tradesmen and city clerks". By 1871, half of the houses on the Christ Church estate were shared by two or more households. Peckwater Street deteriorated into something of a slum. By 1898, it was on the up again, and Charles Booth felt able to upgrade most of the houses, surprisingly from purple ("mixed") to a "fairly comfortable" pink. As Tomkin told him, the street was "vastly improved; used to be dangerous to police going down alone; used to have some ticket of leave men [released prisoners] here, none now." After WWII devastation, Peckwater Street was swept away by St Pancras Borough Council and replaced by the **Peckwater Estate**, seven blocks of flats of different shapes and sizes built between 1948 and 1959 around a linear open space, in various combinations of yellow, blue and red brick. Turn along the rump of Peckwater Street, to view the later (1958-59) blocks at this end of the estate: ahead, a small block known as **Beedon**; on the right **Avington,** and beyond it one end of 8-storey **Arborfield** (the sign on the last block states "Aborfield"). The names were borrowed from villages in Berkshire, the county selected by the Council as a source of names for 1950s blocks in this part of the borough. Around a corner to the left is a recent NHS complex in yellow brick, including, at No.6, the **Peckwater Centre** of the Camden Primary Care Trust. Currently accommodated here is the Bridge Project, a service to people with mental health problems. **No.4,** beyond, is occupied by the Caversham Group Practice. Returning to **ISLIP STREET**, continue east, with 4-storey **Appleford** to your left (Appleford, near Didcot and now in Oxfordshire, was in Berkshire before local government reorganisation in 1974).

Original terraces survive opposite at **Nos.79-119**, their front doors approached by increasingly long flights of steps. Observe the variety of design in the houses' first-floor windows – some square-cut, others with pediments, either triangular or segmental. **No.79** was home in 1988 to Elizabeth Wilson, a lecturer at the then Polytechnic of North London, and well-known writer on feminism and fashion. A later Islip Street resident was Belinda Quirey, the dance historian and teacher who died in 1996.

Back on the north side is a children's play space, dating from 1971-2 when 'Islip Street Gardens' were transformed into an adventure playground, promoted by the Camden Committee for Community Relations. Here youngsters playing football were filmed as part of the 1980 Madness video (see above). Lee Thompson, the band's sax player, lived as a boy in **The Forties**, the next block on the left, which was completed in 1948. St Pancras Council's policy immediately after WWII was to give its blocks historically relevant names. This block takes its name, not from the decade of its erection, but from Fortys (or Fortess) Field, the meadow to the north that underlies part of Fortess Road (p 134). The architect was A J Thomas, the designer of much council housing in interwar St Pancras. The old-fashioned appearance of the Peckwater blocks led Cherry & Pevsner to describe them, wrongly, as "pre-War".

Original terraced housing continues on the south side of Islip Street. James J Carroll, who lived at **No.91** in the late 19th century, was a maker of American organs, harmonium-like instruments in which the air was sucked inwards to the reeds. The corner shop beyond at **No.121A** has served in its time as a butcher's, a greengrocer's, a fruiterer's, a laundry and a car-spares outlet; now it once again sells food, as the Islip Mini Store. No.121, in 1900, housed the St Luke's Institute for Young

Men, presumably an offshoot of the local parish church (p 105). On the opposite (northwest) corner of the junction stood the Garibaldi public house, a victim of the Blitz. The eponymous Italian revolutionary had been fêted in London on his visit in 1855 to accept the Freedom of the City.

Turn left along the northern extremity of **BARTHOLOMEW ROAD**, a long L-shaped road running north to Leighton Road (p 117) from the St Bartholomew's estate (which we reach later). When first laid out, the roadway here ended at Peckwater Street (ahead on the left), until it was pushed through to Leighton Road in 1891. Opposite us, at **No.109,** is a former factory built in the late 1870s on the estate's last surviving greenfield site: Henry Brooks, Peel & Co., "founded in 1810". The firm of Brooks was founded by Henry's father, Cox Brooks, and by 1874 was based at Lyme Street (Camden Town) and at Cumberland Market; by then it was a renowned piano-action maker. It moved here by 1882, when it oddly diversified into the making of "patent portable sprinkler stoppers" for perfume bottles, and of "patent collapsible tubes for artists' colourmen" (tubes of the sort more associated nowadays with toothpaste). By 1904 it had merged with Peel & Co and was a large concern, employing 400 men. After WWI, the Bell Piano & Organ Co. moved into No.109, which later long served as a warehouse of Lilia Ltd, makers

ROUTE **7**

of sanitary towels. After standing empty for some five years, the vandalised building was refurbished by Camden Council around 1986 as the Dove Commercial Centre, 18 workshops for small businesses; early occupants included the sculptors Garden of Eden Statues.

Next door, at **No.111**, and on the site of a garage, is Osborne House Business Centre, currently occupied by the Ford Motor Company. At **No.115**, newly built in 2002, is Workplace Co-operative 115, a consortium founded by typographer Robin Kinross and others. Its seven workspaces, imaginatively designed by co-operative members Dan Monck and Duncan Kramer, house several small businesses in the fields of art and design.

Cross over and turn back southward, passing **DOWDNEY CLOSE**, a cul-de-sac of recent origin that covers the site of a borough council depot. The Dowdney name presumably honours the Victorian writer Sarah Doudney (*sic*), who once lived in Bartholomew Road (p 110). The roadway leads to low-rise, yellow-brick housing association accommodation of the 1990s, and on the right Camden's **Family & Youth Resource Centre**. Organisations based here include the Elfrida Rathbone charity, serving people with learning difficulties or disabilities; the educational Leighton Project; Parents & Co., a project serving stressed families; the 7 O'Clock Club, an 'integrated' youth club; and the Somali Youth Development & Resource Centre – the latter's presence reflecting the role of the Peckwater Estate as a refuge for present-day asylum seekers from the Horn of Africa.

South of Dowdney Close are the Council flats of 8-storey **Greatfield**, another Peckwater Estate block of 1949-50. The 31-acre 'Great Field' was also known as Tanhouse Close, which suggests that tanning once took place on both sides of Kentish Town Road (cf. p 97). Next to your right is **Cantelupe**. Roger de Cantelupe was, in 1242-49, both Vicar of St Pancras and Prebendary of Cantelowes manor. The flats cover the site of an erstwhile Aldrich Yard. It was originally intended that the north-south stretch of Bartholomew Road would be called Aldrich Road, after Henry Aldrich (1647–1710), a Dean of Christ Church, a composer of songs and anthems, and reputedly the architect of Peckwater Quad.

Regaining the Islip Mini Store, turn left into gently rising **OSENEY CRESCENT**, laid out in 1860 and largely complete by 1868. The name derives from Oxford's long-lost Oseney Abbey, headquarters of a short-lived bishopric, the See of Oseney, which was a precursor of the Oxford diocese based on Christ Church. Though every Victorian middle-class development needed its square or crescent, the building of a crescent here was encouraged by the topography. The eastern end of the Great Field was triangular, a feature as prominent on modern large-scale maps as it was on a plan accompanying the 16th-century Morant bequest (see white area on Stanford's map of 1862, p 6). A crescent would fit neatly into the available space.

The northeast end of the crescent was almost wholly redeveloped, after severe bomb damage during WWII. Gone are the coffee rooms (once a baker's) that stood on the near corner at No.82 before the war. In their place is **Greenwood** sheltered housing, low-rise flats of 1954, named after Arthur Greenwood, the former Labour minister who died in that year, and designed by Thomas Sibthorpe in a much homelier style than that of the contemporary Peckwater blocks. Madame Clara Suter, "vocalist", was living in 1877 at No.76, a house on the Greenwood site.

A second 'Greenwood' block stands beyond **Nos.72-74**, the only pair of original houses to survive on this side of the road. By contrast, the terrace opposite at **Nos.33-65** is intact. Notice the unusual painted keystone shapes above the ground-floor windows and the rugged porches approached by steep steps. Still shown as undeveloped on the OS map of 1870, this was the last part of the crescent to be built. Thomas Vincent, the piano maker, was an early resident at **No.59**; **No.39**, further up, was home (c.1880) to Edmund Barnes, the St Pancras Vestryman who later became the first Mayor of the Borough.

The north-east side, meanwhile, is lined by Camden Council's **Rowstock** flats, named after another Berkshire (now Oxfordshire) village. **Peckwater House**, on the site of a Victorian villa known as Compton House, and **Wolsey House** on the corner beyond, were erected by Christ Church before St Pancras Council's purchase of the estate in 1955. Wolsey House bears the inscription "1952" and the Oxford cathedral's coat of arms. Until its destruction by enemy action, this corner was occupied by St Luke's Vicarage, designed, as was the surviving church opposite (**Fig 25**), by Basil Champneys. Charles Eastlake said the vicarage had a "mixed character with Gothic and Queen Anne elements". **St Luke's Church** was consecrated in 1869. While the Oxford college provided the site, the cost of the building was met by the compensation paid by the Midland Railway for its destruction of another St Luke's – the neo-Gothic church in Euston Road, erected in 1861 only to be sacrificed to St Pancras station (opened 1867), and re-erected in 1867 in Wanstead as a Congregational chapel. The Oseney Crescent 'replacement' was the first major commission of the architect Basil Champneys, son of the then Vicar of St Pancras, Rev. William Weldon Champneys. Correspondence suggests that John Johnson, designer of the King's Cross St Luke's, had imagined that the job would be his, and that he was peeved at the apparent nepotism. Built in red Suffolk brick, the Oseney Crescent church has a tower 40m high in a North German style, a polygonal apse and clerestory, and a Willis organ (see p 111). 'Father' Henry Willis married his second wife Rosetta here in 1894. Stained-glass windows include the *Six Days of Creation* by Philip Webb, based on Burne-Jones' designs for Waltham Abbey; the *Four Apostles* by Morris & Co. (now in store); and the east windows are by Henry Holiday. In 1956 St Luke's parish was merged with that of war-damaged St Paul's (Camden Square). When, in the 1990s, 'St Luke with St Paul' faced expensive repairs and was declared redundant, St Paul's parish was, unusually, reinstated, worship transferring to the modern parish hall in Camden Square that had replaced the original church there. Listed Grade II* by English Heritage, St Luke's is now in the

S·LUKES·CHURCH·NEW·KENTISH·TOWN

25   St Luke's Church (and Vicarage, right), Oseney Crescent, 1869

care of the Churches Conservation Trust, admission being by appointment only.

Early plans for the Christ Church estate would have had St Luke's encompassed by a complete Circus. This idea was abandoned, and the church is now curvaceously bounded only on its south side, where Caversham Road (right) bends up to meet Busby Place. Continue beyond Busby Place (p 119) along Oseney Crescent's gently descending southern end, where the original terraces survive on both sides. The houses on the east side have round-arched porches, their shape echoed in the Venetian windows, which combine to form an unusual stuccoed ensemble. At **No.33** (right) lived the Yorkshire-born stained-glass painter John Burlison, a partner of Thomas Grylls in the Fitzrovia-based firm of Burlison & Grylls. Both artists had been apprentices of Clayton and Bell; their work is represented in Westminster Abbey and in the local St Benet's church (p 131). Thomas was the son of a Kentish Town organ builder, and the Grylls (or Grills) family is said to have lived in Willes Road (p 89) at one time. Adolphe Lexow, who lived on the left at **No.24** in 1884, made piano actions. Farther down at **No.4** (left) Miss Mary Cossar ran a mid-Victorian Roman Catholic ladies' school. Beyond **No.2** a footpath leads into Cantelowes Gardens, which the inhabitants of this part of the crescent have the good fortune to overlook

at the rear. We regain **BARTHOLOMEW ROAD** at the point where the Midland Railway burrows underneath. Note, on your left, the bricked-up windows in the end wall of **No.107**, presumably a legacy of the railway widening in 1898. The sites above the covered way are devoted today to van hire and used-car sales; in the yard to your left, KT Auto Services now trade where Henry Manning once made bicycles at No.107A. Turn right along Bartholomew Road, this stretch lined only by the generous back gardens of houses in intersecting streets.

Pause at the next junction, with **CAVERSHAM ROAD,** named after the Rev. South's estate at Caversham (Reading, Berks.), bequeathed by him, like his Kentish Town land, to Oxford's Christ Church. Glance up the slope to the right for a good view of St Luke's at the top of the rise, surmounted by its Celtic cross weathervane, and a triumphal conclusion to the estate's main thoroughfare. The bay-windowed houses at this later-built end of the road are terraced, as were most houses built locally after the arrival of the railway. **No.82**, five doors up on the left, was the home in later life, until his death in 1914, of Rev. Septimus Buss, younger brother and lifelong help of Frances M Buss (p 122), vicar of Holy Trinity Church (p 74), former chaplain to the St Pancras Workhouse, and latterly Rector of a City parish. Living in 1970 at **No.83A**, two

doors up on the opposite side, was Tom Barker, the popular Mayor of St Pancras (1958-9), who gave his name to Barker Drive in Elm Village, and who died in that year. A more recent Caversham Road resident was the singer-songwriter Ronnie Lane, bass guitarist and co-founder of the 1960s pop group the Small Faces (later the Faces), here in 1983 when newly afflicted by the multiple sclerosis that led to his death in 1996.

Turn left along the main stretch of Caversham Road, well endowed with trees of various species, passing further terraces at **Nos.54-72** and **Nos.71-75.** The estate's intended showpiece road did not escape the intrusion of the railway, whose covered way cruelly cut across it. As elsewhere, only light development was possible above, hence the builders' yards ahead on the left, one of which served for much of the 20th century as a timber yard of Maple's, the furniture makers.

Just ahead of the railway at **No.69** is the former North West London Synagogue, which moved here from York Way in 1900. Designed by A Schonfield, and seating just 250, the once unmistakably Jewish building had a glass cupola serving as a skylight, topped, like the pinnacles at each corner of the roof, by a Star of David. Early worshippers were drawn from the families of local Jewish businessmen, some 15 of whom were then listed as trading in Kentish Town Road. The synagogue flourished until the early 1970s, known latterly as the Esther Jacobs Hall. The architects David Stern and Partners took over the redundant building in 1983, remodelling it and adding the large rectangular skylight very prominent today.

Above the covered way on the opposite side, a geographically challenged Surrey Ice Creamery operated before WWII in a little building at No.40C, on part of the site of redbrick **No.42**. This post-war factory, triangular in plan, and previously occupied by the Alpha Mosaic & Terrazzo Co., is now one part of Camden Council's Kentish Town District Housing Office. In 1955 all residential parts of the then run-down estate were put up for sale; withdrawn from an intended auction, the 25½ acres were instead offered by Christ Church to St Pancras Borough Council for £263,000, roughly the price of a single one-bedroom flat today. The Council accepted and opted for improvement rather than demolition, most houses being converted into flats. Many were later eagerly snapped up by tenants under the Right to Buy policies of the Thatcher era, so that ownership today is mixed, and it is usually impossible to tell which properties remain publicly owned.

The housing office also occupies **Nos.49&51** in the terrace opposite, with its imposing Ionic ornament. At neighbouring **Nos.35-43**, a post-WWII St Pancras Day Nursery of the LCC, which evolved into

Camden Council's Caversham Family Centre, and was housed in breeze-block buildings until its reconstruction in 2003, in post-modern style, as **Vadnie Bish House**. Vadnie was, until c.2001, a Principal Officer in the Social Services Department's Children and Families Division. She was, as a black woman, a strong role model for others to aspire to senior positions. Sadly, she fell ill and, facing a life permanently on a ventilator, successfully sought leave from the High Court for it to be switched off. Vadnie Bish House was formally opened in May 2004 by Dame Elizabeth Butler-Shloss, the judge who had ruled in Vadnie's favour.

Development of Caversham Road began at its western end (ahead of you), where just seven houses were listed in 1863. This end of the road remains lined by semi-detached villas of the kind put up before intrusion of the railway lowered developers' expectations, 4-storey and with Corinthian detail. Early Caversham Road was solidly middle-class, "highly respectable and let to solicitors, gentlemen and large tradesmen"; it would remain so into the 20th century, by which time some neighbouring streets had gone down-market. Stop at the junction with Hammond Street. **No.31** (just beyond Vadnie Bish House) was home in 1903 to George Bishop, a 'medical galvanist' offering therapy using electric current. **No.32** (opposite) was occupied before WWII by the local branch

of the Charity Organisation Society. At **No.12** (in the very leafy section beyond on the right) lived Jethro Thomas Robinson (c.1829-78), a builder and architect specialising in theatre work and noted for his successive refurbishments of the Old Vic. **No.11,** on the south side, is a rebuild by Castle, Park, Hook & Partners, of the bombed half of a semi-detached pair of houses.

We, however, turn left down **HAMMOND STREET** which, since the destruction of its northern end (p 102), has no houses of its own. The road could have been named after Henry Hammond (1605-60), chaplain to Charles I and Dean of Christ Church during the Civil War; or perhaps (more appealingly) after Mrs Margaret Hammond, the housekeeper of the Rev. Dr South, to whom he bequeathed the local estate on his death in 1716 and who became its owner until her own demise in 1735.

GAISFORD STREET, which we shortly reach, was named after Thomas Gaisford, a Dean of Christ Church for 24 years, who died in 1855. On the right-hand corner is the **Lion & Unicorn** pub, still thriving despite wartime damage, with a small garden in front for al fresco drinking. Above the pub is the Lion & Unicorn Theatre, specialising in performances by newer theatrical groups. Until a few years ago the premises were known as the Royal Arms. Although the coat of arms is still displayed above the corner, the pub has been renamed, less stuffily perhaps, after its two heraldic supporters. The detached villa opposite at **No.45A**, now converted into flats and dubbed Hammond House, was originally called Gaisford House, housing in mid-Victorian times the "ladies' school" of Mrs Dodwell; many such private girls' schools existed locally at that time.

Turn left along Gaisford Street, noting how the terraces have porticoes with Ionic capitals on the south side, and on the north side too as far as **No.60**, where Corinthian ornament takes over. **No.74** was briefly home to Henry Vincent, the St Giles-born leading Chartist, imprisoned for his part in the Newport miners' riot of 1839, whose powers of oratory and Chartist activity in the West Country earned him the nickname the 'Demosthenes of the West'. In later life a Free Church lay preacher and touring public speaker, Vincent moved to No.74 in 1877 with his devoted wife Lucy after 20 years in Mornington Crescent. He died in the following year: exhausted, he took to his bed on returning from a lecture tour in Northern England, expiring 3 weeks later on 29 December 1878. The wood engraver Robert Brooke Utting (late of Camden Road) was living at **No.97** in 1883; **No.103** was the ladies' school of the Misses Grisdale. **No.108**, the last house on this side, is a strange redbrick interloper in this otherwise yellow-stock-brick street. Tree-lined Gaisford Street is among the most attractive on the estate. The railway only clipped its northeast corner, where, behind a high brick wall, an erstwhile Gaisford Garage has given way to a sub-station of the National Grid. On the opposite corner, a flat at **No.127B** was the 1970s home of the comic actor Windsor Davies, best known for his role as 'Sarnt Major' in the TV sitcom, *It Ain't Half Hot, Mum*.

Regaining the north-south arm of Bartholomew Road, turn right. At the next junction, turn right again into leafy **PATSHULL ROAD**. We have now left the Christ Church estate and entered a second, smaller, parallel property, the 13-acre 'Long Meadow' of the Dartmouth family, whose larger holding further north became Dartmouth Park (Route 10). Patshull manor, near Wolverhampton, was said in 1851 to have been "lately sold" to the Earl of Dartmouth, whose son, Viscount Lewisham, lived at Patshull Hall. The first houses on the left, with their bulbous iron balconies, were among the latest to be built and are absent from the OS map of 1870. Opposite are solid stock-brick houses with redbrick trimmings and small iron window-box supports. At **No.83**, in 1877, lived Richard Kent Jr, a septuagenarian retired builder and Vestryman, whose wife Matilda was the donor of the Milkmaid (or Matilda) drinking fountain outside the Gloucester Gate of Regent's Park. **No.76** (left) was home in 1950 to A W Jones, the conductor, flautist and music critic; and from 1971 to Peter Plouviez, once often in the news as Assistant General Secretary of the actors' union Equity.

Three well-known Labour politicians settled in the then newly gentrified street. Living at **No.64** from 1974 was Philip Whitehead, the former television producer, then MP for Derby North, and now an MEP. A near neighbour was the Jewish parliamentarian Greville Janner, now Lord Janner of Braunstone, while a post-WWII resident at **No.67** (right) was the St Pancras mayor Tom Barker. Just beyond the next junction, at **No.48**, lived Bill Rodgers (b.1928), the Labour MP and minister, who as one of the 'Gang of Four' broke away in 1981 to form the Social Democratic Party. Two decades later, his *Who's Who* entry is still headed "Baron Rodgers of Quarry Bank...Life Peer of Kentish Town in the London Borough of Camden".

No.40, beyond, was home around 1950 to the actor, pianist and baritone Reginald Hayes. A Patshull Road resident from 1979 was the TV and film actress Lesley-Anne Down. In the mid-1980s, three adjoining houses in Patshull Road were purchased by Siobhan Fahey, Keren Woodward and Sarah Dallin, the three members of Bananarama, Britain's most successful female pop group ever, with a tally of 23 Top 40 hits.

Ahead of No.48, turn left along **PATSHULL PLACE**, where just two pairs of semi-detached villas face each other across the road. Pause on reaching **LAWFORD ROAD**, known until 1866 as Bartholomew Road North. The street took its present name from John Eeles Lawford, the founder of the Camden Town building firm of Lawford & Sons, and also land agent to the 5th Earl of Dartmouth. While the north side of the road occupied Dartmouth land, the south side lay on the Bartholomew estate, the third and smallest of the estates on this walk. Known in 1804 as the Lower and Upper Meadows, the 12 acres of "freehold lands in Kentish Town which Mr Kettle holdeth of me by lease" had been bequeathed in 1667 by William Cleave, a City haberdasher, to the Priory and Hospital of St Bartholomew. William had inherited the property from his philanthropic uncle and fellow haberdasher, Thomas Cleave.

Three doors to your right, at **No.21**, Barry Tuckwell, the Australian horn player and conductor, lived c.1973. **No.22**, almost opposite, was once another mid-Victorian ladies' school, run by Miss C E Jones. Turn left (and east) past semi-detached houses, typically of 2 storeys plus basement, and with front doors approached by steps. Notice how there is Corinthian decoration on the left-hand (Dartmouth) side of the road, but none on the other. Two pairs of semi-detached

villas at **Nos.41-47** boast filigree iron first-floor balconies that contrast with heavy window-bars below. The council flats at **Nos.49-53** were built on a war-damaged site in 1957. Opposite is the road's main focus of interest. As a GLC blue plaque testifies, **No.50** was the sometime residence of the writer Eric Blair (George Orwell), while he worked at the Booklovers' Corner bookshop on Hampstead's South End Green. The peripatetic author lived in Lawford Road for six months from August 1935 until February 1936, in the year that saw the publication of his novel *Keep the Aspidistra Flying*. Orwell shared No.50 with his friends Rayner Heppenstall and Michael Sayers. The trio occupied three rooms on the top floor, Orwell sleeping in the back where they dined together, mostly on spaghetti, at a large scrubbed table. Downstairs lived a plumber and a tram driver with their respective wives, the latter couple complaining of being kept awake at night by the noise of Orwell's typewriter. In 1984 (significantly) there was an evidently unsuccessful proposal that the street be renamed George Orwell Road.

What is now the 'Village Store' at **No.62** was, for over a century, a dairy. The former Duke of Cambridge pub, on the corner beyond at **No.64**, closed and then reopened in the 1980s, finally succumbing to residential refurbishment only recently. The old pub fascia has been retained, as well as twin inn-signs depicting the balding

military commander-in-chief, a cousin of Queen Victoria. The Duke of Cambridge was the Orwell household's 'local'; it was Heppenstall's job to go there daily, jug in hand, to get in the evening's beer.

Turn briefly left into **BARTHOLOMEW ROAD**, to examine the front of **No.66**. The now residential corner house was long a grocer's-cum-post-office (note the Edwardian pillar box still standing outside); after WWII it became a beer retailer's. A single stuccoed console survives on the façade of the house as a relic of the old shop's fascia. Four doors ahead on the left, opposite the turning with Sandall Road, is **No.74**, where the founder and Director of the National Youth Theatre (John) Michael Croft (1922-1986) lived and died.

Now turn round and walk south. Early development of the Bartholomew estate, which began a few years later than that on the Christ Church estate, was hampered by lack of access. It was hemmed in on two sides by Lord Camden's property, and there was no access to or from Camden Road. Marquis Camden planned to build houses along that road's northwest side, and was initially not disposed to change them. Only when Sandall Road was opened up in 1867 did the situation improve, but the eastward egress there is still an awkward one.

Poor access was a factor in the piecemeal development of the Bartholomew estate, as exemplified in the motley assortment of architectural styles in this part of Bartholomew Road. The lithographer William P Jeans was a mid-Victorian occupant of **No.81**. Beyond, at **Nos.65-67** (left) is a pair of Italianate villas with stuccoed porticoes. No.65 is associated with the poet and novelist Sarah Doudney (1841–1926) (**Fig 26**), born in Portsmouth, the daughter of a soap and candle manufacturer, and a niece of the educationalist and author David A Doudney. Best remembered for her *Psalms of Life* (1871), Sarah wrote both hymns and secular songs; her many stories for girls included *A Romance of Lincoln's Inn* (1894). From a letter she wrote three years later to Douglas Sladen, the literary agent and *Who's Who* editor, we know that Sarah was then installed at No.65. However, the ratepayer at the time was a widowed Mrs Margaret Swingler, which suggests that Sarah was there only as a lodger or guest. This did not deter the authorities from naming Dowdney Close (p 104) after her, misspelling her surname.

There is a further misnomer in the designation of the district covered by this walk as the Bartholomew Estate Conservation Area, although that estate comprises only its smallest portion. Failing to benefit from conservation

was Montague House at No.63, a WWII bomb casualty replaced by a bungalow, behind a wall at the rear of Camden School for Girls (p 123).

Bartholomew Road now turns sharp right, as do we, along its original east-west stretch. **Nos.56-58**, the modern building on the right, is shown on maps as a "hostel". The road westward is lined

26 Sarah Doudney, c.1895

by mostly semi-detached villas in a great variety of sizes and styles, again suggestive of piecemeal construction. Note the decline from 4 to 3 storeys in the houses on the left, and the varied geometric shapes surmounting their windows and doorways, looking like eyebrows above the windows. **No.40** (right) was home in 1874 to Henry Walter Bates FRGS (1825-92), the naturalist who with Alfred Wallace explored the Amazon, returning with 8,000 previously unknown species of insect; his paper on mimicry contributed to the theory of natural selection. William Shand Kydd, the Highgate Road wallpaper manufacturer, lived on the opposite side at **No.33** in Edwardian times. Note the very grand hood to the doorway of the large detached house at **No.31** (left). Farther on we pass **No.22** (right), in 1877 the ladies' school of Misses Woods & Barrett. **No.19** (left) was known in the 19th century as Penrhyn Villa: many local houses had individual names that were later abandoned.

On the corner site beyond is a low-slung, L-shaped, concrete building, housing the **Kentish Town Health Centre**. Designed by Camden Council's own architects, this was opened in 1973 as the Caversham Family Health Centre by Jock Stallard, the local MP. The first of its kind in Camden, it brought together under one roof a variety of previously scattered health-care services, including the Caversham Group Practice and the James Wigg Practice, whose family-run surgery celebrated its centenary in 1987 with the issue of a delightfully produced booklet. The externally uninspiring health centre building is redeemed by a small mural in praise of the NHS, depicting in the background a (much too close) St Luke's Church. It was painted in 1982 by Mike Jones of the Art Workers' Co-operative. In the same year, the Centre was designated as a first-aid station in the event of nuclear war. Proposals unveiled in 2004 for its complete redevelopment proved controversial. Argyle Villa at No.2, on this site, was home in 1901 (the year of his death) to Henry Willis, the celebrated organ builder, previously of Rochester Terrace (p 62), whose Rotunda works was quite close by, and one of whose instruments graces St Luke's, the local parish church. Bear left, past a secluded postwar house at **No.1,** the successor to an earlier, bomb-damaged Elton Villa. Walk towards Kentish Town Road, stopping a little short of it to observe how the timber and builders' merchant's yard on the right was built over the long back gardens of houses on the main road.

Retrace your steps along the opposite (north) side of the road, passing several early villas converted into flats. These are numbered as part of **BARTHOLOMEW VILLAS,** which soon bends northward past Sunning Lodge at **No.8.** Beyond this at **No.12,** and easily missed, is a

modern house with a sideways-pitched roof, built on a war-damaged site in 1963-4. Designed by the local architect Ted Cullinan, and described by Cherry & Pevsner as a "Japanese-inspired essay", it has a galleried first-floor living-room overlooking the back garden and only small windows facing the street. **No.20** was once home to Jabez Inwards, the Victorian temperance advocate, in whose memory the drinking fountain in Kentish Town Road (p 27) was erected. Opposite Lawford Road, a gateway at **No.24A** leads into a creeper-clad former factory. The 1870 OS map shows a passage here, leading to what looks like a leafy communal garden. A small factory was soon to cover the site, listed in 1877 as "Watson's Syphon", and occupied by ventilating engineers Hill & Hey. Electricity meters were later made here by the Bastian Meter Co.; before and after WWI an electro-plating firm occupied the building, by then known as the Bartholomew Works. The present sign, "Holborn Metal Works", recalls its later-20th-century occupants, a welding firm that migrated here, not directly from Holborn but via Islington.

The houses north of Lawford Road are terraced and 3-storey, with iron balconies but no basements. Those on the east side, with Corinthian decoration, include Osborne House at **No.13,** one of the few local houses to retain its old name. An early resident on the corner beyond

was Rev. Alfred J Buss (elder brother of Septimus), who lived in the 1870s at **No.19** before moving to live in his Shoreditch parish.

We now dip once again into **PATSHULL ROAD** (see also p 108), turning left along its west end. This, like the western extremities of all our east-west streets, became commercialised; early villas here were demolished. A Trafalgar Cottage once stood on the far (Job Centre) corner. Short of this, on the left, is an unnamed cobbled 'mews' only ever known as **No.2** Patshull Road. It once led to the 19th-century works of piano maker John Rintoul (who lived at No.12). For much of the next century, the cabinet makers Holland & Sons shared the site with the paint factory of Messrs Smith & Walton. The cul-de-sac now leads to the private-sector London Skills Institute School of English. Also here are Clean Break, a renowned 'new writing' theatre company founded in 1979 by two ex-prisoners from Askham Grange. Clean Break runs courses throughout the year in creative writing (as well as acting, singing, dancing and video), open only to women ex-offenders and others whose lives have been affected by the criminal justice system. On the opposite side of Patshull Road, a Dudley Villa once occupied the corner site at No.1; next door at No.1A was Oxford House (later Oxford Villa), a detached house in own grounds, on the site of which is now the yard of the Anglo-

Italian Motor Service. Nos.1-5 was the pre-WWII address of undertaker Henry Sinclair.

Turn right up Kentish Town Road, which we briefly traverse before turning right into **GAISFORD STREET** (see also p 107). Residential **Northumberland House** (right) stands on the site of a cinema with seats for 500, opened in 1910 as the Kentish Town Cinema, and later renamed the Gaisford. By 1928 it was offering both films and live variety shows, the latter somehow presented on a stage only 6 ft deep. Popular with locals, the cinema underwent several changes of ownership, becoming part of the Odeon chain before its closure in 1960. The cinema was built on a site previously occupied in the 19th century by the mineral-water works of Messrs Gale & Ubsdell, and in Edwardian times by local undertakers Becket & Sons.

No.1, in the surviving terrace beyond, once housed the Beaufort House Collegiate School, run in the 1870s by a Mr G Tuke; nearby was Miss Mivart's ladies' school at **No.9**. Beyond, on the left, the intrusive 1970s maisonettes at **Nos.6-10** were deliberately designed to contrast with their Victorian neighbours, although Cherry & Pevsner suggest this is "modernism combined with a contextual approach". The architects Colquhoun & Miller were responsible for much of the infill between Gaisford Street and Caversham Road,

with Richard Brearley as project architect. The large opening was meant to lead to a tenants' hall at the rear that never materialised. The site had been occupied after WWII by a base of the Air Training Corps, in two linked buildings extending through to Caversham Road. Former No.10, on the site of the maisonettes, housed Rev. Zephaniah Banks Woffendale, the Presbyterian minister who in 1886 founded the Aldenham Institute in Somers Town.

The surviving terraces to the east, with dignified stuccoed porticoes and crisp volutes, have taller centrepieces. Their construction (under way in 1859) was not without incident. Gillian Tindall relates how a barely completed chimney stack collapsed, along with the scaffolding, injuring several building workers, and prompting an inquiry by the developer, Temple Elliott. Ironically, the latter was soon to write an unpublished book, bemoaning Kentish Town's "descent" from village into suburb.

Backtracking slightly, turn north up narrow **WOLSEY MEWS**, which leads through the site of Morgan's Farm (p 30). We have now returned to the Christ Church estate, hence the name of the mews. The mews remains partly cobbled, though many of its granite setts have been insensitively replaced with swathes of asphalt. Walk up, past the flats of **Christchurch House** on the left,

brick-built above commercial premises in Kentish Town Road, and approached by an extraordinarily long flight of steps. Facing you, on reaching Caversham Road, is former No.14 Wolsey Mews, now renumbered as 230A Kentish Town Road, and home to the **Crossroads Women's Centre**, a base in 2004 for a dozen women's organisations, ranging from Women Against Rape through Wages Due Lesbians to the English Collective of Prostitutes. The building, still sporting its taking-in doors, was in 1900 a small factory making rag dolls. Continue up the Mews to **Nos.25-26** on the right, partly occupied today by a building contractor, and including at No.26 (though unlabelled as such) the 'Old Dolls Workshop'. This former factory also made dolls in Edwardian times, having been built in the back garden of the proprietor, Henry Hazel, "wholesale doll manufacturer" of No.2 Caversham Road.

Ahead lies Islip Street; we have come full circle. Turn left and then right to regain Kentish Town station.

Into the Torriano estate

Circular walk from Brecknock Road/
Camden Road junction

For modern map see back cover

Here we explore the Torriano estate, part of the old Manor of Cantelowes once belonging to Joshua Prole Torriano. Our walk begins and ends, however, on the northern fringes of Lord Camden's estate which we also visited in Route 4. Camden Road continues from Camden Town into this Route. We shall see that the original housing along it dating from the 1840s and 1850s was aimed squarely at the professional middle class while houses in other roads on the Torriano estate behind, also begun in the mid-19th century, were aimed at people who were only slightly below them on the social scale. But the coming of two modes of transport for the common man – the railways in the 1860s and a tramway up Camden Road in 1872 – not only lowered the tone of the district but enabled lower-income workers to look for living quarters further from their place of work. Sufficient reminders of the earlier period nevertheless remain to make it well worth while to explore this area, which is an intriguing mixture of old and new.

Take one of the frequent buses from Camden Town along **CAMDEN ROAD** and alight at the Brecknock Road stop. Walk back to the crossroads at which stands **The Unicorn**, built in 1840 as the Brecknock Arms (**Fig 27**) and named after the ground landlord, John Jeffreys Pratt, 1st Marquis Camden, who was created Earl Brecknock in 1812. In the tradition of the times, this was more than a simple alehouse. With its spacious paddocks it became a popular pleasure garden, with attractions for all the family. In 1840 there was a 'Grand Pedestrian Match' on 21 September when, it was announced, "Harris will walk 170 miles in 1000 hours in the Bowling Green and Tea Gardens"; whilst in 1855 the veteran 70-year-old balloonist Charles Green made his 514th ascent in his monster balloon with his friend Paternoster.

But the event that put the Brecknock Arms on the map was not one it had sponsored. At 5 a.m. on Saturday 1 July 1843, a duel took place in the fields behind

27 Looking along Brecknock Road from Camden Road, c.1907 (Brecknock Arms on extreme left)

Brecknock Road, Camden Road N.

the tavern. Lieutenant-Colonel Fawcett was shot and mortally wounded by his brother-in-law Lieutenant Munro, who immediately fled the country. As the staff at the Brecknock flatly refused to help the injured man, he was carried to the Camden Arms in Randolph Street, where he died two days later. The affair caused widespread public revulsion, and *Punch* produced a memorable cartoon entitled "The Satisfaction of a Gentleman". Munro was not caught until 1847, when he was charged with murder and found guilty, but after a few days in the condemned cell, pardoned. However, duelling itself, long illegal, had been dealt a mortal blow – as had the varied attractions of the Brecknock Arms. One by one the rifle range, bowls and wrestling faded away and the famous paddocks were let for building.

The grey modern flats adjoining the Unicorn, at **No.217**, cover the site of a villa at former No.225, home in 1875-77 to the French labour activist, Paul Lafargue (b.1842) and his wife Laura. Laura was the second daughter of Karl Marx. Paul, medically trained, had become a vigorous campaigner for shorter working hours. The couple when in London ran a photographic shop to make ends meet. They moved in 1882 to Paris, where a year in a French gaol for subversion gave Paul the time to complete his *The Right to be Lazy*, a searing attack on the work ethic. Lafargue in later life became a great friend of Friedrich

Engels. In 1912 Paul and Laura, deeming themselves too old to be useful, died together in a suicide pact by injecting each other with potassium cyanide.

On the same Camden Road site, and at much the same time, the actress Ellen Terry (1848–1928) lived with her children. They had taken rooms at erstwhile No.221 in 1876, the year after her divorce from her first husband, G F Watts, and following her West End success as Portia in *The Merchant of Venice*.

Now turn alongside the pub into **BRECKNOCK ROAD**, likewise named after Earl Brecknock. It is part of the ancient route from the City to Barnet and the North, known as Maiden Lane until the 1850s. In this isolated spot, a notorious haunt of footpads, stood the Turnpike. When the Brecknock Arms was built it may have been surrounded by fields, but it had an intriguing older neighbour. In 1828 James Hargreave Mann, scion of a military family, built here with James Sargon a large industrial complex for the manufacture of floor-cloth and varnish. The works, called Highfields after the field name of the site, continued in operation until 1848, after which the area was developed for housing. James Mann himself had been married in the parish church in 1815 and subsequently served as a St Pancras Vestryman. He was an industrious chairman of the committee overseeing the building of the National Scotch Church in Regent Square in 1823,

and nine years later had the unenviable task of ejecting the Rev. Edward Irving as "unfit to be minister in charge". James Mann later lived with his family at Old Chapel Place (p 22). A contemporary engraving (**Fig 28**) shows the Highfields Works to have been an imposing Classical block with ancillary structures. In 1841, the residents were the floor-cloth maker William Monant with his wife and four children, and Mr Stalbridge, the 'gardener' with his family. Today, an iron gateway leads to **BRECON MEWS**, stylish flats of 1999 which occupy Manville Yard (1853), the former stabling for James Mann's horses.

The next turning to the left, between the two blocks of erstwhile Manville Terrace, is **HARGRAVE PLACE**, formerly James Street, off whose south side there once ran a narrow tributary called Hargrave Street, 'Hargrave' presumably being a corruption of James Mann's middle name. These streets were laid out in 1848, and building began two years later. The builder was probably David Marshall, whom we find in 1851 at No.2 James Street, employing four men. In the census return of that year, all the completed houses in the street were full of builders' tradesmen. On the corner at No.8 is the **Admiral Mann**, with an excellent sign board, and a good interior. This commemorates Admiral Robert Mann (1748–1813), James' kinsman. Mann was an older colleague of

Nelson, but lacked his luck and flair. At Gibraltar in 1796 he disobeyed Sir John Jervis' instruction to come to his assistance in the Mediterranean, and sailed home to Scotland. Forced to come ashore, he then became a member of the Board of Admiralty. St Vincent ("the very ablest sea officer his Majesty has") never forgave him, branding him as "one of the three useless Neptunes".

Returning to **BRECKNOCK ROAD**, we pass **Highfields Villas** (Nos.43-49), three much altered blocks of 1850. The tiny **Nos.51&53**, Gloucester Villas, mark the junction with Leighton Road, originally Gloucester Place. Cross over and walk past **Charlton Court**, Camden's concrete and red-brick development of 1986. This occupies the site of many of the original Leighton Villas of 1855. Milton Rosmer (1881–1971), actor, theatrical producer and pioneer of radio drama, lived at No.77 in 1916, the year in which he appeared in a silent film version of Oscar Wilde's *Lady Windermere's Fan*. No.93 was replaced by a post-war brick block called **The Crest**.

28 Mann and Sargon's factory known as Highfields Works (T H Shepherd, 1829)

The corner house of Torriano Avenue was built as a bakery, where Master Baker William Chew was in charge in 1861. Cross over the northern stretch of Torriano Avenue to the **Leighton Arms** at No.101, a mutilated hostelry of the 1850s, with its traditional armorial inn sign.

We are now on the eastern edge of the Torriano estate, which consisted of five fields containing about 42 acres. These belonged in 1783 to the descendants of John Cox the Elder of London, a soap maker, one of whom was Joshua Prole Torriano of Ruxley Place, Thames Ditton. In 1844 Sir David Leighton of Charlton Kings, near Cheltenham, Major-General in the Honourable East India Company's independent army, married Isabella, a daughter of Honoria Torriano, and so came to own half the estate.

Remaining on the south-west side of Brecknock Road, we reach a row of ample wide-fronted and gabled family homes built in 1911 and known as **Carleton Gardens**. The name comes from the marriage in 1804 of Mary Carleton to the son of George Foster Tufnell who owned the Manor of Barnsbury in Islington. (Carleton Road lies opposite, in the Borough of Islington.)

Turn left between the two blocks and walk to the Regency house known as

ROUTE **8**

Montpelier, No.115. This is even older than the floor-cloth factory, appearing on maps of 1825 as Montpelier Cottage. It may well have derived its name from Dr Rowley's description of Kentish Town as the "Montpelier of England" (p 137) although Montpelier was a fairly common appellation at the time. In 1829 we find Edward Wood, a varnish maker, transforming it into Montpelier House, with staff housing, outbuildings and offices. Wood (1778–1855) was a shareholder in the Regent's Canal Company and builder of the Coal Wharf at Camden Town. In 1851, now retired, he was living at Montpelier with his wife Elizabeth, daughter Mary, four grandchildren and five servants (groom, laundress, cook and two housemaids). Early maps show the house standing in an extensive landscape with "grand views to the north over Islington". These were obscured for ever in 1911 by the building of Carleton Gardens. The house remained in private hands until WWII. In 1940 it was owned by Trustees who had acquired the property for a Welfare Centre, a project which was abandoned. They offered the grounds around the house for wartime allotments. This offer was gratefully accepted by St Pancras Council, whose Councillor responsible for wartime allotments was Miss Barbara Betts, later Barbara Castle MP. Meanwhile, for the duration, Montpelier was used as a Rest Centre, and

in 1945 became an Old People's Home, by 1969 transformed into 11 flats. Seven years later, the house was threatened with demolition, but a strenuous campaign by local residents prevented this and it was restored for community use. The grounds were laid out as a public garden and children's play area named **Montpelier Gardens**. The house is currently home to the Montpelier Nursery, run by Camden Community Nurseries; and the One One Five Behaviour Support Service Resource Base, a facility for excluded school pupils.

Walk through the grounds and find, just before the playground, the exit that leads down to the red-brick church in **LEIGHTON CRESCENT**. (If Montpelier Gardens are closed, walk back to the junction of Brecknock Road and turn right down Leighton Grove to Leighton Crescent.) Leighton Crescent, on the west side of Leighton Grove, was laid out in 1856. In the triangular site behind, another pair of houses, Nos.9&10, was built at the same time and to the same design. The remaining houses, Nos.13-23, were completed in 1876. **Nos.1&2** were rebuilt in 1956. The watercolour painter John Skinner Prout (1806-1876) died at his home at **No.4**. **Nos.11-14** were redeveloped as flats by Camden in 1975-80 to a "notable design" by E Cullinan, P Tabor, M Bedale and M Chassay. Observe the attic strip under the overhanging roof. In 1897 an American

humanist, Stanton Coit, was living at No.7 and had bought Nos.8, 9&10 as well. He formed a Neighbourhood Guild in 1899. Nos.9&10 had already been enlarged to provide meeting rooms. In 1896 a German Evangelical Lutheran church – now the **Luther Tyndale Church** – was established here, and also a German school. The well-known German bakers, Louis Launer of Goodge Street and John Dunsbier of Coram Street, were supporters. In 1914, the headmaster was Rev. Karl Heinrich Knippenberg with a mixed school of 40 pupils. At the outbreak of WWI all German schools in London were closed except St Mary's in Cleveland Street (Fitzrovia), and the ownership of Nos.9&10 (by then known as the Leighton Halls) was transferred to Trustees. Then, in 1938, the two old houses were demolished and the present church was completed to a design by architects Newbury and Fowler, the builders being Hammond and Miles of Ilford. The simplicity of the church with its copper spirelet and warm red brick makes an interesting contrast with the heavy late-Victorian houses. The Crescent has fortunately retained its well-treed central garden. Originally privately owned, it was transferred by the Brownlees Trust in 1954 to St Pancras Borough Council for £1000.

Walk downhill. At the foot of Leighton Crescent, turn right along **LEIGHTON GROVE**. This was completed between

1884 and 1886. Nos.19&20 and Nos.21&22 were rebuilt in 1958 as **Ivy Court** and **Ash Court**. Note the machicolated parapets to the earliest houses at the bottom of the street as you turn left into **LEIGHTON ROAD**, which follows the line of an old footpath from Kentish Town Road to Islington. The first section from the Assembly House appears first on Thompson's 1801 map and was known from 1816 as Gloucester Place. It became a road in stages and was fully built up by 1853. Confusingly, both sides of this more easterly stretch of the road were called Torriano Terrace until 1863, when all the named subdivisions were abolished. On the south side, Bartholomew Road enters. It was extended here in 1891 to provide an additional 'means of escape' from the Christ Church estate (p 100). This new road swept away No.108, which since 1863 had been Miss Frances Holland's Ladies Seminary. In 1871 she had the company of her two sisters and another teacher, two servants and eight boarders. On the south side, notice **Nos.128–134**, nicely paired villas with pediments, while the north side has more condensed terraces – real town houses with basements and original ironwork.

At a slightly staggered crossroads, **TORRIANO AVENUE** intersects. The road was laid out in 1848 and the first houses were under construction the following year. The Avenue provided an important connecting link, via Leighton Road, from Kentish Town to the new Camden Road, towards which it descends on the right. Perhaps unfortunately for its future inhabitants, it was also to provide the shortest route and widest thoroughfare for the cattle which, after the opening of the Midland Railway in 1868, would be driven 'on the hoof' from the Kentish Town Cattle Dock (by Kentish Town station) to the new Metropolitan Cattle Market in Islington.

For the moment, turn left up Torriano Avenue's northern end, where it climbs to meet Brecknock Road. On the east side observe the premises of McCrone Scientific Research, technically **No.155A Leighton Road** but with a main entrance here. Built of dark brick matching the flank wall of No.155, its two gable ends with portholes prepare us for the more familiar stucco pediments on the former Torriano Villas of 1851 that lead up to the next right-hand turning (into Charlton Kings Road). On the Avenue's west side are two archway entrances leading into **TORRIANO MEWS**. This back-land was originally developed as two separate areas: Torriano Mews to the south with 2 houses and 19 stables, and further up the hill, Torriano Yard with 1 house and 2 stables. Today, both have been rebuilt and converted for commercial use. The publishers Frances Lincoln Ltd are at **No.4**. At **No.99 TORRIANO AVENUE** is the Torriano Meeting House – formerly the Torriano Project – a beacon of culture for the neighbourhood, where local poets have met for over 20 years. It also houses the Hearing Eye press, publishing a well-known series of poetry pamphlets. In early 2005 its future is in some doubt. At **No.119**, in 1891, Moritz Immisch was living with his St Pancras-born wife and daughter. Immisch, a German-born clockmaker turned electrical engineer, pioneered the production of battery-powered riverboats. In 1887, with William Coutts Keppel (Viscount Bury), he set up the world's first electric hire-boat fleet. By 1904 there were 23 Immisch launches on the Thames, with 20 battery-charging stations at intervals along its banks. Notice at the top of the street the attractive porch to the blue-painted **No.135**.

Return to **CHARLTON KINGS ROAD**, and turn east along it. Charlton Kings, near Cheltenham, was the country seat of Sir David Leighton. The road's 23 two-storey cottages, with access to a generous back-land site, were completed in 1855. On the north side, five houses were taken for an entrance to Charlton Court in Brecknock Road. On the south side (right), **Nos.15&17** have been added – a commendable example of 'good neighbourly' design – perhaps on the site of an old cottage that stood out resolutely against the original house-numbering system.

In 1883 the pianoforte makers Allison & Allison (founded 1863) moved here from Somers Town. They initially occupied **No.10** (left) and land behind the covered entry, before expanding into 'The Allison Piano Factory', or Apollo Works, on the opposite side, where they remained until 1940. Their pianos were advertised as having "new patent check escapement action". When Charles Booth visited the area in 1898 to update his poverty map he noted that a good many Allison employees were living in the street. From 1941 to 1949 Wurlitzer Cinema Organs and Automatic Phonographs became tenants of the Allison works. At this time, the site was also occupied by W E Grose, a refurbisher of player pianos, and E P Dixon's joinery. Later, some of the premises were used by Raphael's optical works. No.10, with its works behind, still exists, now used by the builder W E Jarman. The Apollo Works opposite at Nos.1-5 is now the **Apollo Studios**, whose several units house a wide variety of businesses; the Labour Party manifesto for 1997 was produced and printed here.

Regaining **LEIGHTON ROAD**, turn briefly left up its easternmost end, observing on the north side the four suburban semis (**Nos.187-193**) that were erected on a former builder's yard in 1938. Opposite is the much more appealing detail of the former Gloucester Gardens Terrace (1850-51), with carefully contrived

later roof extensions. The novelist and poet Kingsley Amis lived (c.1983-85) at **No.186**, the last house before the Brecknock Road junction − after splitting up with his second wife, the author Elizabeth Jane Howard, and before moving back in with his first wife (and her second husband). Turn round and return to the staggered junction, passing Highfields Terrace (1847-50), with its delightful surviving ironwork. Crossing over at the zebra, continue west past a corner building that proclaims its alcoholic origins. This was the Torriano Arms, opened in 1851 and closed in 1993.

Beyond the former pub, turn shortly left to stroll down a gravel lane, unadopted by Camden Council, that leads to **TORRIANO COTTAGES**, an unbarred enclave of 15 Victorian cottages with some more recent additions, retaining an extraordinarily rural atmosphere. What a vision of the countryside in the midst of the town! Most of the cottages were built in the 1860s, with the notable exception of **No.15**, which dates from 1965, designed by the architect Philip Pank for himself. Other, undistinguished modern houses were built in its wake. Follow the lane round to the left and then up the slope, with the two cottages called **Torriano Gardens** to your left.

Re-emerge into **TORRIANO AVENUE**. On the left is the present-day **Torriano** public house, formerly a long-

established off licence. Whilst, as we have seen, the upper part of the Avenue has changed little, this main southern section is now so fragmented that it hardly reads any more as it was planned. Turning right, note the original houses, much altered, on the opposite (east) side. Then, on the right, we come to the first major deviation from the original plan. Board Schools were not even an idea in 1851, and it was only after the demise of the School Board for London that Torriano Elementary School for Boys, Girls and Infants was built. It is now **Torriano Junior School** with about 240 pupils. It still features the separate entrances in the high brick wall and their carved stone lintels. The school was constructed by the LCC and opened on November 1910, with 400 boys and girls in the mixed elementary school and 245 in the infants. The main feature of the school before WWII was the great bell on the roof, which was rung for a full 5 minutes before the morning and afternoon sessions. In 1939 most Torriano children were evacuated to a village in Leicestershire and the school was used as a fire station, the engines being kept in the playground. The school reopened in 1945. The buildings have been described as "rough cast with gables in the Arts & Crafts spirit". The alteration and additions of 1998 have rightly respected the quality of the original design. Beyond the junior school and school keeper's house, at No.27 lies a small block of flats, **Florence Court**. Farther on, set back from the road, is the present **Torriano Infants School** (1980, with more recent additions), with places for 230 pupils up to age 7. Finally, at the corner of Busby Place, two pairs of original villas remind us of what has been lost on this side.

It is now time to look at the east side of the road, and here the transformation is complete. The area in 1945 had been so seriously damaged by bombing that the LCC declared it a clearance area. St Pancras prepared a comprehensive redevelopment scheme, the **Torriano Gardens Estate**. The architect was A J Thomas, who had designed many of the Council's pre-war housing schemes, and in 1937 the new Town Hall in Euston Road. The character is Neo-Georgian, heavy windows, good red brickwork – a design which, if not wildly progressive, has weathered well. The blocks, completed between 1949 and 1954, were given local field names: **Carters Close**, **Long Meadow, Barn Close**, **Tanhouse Field** and **Landley Field**. Maintaining such residential areas requires the active cooperation of councillors, the Local Authority and residents. Torriano Gardens seems to have been fortunate in this respect. In 2003, a communal garden was created on a neglected 'Groundwork' space alongside Torriano Avenue. This was a Charity Challenge scheme, enthusiastically carried out by the residents with the help of the University of London Training Corps and many others. With its flowering plants in railway sleeper boxes, it has benefited the residents – and the street.

At the crossroads, take a left turn up narrow **HAMPSHIRE STREET** (Hampshire Grove until 1884).This is the truncated remnant of an L-shaped street first built in 1851, partly on the site of Mann & Sargon's floor-cloth factory. It once turned north to meet James Street, the present Hargrave Place (p 114). Parallel to Torriano Avenue there were 17 terraced houses, and a long narrow block described in 1870 as a 'swimming baths'. Booth noted, in 1898, that two or three prostitutes lived on this west side of the street, and that navvies and sewer men were opposite. On the east side, backing into the gardens of the houses in Camden Road, various commercial buildings were built. In 1897 a Wesleyan Mission Hall is recorded. Hampshire Street was badly bombed in 1940. On 26 January 1944, 13 derelict houses were used by the Light Rescue Service for an exercise in demolition work. The remaining 4 houses were compulsorily purchased and demolished in June 1953, most of the site being incorporated in the Torriano Gardens Estate. Today it contains such businesses as the A V Laundry and the Hampshire Street Studio, run by Cosprop (p 63), and which includes an editing suite.

Return to Torriano Avenue and at the junction cross over into **BUSBY PLACE**. This is named after Dr Richard Busby, the famous disciplinarian headmaster of Westminster School in the 17th century, who was also a Student of Christ Church, Oxford. We are now on the boundary of the Christ Church estate (p 100); Busby Place, formed in 1858, was the much-needed access road from the latter onto Camden Road. The historic street sign can still be seen at the entrance from Torriano Avenue. Of the houses that remain, **Nos.5-13** on the north side are original, dating from 1866-68, and **No.15** has been rebuilt.

The first bombs to fall in St Pancras in WWII hit Busby Place at 10.20 pm on 8 September 1940. St Luke's Vicarage on the corner (p 105) and two adjoining houses were destroyed. In 1952 Christ Church built Wolsey House on their site. At **No.17** was St Luke's Hall, for many years the headquarters of the 1st St Pancras Scout Troop. This hall is now being rebuilt as a community hall by Archworks and Ian Haywood Partnership. Note the two traffic bollards outside, one with the St Pancras coat of arms. Only **No.2** survives of the houses on the south side of the street. Nos.4-26 were rebuilt in 1867 and demolished in 1965, but new houses are currently being built here. On 9 September 1944 a special street party was held in Busby Place as part of the 'Holidays at

ROUTE **8**

Home' campaign, an attempt to dissuade citizens from travelling at a critical stage of the military campaign in Normandy.

Returning to Torriano Avenue we pass the new houses **Nos.28&30**. These mark the entry to the former Busby Mews. This was a short cul-de-sac, leading from Busby Place to the back-land between Camden Road and Oseney Crescent. Originally called Cumberland Grove and then Cumberland Mews, it became Busby Mews in 1879. It contained four stables with houses over, built in 1868. These were occupied by domestic coachmen and their families, and serviced the houses in Camden Road. Later, as times changed, Tresco Car Hire operated from No.4 from 1947 to 1951. These houses were demolished in 1955 to make way for the Jews' Free School in Camden Road.

Busby Mews provided access to land behind Camden Road, which in 1909 became much-needed playing fields for the North London Collegiate School (p 122). There were three green hard courts for netball, and "energetic if hazardous" hockey and tennis were played on a narrow, tree-shaded open space. Changing rooms were added later. The playing fields were abandoned when the North London Collegiate School moved out in 1940. The open space was then used as a barrage balloon site – and a dreary waste it remained until the formation of Cantelowes Gardens (p 122).

Reaching **TORRIANO AVENUE**, cross over to the east side, noting the block of houses (**Nos.2-6**) and the pretty detached cottage, with a more recent porch, built in the garden of **No.203 Camden Road**.

Regaining **CAMDEN ROAD**, turn briefly left to observe the lions guarding the porches of the Corner House Hotel (**Nos.201&203**) and walk up to **No.207**. In 1884 Horatio Grece Regnart (**Fig 29**), the co-founder of Maple's (the former furniture emporium in Tottenham Court Road) was living here. He had joined John Maple in 1855 and was still the president of the company when he died in 1912. By then he was Sir Horatio, and had been an influential member of St Pancras Borough Council. As one of its first Aldermen, he presented the massive silver-gilt and bejewelled mace, which is the one most frequently used on Camden ceremonial occasions today. Externally, No.207 is in a good condition and unlike most of the houses is relatively unaltered, giving a good indication of how Camden Road would have appeared in better days. As building moved away from Camden Town, the developers became greedier and the houses became larger, quite unlike the earlier chaste Listed villas further down the hill. But these later houses were

29 Sir Horatio (Horace) Regnart, caricatured by Spy in Vanity Fair

ideal for large Victorian professional families. The surgeon Henry Knaggs lived at No.187 in the 1870s. James Park, a ship owner, made No.151 his home for many years, and after the opening of the Metropolitan Cattle Market in Islington in 1855 this street became extremely popular

with the Worshipful Company of Master Butchers, at least twelve of whose members are recorded as living here.

Many other uses were soon found for these large houses. Several private schools flourished. At No.161 a 'Medical Care Home' is recorded. From the beginning there would have been houses in multiple occupation, and it was then but a short step to the dreaded boarding house, several of which appeared quite early on.

Turn round and, re-crossing Torriano Avenue, continue down the right-hand side of Camden Road. As you will see, all the original houses in this stretch have been swept away. Gone, too, are the villas of the former Camden Crescent, which once lay on the site of the open space further down. It was Camden Road's misfortune that the central feature of this great artery was the last to be built, completed only in 1855.

This side of the road, originally named Camden Road Villas, enjoyed a mere decade of peace before the urban invaders arrived. In 1863 the Midland Railway (Extension to London) Bill passed into law, and for the next five years the navigators dug their way through and under Kentish Town. As the line was in a deep cutting, disruption could have been worse, and when a new station called Camden Road opened for traffic on 1 October 1868, all that was visible above ground was a neat single-storey brick building at the junction with Sandall Road

ahead; two villas (Nos.139&141), however, had been lost in the process. More serious was the air pollution by steam locomotives as traffic on the railway increased. This soon caused concern for the health of children attending the nearby school and of those who lived in the area.

The next invader did not destroy houses but was thought to lower the tone of the neighbourhood. The London Street Tramways started running their green horse-drawn cars between Euston Road and the Brecknock Arms on 26 February 1872. Under the 21-year clause promoted by the astute St Pancras surveyor, Booth Scott, this tramway automatically passed into the hands of the LCC on 1 March 1895, and was electrified in 1909. Meanwhile, the Midland Railway had prospered, and in 1898 widened their main line into St Pancras. This widening was to the east of the original formation and entailed the loss of three more houses in Camden Crescent.

The coming of the trams had a disastrous effect on the suburban services of all the mainline railways. On the Midland in 1916, a combination of falling receipts and the need to clear the lines for wartime coal traffic forced total closure of Camden Road station on 1 January 1916. The trams, in their turn, gave way to trolleybuses in 1938.

Partly as a result of these changes, this west side of Camden Road fell into decline,

and in 1939 the LCC used compulsory powers to redevelop the area for public housing. For convenience, the subsequent development will be considered under two headings. The first is at this northern end, where 17 of the original houses were removed in 1955 to make way for the Jews' Free School (JFS). This school arrived somewhat unexpectedly in Camden Road after 226 years of distinguished educational work in London's East End. It was a controversial move. When, in 1939, the LCC obtained a compulsory purchase order to build five blocks of flats to house 1073 people, there were strong protests. But the war intervened and in 1953, when the demand for housing was even greater, the LCC changed its mind. Instead of housing it would give a large part of the land to a school, albeit a distinguished one, from the East End. St Pancras felt it had to make a protest and refused to grant planning permission. A local public enquiry was held, after which the Minister decided to allow the erection of the school, which began in 1956. On Sunday 7 September 1956, the new buildings were dedicated by the Chief Rabbi, who fixed a Mezzuzah on the door-post of the main entrance. The following day JFS Secondary School reopened with 360 pupils. The school flourished at Camden Road. It became an enlarged comprehensive school in 1965 and grant-aided in 1993. But once again, its clientele were on the move outwards, and the decision was taken to relocate to Kenton in 2002.

In its place is a massive housing estate known as **North Point**. It is a joint venture in which the Ujima Housing Association, the Registered Care Homes Association, Camden Council and the Housing Corporation have all played a part. The architects were Jefferson Sheard.

Continuing further down the road, we come to the second area, **Cantelowes Gardens**. The main public open space in this locality, it has had a chequered history. Taking its name from the historic Manor of Cantelowes, the park owes its origin to the ½-acre communal garden that was created for the householders of Camden Crescent in 1855. Like many London squares, access was restricted to authorised keyholders, until 1937 when the Marquis of Camden agreed to dedicate the garden as a public open space (provided it was not used for public meetings). Plans were abandoned at the time of the Munich Crisis, and during WWII the garden was used as a dump for 600 cubic yards of sand (for sandbags and fire fighting). The Crescent gardens were reopened on 30 July 1947 by the Mayor of St Pancras, Councillor F W Powe JP. Meanwhile, the houses surrounding the gardens had been compulsorily purchased by the LCC in 1939 for redevelopment and had subsequently been demolished, the last inhabitants leaving in 1951. Six years

later, in conjunction with the building of the JFS, the Crescent gardens were added to part of the former playing fields. In 1978, after refurbishment, which included a skateboard facility, it was reopened by Prince Charles and hosted a 'Cantelowes Jam', a skateboard and BMX bike festival. When the JFS left in 2002, the boundaries were enlarged and in 2003 discussions were held locally to plan further improvements in facilities and planting. It is a most valuable open space, and heavily used, despite a notable lack of seating.

When you have fully appreciated the amenity of this green, car-free zone, walk back to the entrance and turn right. The Total petrol station is but the latest of several fuel-dispensing structures to have occupied this site, formerly the Midland Railway's Camden Road station. After this closed in 1916, the station building remained in alternative use until well after WWII. At the junction turn right into **SANDALL ROAD**, which was laid out in 1867 on land belonging to the Earl of Dartmouth (p 138). It takes its name from Sandall, near Doncaster, on the Earl's Yorkshire estate. It became a valuable link between the Bartholomew estate (p 109) and Camden Road. One side of the road is hard up against the retaining wall of the railway cutting. When the line was widened in 1898, the first house (No.2) disappeared, as did, apparently, a bridge across the railway to the back-land (now

Cantelowes Gardens). **No.4** has been rebuilt as flats, while **Nos.6-12** are terraced houses of 1868.

The other side of the road is of greater interest. Nos.7-15 were destroyed by bombing in 1941. The St Pancras Council flats, **Sandall Road 9-15**, built in a typically chunky 1950s style, were designed by Nicholls & Hale and completed in 1953. At No.5 was the Railway Tavern, built in 1870 and run by John and Jane Dillow from 1877 until its closure in 1910. The original Nos.1&3 were a furniture warehouse and showroom called The Emporium, owned by Thomas Bowman of Camden High Street fame. In 1870 he sold it to the burgeoning North London Collegiate School for Ladies for £3000. The 2-storey warehouse was converted and extended by E C Robins and opened by the Prince and Princess of Wales on 18 July 1879. A further large extension was designed by J T Lee, along the frontage of former Sandall Mews (Camden Road Mews until 1901), and opened in 1908. The extension included the magnificent Clothworkers Hall and the conspicuous tower.

The North London Collegiate School for Ladies (NLCS) had been founded by Miss Frances Buss in 46 Camden Street on 4 April 1850. Numbers rose rapidly to 200. In 1864, senior pupils were for the first time allowed to sit the Cambridge University Entrance examinations. The school then moved to No.202 Camden Road and finally to Sandall Road. Meanwhile, Miss Buss had perceived the need for a second school to cater for the needs of a less wealthy section of the community. This school, to be called the **Camden School for Girls** (CSG), opened on 16 February 1871 at No.46 Camden Street, with 40 girls and Miss E J Elford as Headmistress. It moved to Prince of Wales Road in 1878, to the premises recently evacuated by the Governesses' Asylum (p 91).

In 1938 the NLCS decided to move to a larger site at Chandos in Canons Park, Edgware, and this it did on 18 June 1940. Its Kentish Town premises were subsequently used as an Emergency Rest Centre for bombed-out families and an Air Raid Precautions Post. In January 1941 enemy bombs destroyed the Clothworkers Hall and most of the Sandall Road frontage. Fortunately, the buildings were empty on the night the bombs fell. The Army took over the premises from 30 May 1947.

The CSG had been evacuated to Lincolnshire, but returned to its home in Prince of Wales Road in 1943. The buildings there were no longer adequate, and serious proposals for reconstructing the Sandall Road school began in 1947, although the situation was far from encouraging. At one point, the Sandall Road site and its ruined buildings were offered for sale. Aided status was finally obtained in 1951, and on 1 April 1954 work began to repair and renew the buildings here. In 1956 the CSG moved into the new premises, which were officially opened on 18 October by the Duchess of Gloucester. Further improvements were made between 1965 and 1967 when architects Stillman & Eastwick-Field, with great ingenuity, provided 4-storey teaching wings and an assembly hall, portions of which can be seen from Sandall Road. In 1973 a capacity meeting was held in the hall as part of the school's fight against threats to its independence. That same night, the roof collapsed, a victim of high-alumina cement failure. But the roof was speedily reinstated and the school remained on the historic site.

In 2004, major new school buildings were completed by Mullaly & Co. on the Camden Road frontage. They provide long-awaited facilities, but they lack visual conviction. It is perhaps as well that the blue plaque to that most remarkable educator Frances Mary Buss should be placed on the remaining fragment of E C Robins' work in Sandall Road.

As we return to Camden Road to catch the bus, we may well ponder the words of the Victorian census enumerator, as the St Pancras-bound express roars underneath, "Here comes the Midland Railway station – nobody sleeps here".

Leighton Road to Fortess Road

Circular walk from Kentish Town station
For modern map see inside back cover

This circular walk is on land bounded by Brecknock, Fortess and Leighton Roads. This area was farmland until the 19th century, primarily owned by two estates: to the north by St John's College, Cambridge and to the south by the Torriano family. In addition, 3 acres of land was part of the Eleanor Palmer Gift, bequeathed to the poor of Kentish Town by the wife of John Palmer, a daughter of a cofferer of Henry VII. This land was by the Fortys Field, which gave its name to Fortess Road. This road opened c.1814 (as Junction Road) from Kentish Town to Upper Holloway to serve as a public carriageway that would avoid the difficult climb through Highgate. Substantial houses were built along it from 1820, at a time when Kentish Town was still considered a desirable address for gentlemen. The 'pure air' of Kentish Town had been extolled by an 18th-century inhabitant, Dr Rowley, who lived close to the Assembly House inn, whose many leisure attractions long acted as a magnet for day trippers from London.

Running directly east from the Assembly House, a footpath across fields to Islington was laid out as the present Leighton Road,

ROUTE **9**

123

in whose western reaches a number of good-sized houses were built in the 1830s. The streets between Leighton Road and Fortess Road were gradually built up from south to north during the succeeding decades of the 19th century. The character of the streets built later – the St John's College Cambridge estate being developed mainly from the mid-1860s to the 1880s – deteriorated as Kentish Town declined in status after the coming of the Midland Railway in 1864 and the relentless march of bricks and mortar over the surrounding fields.

The walk begins at Kentish Town station, where we turn right into **KENTISH TOWN ROAD** and very shortly cross Leighton Road to the **Assembly House** pub at Nos.292&294. The early name of the inn, the Black Bull, was first recorded in 1721. By 1793 it had become the Assembly House, although John Richardson has recorded another name for the pub taken from an illustration of c.1851 of 'The Flask, Kentish Town', which is very similar to the illustration of the inn in King's *Panorama* (p 12). King also shows an oval marble-topped table standing under an elm tree, donated by Robert Wright in 1725 in gratitude for his return to health. An inscription around the edge of the table recorded that he was no longer an invalid, thanks to his daily walks to take breakfast at the inn.

The old inn (**Fig 30**) stood back from the highway facing the main road, with a large cobbled yard and a horse-trough in front. An advertisement of c.1780 states that the inn had "a good trap ball ground, skittle ground, pleasant summer house, extensive gardens" and that there was "a good ordinary [Sunday roast] on Sunday at 2 o'clock". King in his *Panorama* also describes the annual "beanfeasts", and the parlour where entry was restricted to The Social Villagers. This society consisted of the 'aristocracy' of the village and had been founded by James Sheridan Knowles (1784–1862), the most popular verse playwright of his generation, who in 1817 wrote a canto entitled *The Senate, or The Social Villagers of Kentish Town* which described in verse these raucous all-male social occasions.

The inn has had a long and varied history. On 8 December 1784 the landlord, Thomas Wood, was tried at the Old Bailey, accused of highway robbery by Sir Thomas Davenport. Many leading residents of the village, including Gregory Bateman (p 64), who then owned the Assembly House, gave evidence as to Wood's good character and he was acquitted. But Sir Thomas was not content and continued with his accusations until 1787, when Wood died "raving mad". Between 1810 and 1842 twenty-two courts of the Manor of Cantelowes were held at the inn. In 1971 it hosted the filming of *Villain*, starring Richard Burton, described in Halliwell's Film Guide as "very unpleasant and unentertaining". In 1849 the Assembly House was badly damaged by a storm and its tree was struck by lightning, but the days of coaching inns had already passed, and three years later the pub was rebuilt on its present site, losing its old cobbled yard and the facilities required of a coaching inn. Mr Wright's table was taken into the pub, where John Richardson among others can remember seeing it about 20 years ago. Alas, it appears to have been stolen since, possibly by a dishonest landlord.

The splendid, Grade-II-Listed, late-Victorian pub now standing on the site is yet another rebuild, erected in 1898 by Thorpe & Furniss, a prominent specialist firm at the time. Pevsner describes it as one of the best examples of the period, with well-preserved interiors of etched glass and mahogany and a "robust corner turret". Note, at the far side of the building along Leighton Road, the small statue of a little boy holding up the date.

Walk north along Kentish Town Road to **Nos.298-302** with bold, brick quoins and now made into shops. This is the former police station. Built in 1862, the station housed Y Division until it moved to Holmes Road (p 83) in 1896. It replaced a row of cottages which in the 18th century was called Hayman's Row after the name of the underlying field. Hayman's features in an early bequest to the poor of St Pancras by John Morant,

Merchant Adventurer, which was noted in 1547, although the bequest itself may have been earlier. The building stands on the north side of the large cobbled yard that disappeared with the old Assembly House, on the south corner of **LEVERTON PLACE**, into which we turn, right.

The old house on the north side is known as **Village House**. Its former front garden has long been occupied by commercial buildings; the present, glass-fronted estate agent's dates from 1988-89 and is by Jestico & Whiles, well known for their work in Camden Town. Village House is one of the few remaining 18th-century properties in Kentish Town; King's *Panorama* records that in the early 1800s it was the residence of a Captain Finch. A later resident called Borthwick was also a captain, who in 1818 advertised himself as a professor of music of great "talent and celebrity". The parents of 13-year-old Miss Jones apprenticed her to Borthwick for seven years on the understanding that he would train her in dancing and music, but her mother discovered that his intentions towards Miss Jones "were of an improper nature".

The building beyond the turning alongside Village House was a smithy in the 19th century. Go left into the turning. This is **FALKLAND PLACE**. Known as Assembly Row until 1860, it is one of

30 The original Assembly House

the few ancient by-ways left in Kentish Town, retaining the peaceful atmosphere of an earlier age. The small thoroughfare is shown on the 1801 parish map with a terrace of small cottages on the west and a large farmhouse, occupied by Richard Holmes, with outhouses and garden, midway up the east side. Next to it were two cow liers, with further fields stretching eastward to Maiden Lane, now Brecknock Road. On the 1870 OS map the farm had disappeared, as the land was beginning to be developed. The road frontage to the east was taken up by a row of fair-sized cottages, four of which survive at the north end of the lane. The site of the other houses, bombed in WWII, was made into a playground for small children in the 1980s. Small, tightly packed properties on the west side were pulled down, and the space is now a public garden.

On the corner with **FALKLAND ROAD** (left) the houses were demolished in the 1890s and replaced by Falkland Hall, after Falkland Road had been opened up in 1894 to allow access from Fortess Road. The Baptist mission formerly at 20 Fortess Grove (p 136) moved into the Hall in January 1896 and a wide range of meetings was held here, including well-attended mother's meetings and from 1901 the so-called "Cripples Own", a branch of the Ragged School Union. The Highgate Road Chapel (p 58) kept Falkland Hall going until 1956 when it was sold. In the 1990s Nos.2A&2B were built on the site; this western end of the road is discussed later (p 137).

We now turn right. Falkland Road was built c.1864 and was one of the earliest roads to be developed when St John's College, Cambridge began to capitalise on its Kentish Town land in the 1860s. Most of the street names on the estate have some connection with the college. Viscount Falkland, for instance, was a former student who had died at the Battle of Newbury in 1643. Some of the stuccoed houses are now painted in rich, bold colours. Rabbi Julia Neuberger, Liberal Democrat life peer and healthcare champion, and her husband bought a 3-bedroomed house in this road for £23,000 in 1969 and sold it 4 years later. Today, an average price for a house in this road would be £600,000 to £700,000.

Turn right into **LEVERTON STREET**, also very colourful. This south end of the street (it continues north beyond Falkland Road) was first built as a cul-de-sac on the garden land of the old Assembly House, when the pub was being built in its present position in Leighton Road. Walk south, passing Leverton Place on your right. The Grade-II-Listed houses are small and only one window wide on the ground floor; most are well preserved and some still retain attractive pot holders.

Reaching **LEIGHTON ROAD**, turn left. By 1793 the Assembly House property and five fields to the east were owned by Joshua Prole Torriano and other members of his family who had inherited it from an ancestor, John Cox the Elder of London, a soap maker. Joshua proceeded to develop it, starting with Leighton Road. This first appears on the Thompson map of 1801 as a short road, laid out along the footpath to Islington, south of the old Assembly House bowling alley and pleasure garden. In its infancy, Leighton Road was known as Evans Place, after the owner of the livery stables that stood on the south corner of its junction with Kentish Town Road. It was renamed Gloucester Place soon after Princess Mary's marriage to the Duke of Gloucester in 1816. Finally, in 1863, a decision was made to call all the various developments in the road by one name: Leighton Road. The name derives from Sir David Leighton of Charlton Kings in Gloucestershire, whose wife, Dame Isabella Chow Torriano, had inherited part of the estate from her mother's brother, J P Torriano. (The Leightons' land agent was Professor Thomas Leverton Donaldson, who developed the estate.)

On this north side of Gloucester Place J P Torriano sold off the land in long narrow building plots, extending the whole breadth of the Assembly House grounds as far as today's Lady Margaret Road, where the early road ended. In the 1830s a picturesque enclave of middle-class houses was thus formed.

Early in the 19th century development also began on the south side of the road. Here the small cottages at Nos.2-18 have gone, replaced by the railway and the site now occupied by Meers Engineering Co. The 1851 census shows that many were occupied by artisans connected with the piano trade. Between **No.18** and **No.20** a short drive once led to diminutive Hope Cottages.

Walk east, passing early-19th-century stuccoed villas and then a long brick wall with a blocked-up doorway, until you reach the entrance (on the left) to **Maud Wilkes Close**, Nos.21-25, a housing project begun in 1999 by the St Pancras Housing Association, comprising 18 self-contained flats and 12 houses. Its pleasant, friendly open aspect is a fitting tribute to Maud Wilkes, the first superintendent of St Margaret's Nursery that was once here.

Turn into the estate and pause to consider its history. The parish map of 1800 shows a short drive, entered through the doorway we have just passed, leading to a property standing in open land. Fronting the road to the east of the drive, a small Wesleyan chapel seating 257 people was erected and opened in 1828. The congregation moved in 1864 to a larger, grander chapel in Lady Margaret Road (p 128) and converted the chapel here to a mission hall, to cater for the many navvies in the area brought in by the Midland Railway. This was sold in 1880 to the Presbyterians, and a schoolroom was built at the back.

The gentleman's residence at the end of the drive was known in the mid-19th century as Bower Cottage, when it was occupied by the prosperous builder Charles Crane and his family. He had earlier built and lived in Sussex House on the site of the old National School in Monte Video Place (p 67). He achieved a certain national notoriety when *The Times* of 19 June 1866 reported his altercations with a neighbour, a disbarred barrister called Pike. Their quarrels involved throwing dead chickens over the garden walls. In 1867 the newly established St Pancras Board of Guardians leased Bower Cottage to use as one of four Poor Relief Stations. Leighton Road was no longer considered a desirable locality, as the Midland Railway had arrived on the other side of the road in 1864. Mr Pike, for instance, bought his property for £900 in 1840 but resold it in 1880 for only £500.

The Poor Relief Station acquired a soup kitchen, and in the mid-1870s Casual Relief wards were built in the garden, much to the chagrin of Charles Crane's executors. By the end of the century the Casual Wards were removed to Holmes Road (p 98) and the overnight accommodation was demolished. In 1903 a large red-brick building was erected on the Leighton Road site: the LCC's St Margaret's Nursery, a receiving centre where children from many parts of London were assessed when first taken into care. After assessment, the children were taken to a 'country home' at Leavesden in Hertfordshire, known as Leavesden Industrial School (and by locals there as St Pancras School), where the boys were taught various trades and the girls trained to enter domestic service.

During the 20th century the receiving centre at Bower Cottage became more of a permanent home for the children. The old soup kitchen was incorporated into the institution. Space for the children to play was needed, and Nos.15&17 to the west and Nos.23&25 to the east of the mission hall were bought and demolished in the 1920s. A large Lodge, partly used as a nurses' home, was erected facing the road in front of Bower Cottage.

During WWII the mission hall became a British Restaurant, catering for those involved in Civil Defence, and also a First Aid post for bomb casualties. It was demolished together with the schoolroom in the 1950s. Smaller numbers of children in the Nursery (by now sometimes referred to as St Margaret's Hospital) meant that the building could be used for other purposes, and for 10 years it also housed the offices of Camden Area 5 Social Services. Eventually, the Nursery closed, and the last occupants of Bower Cottage were Albanian refugees in 1998, before its demolition in 1999.

Continue walking east. Pevsner picks out for comment the Grade-II-Listed houses opposite. Double-fronted **No.28**, with its Greek Doric porch, survived attempts to demolish it so as to enlarge the former Post Office Sorting Of next door at **No.30**, an exuberant 1-storey Edwardian building erected in 1903. Note the prominent royal insignia and "Postmen's Office" inscription. In February 1995 the pillar-box outside disappeared; it was eventually traced to Stacey Street, Hornsey and returned to its old position.

Alongside is **No.32**, a new building housing the London Centre for Psychotherapy (LCP). Next door is an entrance to the Caversham Group Practice (p 103), built on the site of the original No.34, which in the 1870s housed a small private school, in common with several other properties in early Leighton Road. In 1929 this site had become a garage and workshop for the City Motor Omnibus Company and for its New Empress coaches, which once provided a popular twice-hourly service to Southend. When, in 1934, the firm lost its local bus routes to the newly-formed London Passenger Transport Board, it became the City Coach Co., subsequently relocating to Wood Green. On this side of the road, **Leighton House**, on the corner at No.37, is one of the largest of the early houses. From the 1920s it was the headquarters of St Pancras North Unionist Club, becoming

in 1971 the Holborn and St Pancras Conservative Association, based here until the early 1990s.

Turn left up **LADY MARGARET ROAD**, which was named after Lady Margaret Beaufort, Countess of Richmond and Derby, mother of Henry VII and the founder of St John's College, Cambridge, which owned the land north of Leighton Road. The houses date from the 1860s. Lady Margaret Road was one of the settings for the 2002 film *About A Boy*. In 1986-88 the architect Richard Burton made use of the long garden behind Leighton House bordering Lady Margaret Road to build a house and studio, **No.1B**, immediately on our left. It is "a house of … ingenuity, richness and ecological consciousness" (*Architectural Review*). Follow its garden wall to the circular front door, built into one side of a London plane tree.

In 1867 the *Illustrated London News* referred to the church on the opposite side of the road as another "ornament of the neighbourhood", although Pevsner thought it "ugly and uninspired". Look at its imposing spire before crossing over to it. The church was built in 1864-67, designed by John Tarring for the Wesleyan Methodists, who moved to this site from Leighton Road. The building eventually became too large for them, and in 1969 they exchanged it for that of the Roman Catholic congregation in Fortess Road. Now dedicated to **Our Lady Help of**

Christians, and Grade-II Listed, the church has an interesting galleried interior. Just along from the church, **No.16** was the birthplace of Harold James (Jim) Dyos, the historian who wrote the pioneering local history study *Victorian Suburb: a study of the growth of Camberwell* (1961).

Return to Leighton Road, passing the site of an early house on your left, which in the 1870s was a ladies' school. It is now part of the grounds of **Kennistoun House**, built for St Pancras Council in 1934 (Kenniston being one of the earliest known names for Kentish Town). Turn left along **LEIGHTON ROAD** and walk a few yards to view a small plaque attached to Kennistoun House and dedicated to Don Cook. He was the leader of this building's tenants during the St Pancras rent strike of 1959-60 when they and thousands more across the borough protested against the large rent increases imposed by the Council. Organised marches attracted national press coverage, and rents were withheld until the Council finally threatened the tenants with eviction. Don Cook barricaded himself into his flat, but he was evicted early in the morning of 22 September 1960. A subsequent march led to an unsuccessful attempt to reoccupy the flat, and 450 police fought with over 2000 demonstrators outside St Pancras station; the Home Secretary then banned all secular marches within the borough of St Pancras.

On the south side is a brick-faced row of early cottages, **Nos.34-54**, built by 1834, with round-arched doorways. **No.36B**, another building named Leighton House, is an infill, as is **No.56**, built in a sympathetic style. Look out for **No.52**, which has original doors and windows. Carry on walking. On the left, the site of No.57, adjacent to a small driveway, is now called **Dunne Mews**. By peering over the security-guarded entrance door, you can see a row of 1-storey houses to the right of a path leading from the entrance, part of the sheltered housing accommodation now occupying the site. It was occupied for a century from the 1870s by dairymen.

Next door is the **Gloucester Arms** at No.59, which originated in the 1840s, although the current building is an early-20th-century rebuild. Its side wall announces a "scenic painted beer garden", which dates from the 1960s. It is a little faded now. The coat of arms on the inn-sign belongs to the City (rather than the Duke) of Gloucester, and its Latin motto meaning "unconquered faith triumphs" has been misspelled. **Margaret House** and **Rosemary House** beyond the driveway, and separated by a grass space, were built for St Pancras Borough Council in 1952 and 1953 respectively on the site of the original houses.

On the south side **Nos.58-80** form another terrace of early houses, mostly brick-faced; Nos.64-70 are Grade-II

Listed. They originally had long back gardens, which were lost as Leighton Place behind was developed. The present **Kenbrook House**, named after a nearby stream, was built in 1938 by St Pancras Council over another early terrace, Nos.84-100. A Goad insurance map (c.1900) shows beside No.84 a driveway leading to the site of an intended factory, No.86A (now Nos.3&5 Leighton Place), at the foot of its garden, and another factory shown as No.84A, very close to the short back gardens of the houses in Peckwater Street (p 102). A few years later, No.82 was demolished to enlarge the driveway, which received its present name of **LEIGHTON PLACE** in 1932 along with a new number sequence to replace the old Leighton Road numbering.

Cross the road carefully and walk south down Leighton Place. The first building to note is **Nos.3&5** on our left. When first built in 1900 it was occupied by makers of organ keys Richard William Cork; the firm celebrated its diamond jubilee in the same building in 1937. C A Dettmer & Sons, piano-string makers (cf. p 90), were here before and after WWI. The Nordoff-Robbins Music Therapy centre, now removed to Lissenden Gardens (p 51), was based here in 1986. To the east, a rather grim playground behind Kenbrook House has replaced an erstwhile small orchard.

The first warehouse built on the new estate in 1898, No.84A, now **No.7**, lies

at the bend in the road. It was occupied until 1912 by Pull & Field, piano manufacturers. The mapmaking firm Geographia was installed here during WWI, and in WWII St Pancras Borough Council used the building as an Air Raid Precautions base. Camden ITEC, founded here in 1986 by Priscilla Waller, is an Information Technology Centre and provides work-based training for young people in computer skills, literacy and numeracy.

Proceed to the end of the cul-de-sac, noting the row of handsome warehouses on the left, several once associated with the piano trade. However, **Nos.13&15**, dating from 1920, were the workshops of Rowland Ward, taxidermists, whose showrooms were at No.166 Piccadilly; the firm was awarded the royal warrant in 1947 as 'naturalists' to the King. From 1912 they had been at **No.18**, which bears in paint the name "R F Stevens" − a firm of harmonium manufacturers, who were based in several of the warehouses in Leighton Place, but never here.

The road is otherwise lined by 1930s houses, including the terrace at **Nos.8-16**, built in 1932 when Leighton Place was given its name. Return to Leighton Road, carefully cross to the north side and turn right to reach **WILLINGHAM TERRACE**. The shops beyond it, in Leighton Road, were built around 1850; an early post office later stood on the corner. Turn left into Willingham Terrace, now a service road. The origin of the name is unknown, but St John's College, Cambridge did own land in Willingham, a village in Cambridgeshire. A short way up on the left are the flats of **Willingham Close**, officially recognised by the Post Office in 1952. Willingham Terrace once pursued a right-angled spur to the west along the site of the north side of Willingham Close. The buildings on its north side, which may well have been stables with accommodation over, were bombed in WWII, as were the small early houses on the east side of Willingham Terrace, which were swept away; the site is now occupied by lock-up garages.

North of Willingham Close, the path becomes a continuation of the old road, flanked by the garden walls of the buildings in **FALKLAND ROAD**, whose westernmost end we shall explore later (p 137). On the left corner is a house converted from the recently closed Falkland Arms pub, erected in the 1860s at the same time as the houses here. Cross the road and stand outside the neighbourhood shop on the corner of Montpelier Grove. Look west along Falkland Road as far as the church hall that stands just short of the Roman Catholic church on the corner. The hall, now known as **Our Lady's Hall**, was erected on the site of the school built for boys, girls and infants by the Wesleyans in 1880 with the proceeds of the sale of

their mission hall in Leighton Road to the Presbyterians.

The roads north of Falkland Road are part of the St John's College estate, developed after 1864 with houses designed to appeal to less prosperous tenants. Proceed up **MONTPELIER GROVE** (Montpelier Road until 1938). The name derives from the neighbouring large house (p 116) that stands behind the houses on the east side of the road. Below the first floor of **No.13** is a covered passage leading to the entrance to the Montpelier Gardens.

We, however, turn left along **DUNOLLIE ROAD**, named after the ruined castle near Oban and near which John McNab, one of the builders who developed the area in the 1870s, was probably born. Dunollie Road has small but quite tall houses. On its south side is a pocket of houses called **Dunollie Place**. Charles Booth, walking the area in 1898, noted that "a clothes line close by showed sorry linen and a torn waistcoat that told clearly of working-class occupants".

Cross Lady Margaret Road and continue into **ASCHAM STREET**, named after Roger Ascham, tutor to Elizabeth I and a patron of St John's College. The houses were developed by Philip Luzmore, who was also the principal leaseholder of properties in Leverton Street, ahead. The centre of the block on your left was by the 1890s taken up by a factory, originally a Victorian dye works. In 2004 the residents

of several local streets feared having their gardens concreted over because of arsenic pollution from the old Ascham Works. As early as July 1988 a local action group, in their broadsheet *The Daily Hazard* (No.59), had complained that developers had scant regard for the spread of pollutants when the site was being prepared for the building of sheltered housing. Now called **Ash Court**, this is a private 62-unit nursing and residential home for the elderly run by Forest Healthcare Company, formed in 1994. The name of the court is presumably a play on the street name.

At the corner of Leverton Street take a look at the **Pineapple** pub, opposite. It dates from 1852 and has a façade, and interior, liberally decorated with representations of the fruit. In a stable block behind the pub a giraffe called Zara was kept in the 1890s while its home was being built at Regent's Park Zoo. The pub was saved from closure by the Powell family, father and daughter, who took it over in 2002 after a battle with developers who wanted to convert it into flats. They were supported by local residents and also by local celebrities such as Jon Snow, Ken Stott and Rufus Sewell. The pub is now Listed Grade II.

Continue down **RAILEY MEWS**, to the side of the pub. The property on the corner, with a well-preserved exterior painted dark green, was originally the workshops of the Railey Works Company. The 'Railey Works' at No.1B housed the peripatetic Dettmer & Sons, piano-string makers, from after WWI until the 1980s. Follow the Mews as it turns right. The row of buildings on the west (left) side was built as stables with accommodation above, and for much of the 20th century housed small workshops before being converted for residential use. The building plots follow the curving line of the boundary of the Fortys Field estate in Fortess Road (p 134), the houses at both ends being considerably deeper than those in the middle. Despite the lack of back yards the houses have been gentrified, encouraged by the pleasant open aspect of the east side provided by the back gardens of properties in Leverton Street. Continue, noting on the last building the hoist, whose chain currently holds up birdfeed. Over the wall beyond you can see the back of Fortess Terrace (p 135). The mews bends again, past modernistic **No.17**.

Continue into Ospringe Road and the junction with Lupton Street (see later), left. Above us rises the imposing Grade-II-Listed **St Benet and All Saints**, architect Joseph Peacock. The original nave was consecrated in 1885. The chancel was built in 1908 and a replacement nave in 1928; both were by Cecil Hare. Pevsner suggests that the chancel and south chapel are "still in the Bodley tradition, Dec[orated] with elaborate tracery" but that Hare's nave

was an "original spare version of Gothic". The first building was constructed on a giant dust heap, and in 1907 had to be expensively underpinned. The church is High Anglican and in the care of the Society of the Holy Cross, whose purpose is to strengthen the spiritual life of its members. Inside, the white plastered walls and the church furnishings provide a friendly atmosphere. The rood (1912) and the baroque painted statue of the Virgin and Child are by Hare. There is also stained glass by Clayton and Bell and by Burlison and Grylls, who also the designed the pairs of archbishops in the nave. One window, *The Building of the Temple*, is by Burne-Jones and was brought here from Kentish Town parish church (p 34).

Camden Council's 1979 report claimed the church was too large for the congregation; the plan was to build a smaller nave for worship and use the ground released for sport and recreation. Nothing has come of this, perhaps because St Benet's has acted as Kentish Town's parish church since the parish church in Highgate Road closed in 1993. However, the church is in need of attention.

Turn left out of the church and bear left along **OSPRINGE ROAD**, which takes its name from a former hospital and land owned by St John's College at Ospringe in Kent. Continue walking until you can turn for a good view of the east end of the church and of the Crucifixion high up on

the wall. **Church House**, tucked away to the east of the church, was built in the 1970s in stark contrast to the enormous vicarage it replaced; the latter used to stand on the site of the present post-war flats called **Lambourn Close**. These were named, like several other Kentish Town Council blocks, after a place in Berkshire.

Turn right and walk south along a stretch of **LADY MARGARET ROAD**. The houses on the east side (left) have large porches, most with a room added above, some rather unwisely in brick and plaster. The houses on the west side have imposing columned entrances, but otherwise their rambling design makes each façade look like the *back* rather than the front of a house. Continue to the corner with **COUNTESS ROAD** and look left and right along this typical residential road. Built in the 1870s, it was known as Frost Road until 1880, when it was renamed in honour of the Countess of Richmond and Derby − Lady Margaret again, with another title.

Now retrace your steps to the front of the church, where we enter **LUPTON STREET**, and stop at the sunken garden to the north of the church. The garden's flower beds are edged with old railway sleepers. It was developed in 1966 by a group of young people from the Manpower Services Commission on the site of No.2. One of the largest houses on the estate, the Liddon Memorial High School, was

ROUTE **9**

131

opened here in 1892 by the Sisters of the Church, a Church of England community founded that year in Kilburn by Mother Emily Ayckburn. The school was probably named after H P Liddon (1829–1890), a clergyman whose High Church sermons and writings strongly influenced Victorian religious thought. The Sisters aimed to "secure religious teaching for the little ones of the neighbourhood", as no religion was taught in the Board Schools established by the 1870 Education Act. They were still here in 1901, but by 1906 the school was kept by Miss Lavinia Burdett. She, if not the school, remained here until at least 1926. From 1953 the house was used as the vicarage, with the Rev. Frank Oakley in residence, until its demolition in 1966. By that time it was in a sorry state. The church and its grounds are still having problems with underground springs. At the back of the garden is a forlorn building dating from 1881. Built as the church's mission hall, and later described as its Sunday school, it is no longer used as such. Next door, at **No.4**, in 1906 lived Alice and Agnes Douglas, two of the many music teachers who appear in the directories for this area.

On the west side of the road, Nos.15-25 were demolished to enlarge the **Eleanor Palmer Primary School**, built in 1969. The school commemorates the eponymous charitable lady (p 123), although it does not stand on land that belonged to her.

Admire, on the front gates of the school, the figures of fish, birds, children, houses, toys, etc., shaped out of blue coloured tubing with the help of mosaic. Outside the school, the Council has provided an area isolated from passing traffic where parents can wait for their offspring. The school is within Camden's first 'Home Zone', part of a government-funded national initiative launched in 2002, which is designed to transform the area into a pedestrian-friendly community space, with traffic calming measures, street art and benches.

Continue downhill to the junction with Brecknock Road, the houses on the southeast corner of which were bombed in WWII. The site is now covered by an unnamed block of flats owned by the Council, numbered **Nos.24-58**. Lupton Street, known thus since 1882, derives its name from an early benefactor of St John's College, Roger Lupton, Provost of Eton. When built c.1880 the street was at first known as St John's College Park. When this name appeared earlier, on the Stanford map of 1862 (p 6), it was assigned to the whole of the St John's estate to the east of Fortess Road, then shown prophetically as "building ground". The proposed street layout was more spacious and quite different from what eventually materialised.

Turn left into **BRECKNOCK ROAD**, which was developed in the later 19th century on the line of ancient Maiden Lane (see p 138). Just before the next junction

on the opposite (Islington) side of the road is Tufnell Park Underground Station. The building on the junction's southeast corner is now called **The Grand Banks** and was built c.1927 as a branch of Barclays Bank, here until the late 1980s. The building subsequently became a trendy wine bar which closed in 2001. Early in 2004 a group of international squatters, known as The Wombles, seized the building to prepare it for use as an "occupied social centre" but they were removed by police some months later. To the left of the steps, a small metal plaque inscribed "SMI Boundary 1883" indicates the parish boundary of St Mary's Islington.

Stop at the junction and look left and right. The construction of a good road from the West End to avoid the difficult slopes for horses of the Highgate Northern Heights had been mooted for many years, but it was not until 1812 that an Act of Parliament was passed for the making of a "public carriageway road from Kentish Town to Upper Holloway". It was opposed by the St Pancras Vestry, who successfully demanded that no tolls would be taken south of Brecknock Road. Opened c.1814, the new highway was known as Junction Road until its southern portion below this crossroads was changed to **FORTESS ROAD** in 1879. It was so named because it followed (in part) the line of an earlier Fortys (or Fortess) Lane, passing the Fortys (or Fortess) Field, land that belonged to the Eleanor Palmer Charity. Turn left into Fortess Road and stay on this (east) side.

Edwardian Fortess Road was a lively shopping street which, together with Kentish Town Road, supplied every household need. Today, the shops are mostly cafés serving a local multi-cultural community. Walk a few yards south along Fortess Road to the shops on the east side. You will pass the site of the original turnpike, removed when the toll system was abandoned in 1864. The houses as far as the first turning left (Raveley Street) were built between 1870 and 1890. Behind the houses on the opposite (west) side, the London General Omnibus Company built stables. A pair of horses was needed to pull each omnibus and a third would be added on a steep incline, such as this one. Each horse bus needed 11 horses working in rotation.

The remainder of the west side of Fortess Road is described in Route 2 (p 43). We concentrate here on the east side, where the shop fronts (added to the original houses) have been extended by a three-sided, mostly glass structure. This enables outside access to the original front doors of the buildings. Note this unusual

31 Philipp Gottfried's baker's shop in Fortess Road (Ernest Milner, 1904). The "rout seats" advertised were benches hired out for large social gatherings.

method of enlarging the front area of the shop as you walk down to **No.136**, the last building to be treated in this way. **No.134**, now the 'Zuni Southwest' Mexican restaurant, was once the baker's shop of Philipp Gottfried & Son (**Fig 31**, p 133). Pass **Gottfried Mews**, whose cobbled surface is in a dangerous condition, and where in 1900 the eponymous German-born baker owned 11 stables. The German name of the Mews did not save it from bombing in WWII. It now leads to a row of lock-up garages and an area of casual parking. **No.114** beyond was kept by the Jersey Milk Company at the beginning of the 20th century.

RAVELEY STREET, built about 1880, was named after an estate owned by St John's College at Little Raveley in Huntingdonshire. On its south side is the Eleanor Palmer Primary School, which we noted earlier. It stands on the site of Paddock Lodge, a gentleman's estate on the St John's College land, shown first on a map of 1829. Leonard Hicks, attorney at law, and his sister were the occupants (along with 3 servants) in 1862; they were probably members of the local landowning family of the same name. By 1884 most of the grounds had disappeared under brick, and the property was being used as a school, the Boys' Public Day School, headmaster Rev. Alfred Allen. This was run by the nondenominational Boys' Public Day Schools Company, but as noted by the Bryce Commissioners in 1895, metropolitan conditions were unfavourable to schools of this kind. It was taken over by the London School Board "temporarily", but was replaced with another school by the LCC in 1905 and became the Acland Central School for Boys. In 1969 the old school building was demolished and replaced by the present primary school.

Beyond its high walls in **FORTESS ROAD** are two large terraced houses, **Nos.100-102**, with imposing steps built c.1880 on the southern edge of the old Paddock Lodge garden. They were originally part of a terrace of six houses, but Nos.104-110 were demolished in the early 1980s to enlarge the school premises. The East Kentish Town Library was at the converted No.104 from 1949 to 1962 before it moved (as Kentish Town Library) to its present site at 262-266 Kentish Town Road (p 30). No.110 was home in 1884 to James, Annie and Isabelle Tweddle, who ran a school on the premises.

Stop at **No.98**, the northern boundary of the Eleanor Palmer Gift (p 123), which comprised three acres situated near Fortys Field. As noted earlier, the estate can be clearly traced on Thompson's 1801 map (see frontispiece), where it is labelled "Great Paddock". Fortess Terrace begins here, a long straight stretch of houses along Fortess Road. In 1820 a 90-year lease was given on Nos.96-98, followed in 1823 by similar leases on Nos.76-94. The ground rents varied from 10 guineas to £13 a year. The twenty householders of Nos.36-74 were more fortunate as they paid only a peppercorn rent for their leases, also let for 90 years from 1823. Since 1852 the profits have contributed to the finances of the St Pancras Almshouses. By 1982 the freehold on all but three residential properties in the Terrace and in Fortess Grove, further south, had been sold, and later in the year the remaining three were sold by public treaty. The estate is now administered by the Fortys Field Housing Association.

Continue southwards. Grade-II-Listed Nos.44-98 have channelled stuccoed ground-floor walls and neat first-floor balconies with elegant lyre-patterned ironwork. Nos.76-84 were bomb-damaged in WWII and were largely rebuilt; only No.74, the end bay at the south, was left intact. This was the home (then No.32 Fortess Terrace) in the early 1850s of the watercolour painter Frank Topham (1808-1877). These houses are now flats and known as **Palmer House**. The front elevation resembles those of the original houses, although you will notice that the ironwork on the balconies has a different lyre pattern from that on the houses to the north. The block was in fact rebuilt behind the façade after the war.

There was originally a service road in front of Nos.54-74 and a long narrow strip of garden bordering the road. Above

Nos.62&64 a pediment carries the legend "Fortess Terrace". Pause at **No.56**, in the shade of three huge plane trees. The house bears a blue plaque to Ford Madox Brown, the Pre-Raphaelite painter (**Fig 32**) who lived here from 1855 to 1862. Born in Calais in 1821, he moved here (then No.13 Fortess Terrace) with his second wife Emma and their young family in October 1855. During the summer of 1857, when "our poor little Arthur sickened and died

in one painful week", Madox Brown painted from his first-floor studio window the watercolour now in the Delaware Art Museum entitled *Hampstead from my window – a sketch from Nature*. In the foreground is Landor Cottage, which then stood opposite, and a plane tree which may be the same as the one standing in the front garden of **No.54**. The novelist and essayist Henry Kingsley (1830-1876) was living here (then No.22 Fortess Terrace) in the early 1870s. An earlier occupant was the court painter George Dawe (1781-1829), who painted both histories and portraits (including one of Sir Samuel Romilly); he died here and was buried in St Paul's Cathedral. To the right, Madox Brown shows a low building, with only the roof exposed. It is possible that this was the building used by the Roman Catholics as their St Mary's mission before their permanent church was built in 1859.

Madox Brown used the *back* garden of No.56 as the background for several of his paintings, including *Stages of Cruelty* (in the Walker Art Gallery, Liverpool). While living here, he also painted *Work*, one of his most famous paintings. He was in constant contact with his Pre-Raphaelite Brotherhood friends and particularly with Dante Gabriel Rossetti and his mistress Lizzie Siddal. Madox Brown was not

32 Ford Madox Brown, drawn by Dante Gabriel Rossetti 1852 (National Portrait Gallery, London)

pleased to find them upstairs together when he and Emma arrived home one afternoon. "I was very cool to them" he recorded, and he remained cool for some weeks. In 1856 after a visit from Thomas Seddon he agreed to resume his seat on the board of the North London School of Drawing & Modelling in Camden Town provided "it be remodelled and the school rescued from the grasp of government". This was a generous gesture, as an earlier entry in his diary of 1854 shows that he had previously been headmaster of the school for nearly a year but saw next to nothing of his promised £60 salary.

Madox Brown and his family left No.56 in October 1862 for a grander house in Grove Terrace (p 56). According to his biographer he did so in a fit of pique because the Roman Catholic church (p 44) had been built opposite, spoiling his view. By 1867 his former home was inhabited by nuns of the Convent of St Catherine, who stayed several years.

At **No.40** (then No.15 Fortess Terrace) Dr Thomas Southwood Smith (1788–1861) lived from 1840 to 1844, although there is no plaque to acknowledge him or his pioneering public health work. A physician at the King's Cross Fever Hospital, he had been involved in the passing of the Factory Act of 1833 and was frequently consulted in fever epidemics and on sanitary matters by public authorities. He lived here with his second wife and family and with two old family friends, the writer Miss Mary Gillis and her sister Margaret, a gifted artist. Margaret did a chalk drawing of Southwood Smith (**Fig 33**) that appears as the frontispiece engraving in the biography by his granddaughter, Mrs C L Lewis. In it, Mrs Lewis recalls that he kept a horse and took her perched in front of him on a railed saddle, for Sunday afternoon rides through the fields of Kentish Town. Another granddaughter was Octavia Hill, the housing reformer and a founder of the National Trust.

During his time at Fortess Road Southwood Smith founded (in 1842)

33 Dr Southwood Smith, public health pioneer (chalk drawing by Margaret Gillis)

the Metropolitan Association for the Improvement in the Dwellings of the Industrious Classes, a philanthropic housing association which was to build the first purpose-built block of flats in London, aimed at artisans, at Pancras Square. He had been a close friend of and physician to the utilitarian philosopher Jeremy Bentham and when the latter died in 1832 carried out his wish that his body be made into an "auto-icon". Seated and clothed, and with a lifelike wax mask over the skull, the body can still be seen today at University College, London. Southwood Smith did not donate the auto-icon to the College until 1850, so it may well have been brought here from time to time, as Bentham's will had recommended that his body be present at meetings where his friends and disciples discussed his philosophy. There is a bust of Southwood Smith in the Highgate Institution.

Continue walking down the hill. The inhabitants of Nos.36-50 originally approached their front doors by a set of steps between No.42 and No.44. Nos.44-50 are still approached from the old steps, but **No.44** is now the last of the late Georgian houses and **Eleanor House** is on the site of Nos.36-42. Eleanor House was built by the Eleanor Palmer Trust and was sold to Circle 33 Housing Association

in 1982 along with the charity's other residential properties.

Turn left into **FORTESS GROVE**, the south end of the Eleanor Palmer estate. The road bends round to the right, passing the entrance to **Fortess Mews** on the left. This continues to be used for industry and is the only property still owned by the Eleanor Palmer Trust. In 1900 the workshops of the successful piano maker T G Payne & Co. were based in the mews. It is not known if the mews' original use was in providing stabling for local residents. If not, where did Dr Southwood Smith keep his horse? Tucked into an alcove made by two walls of the Mews is **No.20**, which from 1881 to 1895 was the mission hall of the Highgate Road Baptist chapel, which bought the hall in 1883 and soon found it too small. The congregation moved to Falkland Hall, Falkland Road in 1896 (p 126). The Grove is a pleasant backwater of bijou, well-kept houses, built later than Fortess Terrace in c.1865, spoilt only by parking problems. At the southwest end, behind the fences at the end of the gardens of the houses there, is the spot marked on the 1870 OS map as the site of Cantelowes Manor (see below).

Walk back to Fortess Road, stop on the corner and look south to the Tally Ho pub and the adjacent Fortess Walk (p 44) on the opposite side of the road. Before Junction Road (now Fortess Road) was built in c.1814, Willow Walk was a small lane off the east side of Highgate Road encompassing three sides of a paddock. Junction Road went straight through the paddock, and the old road was split: its northern arm now lay to the west of the new road and retained the name Willow Walk until it changed into Fortess Walk. The other two arms of the old road lay to east – one running behind the new Winchester Place that fronted Junction Road and the last short section (what remained of the southern arm of the old lane), which was renamed Blandford Place. The properties in Blandford Place and Winchester Place were later felt to impede the flow of traffic in Junction Road and in 1894 all buildings as far east as the back of the gardens in Fortess Grove and south to No.322 Kentish Town Road were destroyed to widen **FORTESS ROAD**, as Junction Road had by then been renamed.

On the east side of Fortess Road, south of the corner where you paused, the two southernmost houses in Fortess Terrace were demolished and replaced by **Nos.28&30,** rather smart, with rounded brick corners and tiled windows. This property became additional accommodation for T G Payne, the piano manufacturers in Fortess Mews. Beyond are **Kingston House** and **Lampton House**, built after 1894 as shops with apartments over. These buildings lie over the site of the eastern arm of old Willow Walk, alongside which had been a large

house, home in the late 18th century to Dr William Rowley, who had the lease of the Fortys Field and kept his horses on the Willow Walk paddock. Rowley was a prominent physician who campaigned against Edward Jenner's introduction of cowpox vaccination. In a work *Cow-pox inoculation* in 1805, which reached a third edition in 1806, he gave particulars of 504 cases of smallpox and injury after cowpox vaccination, with 75 deaths. He wrote that it was "a murderous practice, which carries desolation into families, and compromises the reputation of those who protect or practise it", and even claimed that it had produced an "ox-faced boy".

Rowley was also well known for promoting the amenity of Kentish Town and its pure air. According to Bennett, writing in 1821, Rowley "denominated the village the 'Montpelier of England', and it was his custom in almost every case where he considered a change of air necessary, to recommend most strenuously to his patients a sojournment in Kentish Town". It was common practice in the Georgian period to puff the charms of a spa town by referring to it as Montpelier, not to compare it with the French town as such but rather to convey something of its neo-classical sophistication and sylvan, airy setting.

Just before the junction with Falkland Road we reach **No.14**, one of the new properties erected in 1894, when it was

occupied by the ironmongers W Flint. It remained in the family until 1984 but is now the NW5 Theatre School. Beyond is a driveway that led to the two warehouses where the Flint family kept their stock; these were built after 1894 over part of the site of the Manor Cottages, a row of seven small houses that previously ran along the east side of the old south spur of Willow Walk.

Turn left into **FALKLAND ROAD**. Here **Raleigh House, Burton House** and **Falkland House** were all built on the south end of former Manor Cottages. The cottages were close to one of the supposed sites of the Cantelowes Manor House. This proposed location is supported by captions on mid-Victorian pictures and by successive late-19th-century OS maps. The 1889 map actually pinpoints Nos.8-10 Manor Cottages as its location, while the 1894-96 edition adds the words "the site of". However, John Richardson in *Kentish Town Past* (1997) discusses various conflicting pieces of evidence and concludes that the manor house was actually near present-day Baynes Street, off St Pancras Way in Camden Town.

Raleigh House and Burton House are now used for social housing. A covered way beneath the first floor of Falkland House leads to the recently built, security-guarded **Falkland House Mews**. On the south side of the road is **No.2**, which we noticed earlier while walking up Falkland

Place. It dates from the 1894 road-widening scheme. Pass the Kulubi Centre at **No.2C**, home to Camden Black Sisters, a support group for women of African or African-Caribbean descent.

Return to **FORTESS ROAD** and turn left. In a few steps we reach **No.6**, with an interesting façade in faded red and cream and a Queen Anne roofline. An inscription in tiling shows that this was the old Fortess Road Post Office. Like the other buildings south of Falkland Road it was erected shortly after 1894.

Another few yards on, at the fork where the main road divides, we reach **KENTISH TOWN ROAD**. Here, **No.326** also dates from 1894. The houses southward to Leverton Place are possibly late-18th-century and were known by 1835 as Commercial Place. **No.322** was the base before WWI of the builder Robert Smerdon, who laid out a good deal of Dartmouth Park (see Route 10). Between it and **No.324** is a small drive that led to stables in the 19th century.

Crossing Leverton Place we have almost come full circle. Ahead on the left, past the Assembly House, lies Kentish Town station and the end of our walk.

Route 10
Dartmouth Park
Circular walk from Tufnell Park station
For modern map see inside back cover

The marriage of William Legge, 2nd Earl of Dartmouth (1731–1801) in 1755 to Frances Catherine, the daughter and heiress of Sir Charles Gunter-Nicholl of Woodsome in Yorkshire, brought into his family part of the old manor of Cantelowes that had belonged to the prebendaries of St Paul's Cathedral. His family waited 100 years before they started to develop their Kentish Town estate, known as Dartmouth Park. Our walk will at first follow the east boundary road, now called Dartmouth Park Hill, which is also the boundary between the London boroughs of Camden and Islington. The estate extends west as far as the Highgate Road.

The walk begins at Tufnell Park Underground station. Nearby are bus stops. The exit from the station is at the north end of Brecknock Road (p 132), a road built up in the 1870s on the line of the ancient Maiden Lane that ran from Highgate to King's Cross. When the Great Northern Railway's line from York reached London, Maiden Lane was renamed York Road throughout its length.

Turn right, and at the scissor-like crossroads cross over to walk up **DARTMOUTH PARK HILL**, named after the Earl's country seat, Dartmouth Park near Huddersfield. The Hill is shown as York Road on the 1862 Stanford map of London (p 6), although some late-19th-century maps referred to it as Brecknock Road, and the old name Maiden Lane lingered for many years.

The first building of note, on the right, is the flamboyant Boston Hotel (1899). This, however, is in Islington and we shall concentrate on the left-hand, Camden, side of the road. Former No.9 in 1885 was the mission hall of St Benet's and All Saints, the church some 350 yards south in Lupton Street (p 131). Pass Acland Burghley School, which we shall visit later; it covers the site of the former Ingestre Road. Stop when you reach the railway bridge, built in 1888, at a plaque giving details about the repairs undertaken in February 2004.

Carry on walking and pause at **CHURCHILL ROAD**. The Dartmouth Park estate was first developed at its western side, off Highgate Road, by the 4th Earl in the 1850s. The Legge Family held the land copyhold and could only give leases, normally of 99 years, until 1926 when the estate was enfranchised. Stanford's 1862 map shows much of the Earl of Dartmouth's estate laid out for development. In 1857 the Earl had granted several acres to Lord Alfred Spencer Churchill (his first cousin) and Charles

John Chetwynd, Lord Ingestre, (his wife's nephew), who had gone into partnership as developers. They bought the land on behalf of the Conservative Land Society, whose principal aim was to encourage people to become property owners – so that they might vote Tory or, as its first Annual Report in 1853 put it, "support that constitution to which England owes its prosperity".

The Society's name appears on the 1862 map across four roads leading off Dartmouth Park Hill: Ingestre Road (whose site we have passed); York Villas (now Churchill Road); Spencer Road (now Rise) and Chetwynd Road. The roads ended at the Highgate branch of the River Fleet, which runs in a valley (York Rise) that bisects Dartmouth Park. At that time, and until it was enclosed in a culvert in the 1890s, the river ran above ground from Highgate Ponds to its junction with the Hampstead branch in Kentish Town.

By the time the roads were built up, this vicinity had lost its appeal to the more affluent, as by 1868 the new Tottenham & Hampstead Railway had arrived and was spewing smoke and grime across the south side of Churchill Road. Small, narrow sites in Ingestre Road and Churchill Road were sold copyhold for £10. The early plots in Chetwynd Road, further away from the smoke, were larger.

Look along Churchill Road. This was first known as York Villas but

became Churchill Road in 1878, after its development by Lord Charles Spencer Churchill. There were never any houses on the south side next to the railway line, occupied today, behind a long buff-brick wall, by a car park, playground and gymnasium for Acland Burghley School. The north side was developed early and by 1870 was practically complete. This east end was bombed in WWII, as were the houses on the south side of adjacent Spencer Rise. In the 1950s, St Pancras Borough Council replaced the bombed houses with two blocks of 4-storey flats, with green pitched roofs and prominent chimneys.

Continue walking up Dartmouth Park Hill. A building on the left was occupied in the early 20th century by the St Pancras Ethical Society. Stop at the corner with **SPENCER RISE**, another road named after Lord Charles Spencer Churchill. Prior to 1937 it was known as Spencer Road. It was developed in the 1870s with small artisan houses, but at first included Henry McCarthy's school at former No.135 and the Misses Hicks' Ladies School at No.1 Laurel Villas. Charles Booth, walking the area in 1898 to update his poverty map, said some of the houses were purple, i.e. "mixed, some comfortable others poor".

Farther up **DARTMOUTH PARK HILL**, **No.21** marks the end of 20th-century development. The next five

houses are examples of the good-quality properties that the Earl of Dartmouth was aiming for when he began development. They are once again well maintained after deteriorating in the decades following WWII. Local archives reveal a community of young people squatting in derelict houses in this road during the 1970s, although even by then gentrification had begun.

Nos.27&29 were originally known as Nos.1&2 Chepstow Villas until the whole road was renumbered in 1885; No.27 has some delightful ironwork on its windowsills. No.31 was built in 1876 by Robert Smerdon, probably the most prolific builder on the estate, and called Somerset House. Charles Booth in 1898 noted that it was let out in 2- and 3-roomed tenements and "rather poor, its presence just at this point a little difficult to understand", since otherwise the road was then well-to-do.

Now turn left into **CHETWYND ROAD**. This was the most northerly of the Conservative Land Society's developments. The 4th Earl of Dartmouth married Frances Chetwynd, daughter of Lord Talbot, in 1821, when she was 20. She died in 1823, two months after the birth of their son. The first building on our left at **No.114** is called Tudor Mansions. It is double-fronted with a covered entrance, a castellated parapet and decorated with horizontal lines of terracotta Tudor roses and splendid brick quoins. A small plinth dates the building to 1895. Further down the hill at Nos.96-110 are some grand, 2-storey semi-detached villas, some with large Ionic porticoes. **Nos.108&110** are the earliest, built in 1866. The road descends sharply to the valley of the Fleet tributary, then rises again, continuing towards Highgate Road (see pp 144 & 145).

Return to **DARTMOUTH PARK HILL**. On the corner is the **Lord Palmerston** pub (**Fig 34**), which is marked on the 1869 OS map. The pub was named after the eponymous Viscount, twice Prime Minister, who died in office in 1865. A large forecourt allows customers to drink *al fresco*. Adjoining the pub is a row of six terraced houses, **Nos.35-45**, whose stone string courses and blue, red and yellow brickwork are echoed in the façade of the pub.

Further use of decorative brickwork can be seen in the interior of the next major building we reach: Grade-II⋆ Listed **St Mary Brookfield** church. (Brookfield House, off Highgate West Hill, was the home of Baroness Burdett-Coutts, who once owned much of the land northwest of here on Highgate's southern borders.) Built in 1869-75 by William Butterfield, St Mary's has polychromatic brickwork in red, blue and yellow, typical of his Gothic Revival style. After some unpleasantness, he refused to continue and the Decorated chancel was added in 1881 by W C Street. Sir Ninian Comper provided the rood in 1913 and also the south chapel. When built, the church provided a free place to worship for many of the poor of Highgate New Town who were previously excluded from St Anne Brookfield, on

34 The Lord Palmerston on Dartmouth Park Hill, c.1904.

Highgate West Hill. St Mary's suffered bomb damage in WWII. At the church turn briefly left. Prominent on the hills to the west is the Royal Free Hospital in Hampstead. At the forked junction immediately ahead, Laurier Road (p 142) approaches on the right. To the left, **DARTMOUTH PARK ROAD** descends into the valley of the Fleet, where we revisit it later (p 144). The road was begun in the 1850s as a turning out of Highgate Road called Dartmouth Road. It was extended up the hill to the church in the 1880s when for a few months in 1885 this section was called Dartmouth Road, renamed as part of Dartmouth Park Road later that year. These later houses were built by Robert Smerdon with William Wood, and display a certain unity with their gault brickwork and Gothic porches. Next to the church, in Dartmouth Park Road, is the large detached vicarage built by the architect Temple Moore in 1911-12. Further down on the right, the writer Julian Barnes (b.1946) lived at **No.58A** in the early 1980s.

Return to the church and continue left up **DARTMOUTH PARK HILL**, past **Crestfield**, a tall block of post-war flats with garages underneath. The views towards Hampstead and across London must be outstanding. The site was previously occupied by Dartmouth House, whose spacious formal gardens are shown on the 1869 OS map. Dartmouth

Park Hill winds attractively, recalling its rustic origins. Cattle on the hoof used to be driven down the hill every Monday morning to the cattle market.

Farther up we reach No.55, now **Mary Webster House**. Built in the 1860s as Grosvenor House, it was later home to William Heath Hamer, a physician knighted when he was living here in 1923. He was the schools medical officer for the County of London from 1911 to 1925. He died in 1936. In the early 1980s the house was extended and converted into sheltered accommodation of double bedsits, each with its own kitchen and bathroom, and opened in 1984 by the then Minister of Housing, Ian Gow. The House takes its name from Rev. Mary Webster, a Congregational Minister, who founded the National Council for the Single Woman and Her Dependants in 1965, having sacrificed her career to care for her ageing parents. After their deaths she began writing to newspapers, journals, MPs and peers, drawing attention to the isolation and financial hardship that women carers suffered. As a result of the Council's campaigns carers won their own benefit, Invalid Care Allowance, in 1976. The Council subsequently changed its name to the National Council for Carers and their Elderly Dependants, and the charity is now known more simply as Carers UK.

The reservoirs beyond, and opposite (in Islington), were constructed by the New River Company in 1856. They were built to conform with the Metropolitan Water Act of 1852, which required improvements to the sourcing, storage and distribution of London's water.

Continue uphill to **Nos.77&75**, built in 1872 and still retaining their original boundary walls. At No.75 lived Edmund Clerihew Bentley (1875–1956) (**Fig 35**), whose middle name will always be remembered in the English language as a literary form. His 4-line nonsensical clerihews were first published in a book *Biography for Beginners* in 1905, with two more in 1929 and 1939. He was also well known as a writer of detective fiction with a hero named Trent, the first of them, *Trent's Last Case*, published in 1936. Here is a clerihew about Bentley himself:

> Edmund Clerihew Bentley
> Created Philip Trent, He
> Also defined the norm
> For his eponymous art form.

Passing No.79 (with its corner turret), cross Dartmouth Park Avenue and continue up as far as **Bramshill Mansions**. This block was built as four houses in 1886 by the developer Edward Blunt; in 1904 he had them converted into flats by Fred Edser, who often worked for him. Blunt was particularly associated with the building of local pubs in a flamboyant style popular in the late 19th century, for instance the Boston Hotel (p 138).

Turning round, retrace your steps and

35 Edmund Clerihew Bentley, drawing by H G Riviere, 1915, when Bentley was living in Dartmouth Park (National Portrait Gallery, London)

turn right down **DARTMOUTH PARK AVENUE**. This road was first named in 1877 when houses first appeared along it, although it was projected from the early 1860s when it appears on several maps as "Dartmouth Road". At the top, on your right, is a block of flats built for the Metropolitan Police in 1953 and taken over for social housing in the 1980s. Its name, **The Towers**, was that of a 19th-century detached house formerly on the site. An early resident was the publisher Andrew Chatto (1840–1913), who in partnership with William Windus founded the firm Chatto & Windus, a publisher known for the quality of its book design. Its authors included R L Stevenson, Wilkie Collins, Anthony Trollope, Walter Besant and Ouida. Standing well back from the same side of the road, and approached by a short drive, is **Dartmouth Lodge**. A plain but distinguished 2-storey residence in stucco, it has a hipped roof and sits in what is left of its original grounds (shown on the 1869 OS map).

Houses opposite, to the north of **No.26**, were hit by a flying bomb in July 1944. In 1959 St Pancras Borough Council replaced them with two blocks of flats, **Nos.28-42** and **Nos.60-70**. Built on the slopes of the hill, they are approached by steps set in a landscape of grass and mature trees. Behind these are four further blocks of flats with entrances in Dartmouth Park Hill. They were built using the Reema system, of pre-cast reinforced concrete, which often suffers from inadequate overall insulation and condensation problems. One solution, tried here, is to span the structural cladding panels between beams and columns.

Pause near the corner of **BRAMSHILL GARDENS**, which enters from the right. The origin of the Bramshill name is unknown. The road was laid out in the 1890s, when **Nos.2-30** on the left and **Nos.1-7** (at the far right) were built by Fred Edser. Much of the east (right) side was developed only in the 1930s on the grounds of Dartmouth Lodge, behind. **Nos.15 & 17** were built in 1934 in the International Style with metal windows.

Continue down **DARTMOUTH PARK AVENUE**, noting the mature trees along its length and the interesting planting in the gardens. The houses look much as they did in the late 19th century. Walter de Gray Birch FSA (1842–1924) was living at No.6, on the left, in 1885. The son of the Egyptologist Dr Samuel Birch, Walter was a specialist in Anglo-Saxon, medieval Latin, Spanish and Portuguese languages at the British Museum. A member of many societies, he published numerous academic papers and was the editor of the *Journal of the British Archaeological Association* for 22 years. From 1967 to 1969 the house was used as the Westlea Children's Home and later as a centre for people with learning difficulties.

Reaching **LAURIER ROAD**, stroll briefly to the left, back towards St Mary's church. Here, on the right, **No.47** was built in 1884 by Robert Smerdon as a coach house and stables in the grounds of Legge House, **No.45**. This latter house and **No.43**, both double-fronted and with large, semicircular pedimented porches,

were two of the earliest villas to be built hereabouts. All were numbered as part of Dartmouth Park Avenue until 1924, when this eastern end of Laurier Road gained its present name. Sir Henry Charles Laurier (1841–1919) was Canada's first French-speaking Liberal Prime Minister, who was nevertheless accused by his opponents of being "a supporter of British jingoism". Return to the T-junction, where **No.48**, the big red-brick corner house opposite, was built in 1884. The 1862 Stanford map (p 6) shows a projected 'Linden Road', approaching from Dartmouth Park Hill, then passing through the site of No.48, before striking northwest along the line of its back garden, to join St Alban's Road. On the 1895 OS map there is no sign of the proposed road.

The main part of Laurier Road, down which we proceed, was so renamed only in 1937. It was previously known as Lewisham Road, after Viscount Lewisham, the son of the Earl of Dartmouth, who helped him develop the estate in the 1860s. Continue downhill to the next crossroads, at the junction with **YORK RISE**. The name of the Rise probably derives from York Road, an early name of Dartmouth Park Hill. Running through a dip in the landscape formed by the River Fleet, York Rise bisects the Dartmouth Park estate like a backbone, with intersecting streets as the ribs. The Highgate arm of the river, culverted here in the 1890s, now runs underground near the west side of the road.

Turn briefly left, to observe on the east side, a few yards south of the crossroads, the glass roof of the double-height kitchen of **No.24A**. This house was built in 1975-79 by architect Joanna van Heyningen as her own home, on a plot measuring 11 metres by 10 metres; it won the prestigious International Eternit Prize (small house section) in 1980, and a further prize from the RIBA in the following year. On the opposite side stands curious, tiny **No.39**, appearing almost sunken.

Now return to the crossroads and walk north up York Rise, passing on the right, behind a forecourt, the **church hall** of St Mary Brookfield. A typically austere building of 1954, it is gable-fronted and was erected to replace the Victorian church hall that, with its neighbourhood, was destroyed by bombing in WWII. The hall is a great focus of the social life of the area, a hive of activity with a full-time nursery school and evening dance and badminton sessions.

To the north, at **Nos.24-26**, stands a contemporary concrete-framed block of flats, also built on a bomb-damaged site. The last terrace of houses on the east side, at **Nos.36-50**, has pitched roofs and was built by T Boddy in 1891-93. Along the north side of No.50 is the rump of an ancient track from Highgate that once continued behind the gardens of houses on the north side of Woodsome Road, ending at the back of the Bull and Last public

house in Highgate Road (p 55).

Backtracking slightly, turn right into **WOODSOME ROAD** and walk west, noting the 3-storey houses and pleasing treescape in this quiet residential street. The road was named after Woodsome Hall, near Huddersfield, one of the Dartmouth family seats. **Nos.70-86**, the corner building on the north side, is another block of concrete-framed flats built for St Pancras Borough Council in the 1950s on a bombsite. **No.29**, in the post-war block of flats on the left, was home for many years to Kate Springett, after whom Springetts Wood, south of Spaniards Road on Hampstead Heath was named in 1994. Kate was official bird observer for Hampstead Heath for many years, during which time she taught local people about local bird life. Her legacy is the still flourishing Marylebone Birdwatching Society.

Turning left into **BOSCASTLE ROAD**, we see 4-storey houses (plus basement) dating from about 1870. **No.29**, on the right, is thought to be where 'Count' Girolamo Piero Nerli – an Italian painter (1860–1926) well known in the Antipodes, but remembered here only for his celebrated 1892 portrait of R L Stevenson in Samoa – spent some of his later years in poverty, lodging with his wife at the home of Mrs Louisa Silveyra, a diamond setter's widow to whom he sometimes gave paintings in lieu of rent.

Turn left and walk a short way along **LAURIER ROAD** (see also p 142). Its 4-storeyed terraced houses were begun in 1875 by the builder W Crockett and are of generous proportions. **Nos.1-5** retain their original railings. Before them stands **No.1A**, slightly later, detached and built in gault brick; and nearer to the corner the infill of **Laurier Court** flats and ivy-clad **No.1C**. Built on a bombsite in 1986 by the architects Joanna Van Heyningen and Birkin Haward, it has square windows, and "the only thing it has in common with the other houses in the street is its height". Outside it is a Listed red telephone kiosk. Further along on the left, a flat at **No.17A** was home to Jonathan Porritt from the 1970s to the 1990s, when he was the high-profile Director of the campaigning group Friends of the Earth.

Return to **BOSCASTLE ROAD** and walk down its southern, much earlier end, known until 1897 as Grove Road. The latter, so named in 1879, was in turn a combination of earlier Devonshire Villas and Cornwall Villas. According to Bebbington, the later Cornish village name was borrowed from the first house at the south end of the road, named 'Boscastle' by its first owner, a Cornishman. **Nos.2-6** make an interesting ensemble, the lower, double-fronted No.4 forming the centrepiece. Its Ionic portico is rather feebly echoed on modern **No.2A**. Across the road, notice the bulbous balconies of the houses which were put up in the late 1850s.

The balconies are repeated in the nearby houses in **DARTMOUTH PARK ROAD**, this western end of which was begun in the 1850s. Charles Booth, in 1898, called Dartmouth Park Road "the dividing line of middle-class respectability", with streets to the south full of working-class households. Pause and look along the road to the left. On the near corner, No.12 has bricked-up windows – presumably a design feature, Window Tax having been abolished before it was built. No.22, a few doors beyond, was home in 1983 to Giles Radice (b.1936), Labour MP and Chairman of the Treasury Select Committee. His wife, Lisanne Radice, was the chair of The 300 Group, formed to bring more women into Parliament.

Turn right. Detached **No.2** is an 1850s house of some pretension. In 1884 it was the home of Richard D'Oyly Carte (1844–1901), the producer of the Gilbert & Sullivan operettas. "Lamorna" on the opposite side is a 1930s escapee from suburbia, which looks as out of place here as does No.1 beyond, the buff-brick, aptly named, **First House**. Not only is it the first building in the road: it also stands on the site of the first house to be erected in the road in 1857, by W Hall. In 1864 this was home to the false-teeth maker Claudius Ash (p 86). The present building is by J de Syllas of Avanti Architects, and

dates from 1990-93. It has a double-height roof-lit dining area and a curved, corrugated iron roof.

Just before the main Highgate Road, turn left down a stretch of footway, part of the College Lane–Grove Terrace continuum, past the large Grove End House at No.150 (p 57). Cross over to the side of the Highgate Road Chapel (p 58), turning left into **CHETWYND ROAD**, re-entering the Dartmouth Park estate. The road's western end was built up with terraced housing after 1874 when the lands of Grove End House were sold. It was known as Carrol Road until 1886 when the numbering was complete and it became part of Chetwynd Road. On the north side is the interwar terrace **Chetwynd Villas** and beyond it a long 3-storey terrace built in 1875 by James Randall running along the winding road which dips down to the valley of the Fleet at the junction with York Rise, ahead. Booth recorded in 1898 that the houses in the road had been badly built throughout, and that Inspector Tomkin, who had lived here in one of the smaller houses, had complained about its sanitation.

Turn right into **TWISDEN ROAD**, begun in 1874. Although Bebbington declares the origin of the street name to be "unknown", it is perhaps no coincidence that in 1873 Lt-Col. Henry Legge, a relation of Lord Dartmouth, married Cordelia Twysden Molesworth.

Another member of the Twysden family – Dorothy (born 1612) – had married Ralf Chetwynd in the 17th century. The grim-looking terrace of **Nos.2-14**, on our right, was built in 1875 by James Randall. No.12 was home in the 1970s and '80s to the television actress Maggie Ford. The terrace destroys the harmony of the main east-west stretch, into which we turn left. The houses are all of a piece – gable-fronted, with barge boards and Venetian windows. The septuagenarian A J P Taylor (1906–1990) bought No.32 (right) in 1977, moving in with his third wife and fellow historian Eva Haraszti, the daughter of a Hungarian ironmonger whom he had quietly married in Hungary the previous year. Past Camden Council flats at Nos.25-35, infill built after wartime damage, **Nos.37-47** are the earliest houses in the street. They face **Nos.64-74**, which have original railings and bear elaborate carvings. In the arch above the doorway of No.74 is the decorative inscription "PJ 1878", probably for P J Jegers, who built Nos.44-74 in 1876-77. The road turns again, to the left, to avoid a pond formed by the River Fleet that stood in the way when the road was first built up.

Regaining **CHETWYND ROAD**, notice on the side wall of **No.54** to your left painted on to the brickwork an old advertisement for the local builder, John Hirst, who lived in this house which he built in 1877. Hirst built much of this end of Chetwynd Road (then Carrol Road) including **Nos.28-38** in 1876 and **Nos.41-59** on the opposite side in 1877. Just along from Hirst's former house, at No.46, lived Rev. James Stephens (1878–1932), the first minister of Highgate Road Chapel. He came from Berwick-upon-Tweed and named his house "Tweedsyde". We turn right past a row of shops, which includes **No.58**, now the Antonym Bookshop (specialising in poetry).

We are in the small neighbourhood shopping centre of Dartmouth Park, focused on **YORK RISE**, into which we turn left. Past **No.33** on the left is a small cobbled courtyard, which led in 1885 to Dartmouth Park Nurseries. It now leads to **Bellgate Mews**, a very private late 1970s development, heavily clad in creeper. Turn to look up at the side wall of No.33, on which an advertisement is painted in bold black lettering for a firm of drapers, K & M Larn. In the early 20th century, Kate and Louise Larn kept what was then numbered No.11 and proudly announced their large and varied stock of haberdashery goods, including calicoes and "maids' dresses". The publican of the **Dartmouth Arms** beyond the yard has also decided to advertise what he has to offer in similarly bold lettering on the façade of his hostelry, which dates from the 1860s.

DARTMOUTH PARK ROAD
intersects at the next crossroads. To our right, the Smerdon and Wood houses on either side of the road rise grandly up to the church at the top of the hill where we first observed this road. Just before WWI No.51, the corner house (south side), was a preparatory school and kindergarten kept by Miss E R Symonds. Next door, No.53 was occupied by the builder Robert Smerdon. This remains a select area, no doubt helped by the new road layout which prevents its use as a through route to Highgate Road.

Turn back along **YORK RISE** past The Continental Provision Store at **Nos.16-18**, which is known locally as George's. It has been owned by a Greek family since 1956. Georgiou arrived in London from Cyprus in 1947 and by 1971 he had also taken over the drapers opposite, which was managed by his daughter. The store's small front window full of bread is deceptive, as the shop inside is a lengthy cavern packed full of a wide choice of comestibles.

Return to the corner with **CHETWYND ROAD** and stop at the traffic lights. Note the butcher's shop facing York Rise but numbered **No.69**. This has been a butcher's for over 100 years, and what appears to be the front façade of the corner house is in reality the end wall of the shop. From the early 1900s Richard Selway was established here, until his son Leslie took over in 1938 and stayed until at least 1952. It is said that Richard kept live animals in the grounds of the old garden nursery opposite, where his slaughterhouse may also have been. Note the faded lettering above the estate agent's on the corner opposite, where "Chetwynd" can be made out. Henry Dixon, known for his photographs of London life, died at **No.117** (left) in 1893. He was described on his death certificate as "Photographic Master Retired". 1970s residents of Chetwynd Road included Charles Bowell, guitarist and professor at the Royal College of Music, and the mezzo-soprano Glenda Simpson. During the next decade the writer Julian Gloag lived here.

In the 1970s Chetwynd Road became a rat-run for traffic avoiding the main roads. A group of local residents organised themselves to fight this intrusion and were successful in banning lorries and large cars from using the street by the erection of a barrier at the western end.

Cross the road and continue walking south. Stop at the next turning on the left, **SPENCER RISE**, observing the black-and-white "St Pancras Parish Middlesex" bollard on the corner. The road rises steeply to the east. Note the variety of building styles.

Proceed along the east side of **YORK RISE** to reach two 1-storey gable-fronted buildings, both recently converted from light industrial use. **No.4** has neat security gates that allow the cat to eat food left for it outside the front door but protected by a grille. **Nos.2&2A** are semi-detached and have façades with decorative brickwork,

which dates from 1985 when they were converted to residential use by the Tenants Association of North Camden (TANC) Housing Co-operative, as the plaque attests. Since 2000 TANC has been known as the North Camden Housing Co-operative and continues to provide low-cost rented housing in the Kentish Town area.

Opposite is the **York Rise Estate**. These 119 flats in 5 blocks were built in 1937-38 on land leased and financed by the LMS Railway to the St Pancras Housing Association (as it was then called). The estate was built to rehouse families who had lost their homes because of a proposed rebuilding of Euston Station. The blocks, which stand alongside a railway on land which had in the early years of the century been a miniature rifle range, were given names connected with 19th-century engineering and science: **Faraday House**, **Newcomen House**, **Brunel House**, **Trevithick House** and **Stephenson House**. The architect Ian Hamilton provided good-sized balconies and gardens. Washing-line posts topped with ceramic figures by Gilbert Bayes, similar to those on other SPHA estates, were installed (**Fig 36**). What was left of the delightful dragon, rose and thistle ceramic motifs has now been removed, but

36 Washing-line posts on the York Rise Estate, with Gilbert Bayes' ceramic finials

there are plans to install replicas.

After WWII the freehold was purchased from British Rail, together with a further plot of land. A 7-storey block with 16 flats was built, designed by the architect Alan Chalmers and opened in 1965 as **Winifrede Paul House**, ahead. Winifrede Paul was a Labour Councillor for 20 years and one of the founders of the St Pancras School for Mothers. She died in 1972. In 1967 a social club, for and managed by the tenants, was opened – in the Jim Faulkner Community Room on the ground floor – and is still in use.

Winifrede Paul House stands on the south side of **CHURCHILL ROAD**, whose eastern end we saw earlier. Opposite, at **Nos.1-11**, some 19th-century 2- and 3-storey properties still remain. They were built by various small builders c.1875 and display a hodgepodge of detail.

A few yards beyond, a footbridge to the right leads up and across two parallel railways, the original higher-level Tottenham & Hampstead line of 1868, and the Midland's later low-level addition (see p 15). St Pancras Vestry minutes show that the bridge was erected by the railway company shortly before 1869. It lies on the line of an old footpath, probably that shown running beside the River Fleet on the parish map of 1800. The river passes over the railway alongside the west (right-hand) side of the footbridge, encased in a storm drain.

Cross over the footbridge, observing the pipe to the west, and to the east the school gymnasium that straddles the railway line. Stop on reaching **INGESTRE ROAD**. Named after Lord Ingestre, one of its developers whom we encountered earlier, Ingestre Road is a street that has moved. The original, L-shaped road approached from your left, running west from Dartmouth Park Hill, roughly parallel to the railway, before turning south to join Burghley Road (ahead). The site of the houses built on the south side of its east-west stretch is now covered by Acland Burghley School. In the 1860s the Imperial Sanitary Steam Laundry was established on the corner to your left, sited here (some suggest) for easy access to the River Fleet. Although the river still flowed above ground at the time, it was by then no doubt polluted. On our right is the Ingestre Road Estate (p 40), built on the largely open land of the 'Kentish Town Alps' in the 1970s. Most of early Ingestre Road having been lost to the school, its name was transferred to the service road running west through the new housing estate.

Continue ahead and pause again at the next corner, by **Acland Burghley School**. Burghley Road School was built by the London School Board south of the laundry, on the corner of Burghley Road. It opened in 1884 and within a few years became a Higher Grade School, one of only four Special Schools of Science in

London. In 1905 the Burghley Senior Boys moved to new buildings on the site of the present Eleanor Palmer Primary School in Fortess Road (p 134), later becoming the Acland Central School for Boys. The name Acland commemorates Sir Arthur Acland, Liberal MP and Education Minister in Gladstone's last government. Another name associated with the school was Lyulph Stanley (1839–1925), who gave his name to other St Pancras Central Schools. He was the last vice-chairman of the London School Board, with special responsibility for the Burghley Road schools. The school logbook records that he frequently rushed through the school on inspections.

In 1906 a county grammar school known as Ingestre Road School was opened in one of the buildings here. This later moved and became Parliament Hill County Grammar School. Former pupils who attended the school in WWI recalled seeing Zeppelins flying over the houses nearby. In 1931 the girls' school, Burghley Central, moved to Chester Road, Highgate New Town. The Ingestre Road school was bombed in WWII and was closed for a time. In 1959 Acland Central School and Burghley Central School joined together and used both sites. The present school here was built here 1964-8 by the architects Howell, Killick, Partridge and Amis. Pevsner describes it as "an arresting urban composition on a tight site", although, to the outsider, the large concrete structures look forbidding. The school became a comprehensive in 1977 and the juniors were moved to other local schools. In 1981 the sixth form joined with pupils from three other schools to form La Swap Sixth Form Consortium. In 2000 it was awarded specialist college status in the arts.

Turn the corner into **BURGHLEY ROAD** and carry on walking past Oakford Road on the right (p 43) until you reach the school entrance. This south end of the school is built on land that was owned by St John's College, Cambridge.

Another few steps and we are at the junction with Dartmouth Park Hill and the end of the walk. Turn right for Tufnell Park station and adjacent bus stops.

Sources

Books and pamphlets

Aston, Mark. *The cinemas of Camden.* LB of Camden, 1997

Barnes, Eric George. *The rise of the Midland Railway, 1844-1874.* Allen & Unwin, 1966

Barton, Nicholas. *The lost rivers of London.* Historical Publications, 1982

Barty-King, Hugh. *Maples, fine furnishers: a household name for 150 years.* Quiller Press, 1992

Bebbington, Gillian. *London street names.* Batsford, 1972

Bentley, Edmund Clerihew. *Biography for beginners.* T W Laurie, 1903

Bentley, Edmund Clerihew. *Those days: an autobiography.* Stratus, 2001

Black, Gerry. *JFS, the history of the Jews' Free School, London since 1732.* Tymsder Publishing, 1998

Blacker, Ken. *London's buses,* Vol.1. H J Publications, 1977

Burchell, Doris. *Miss Buss' second school.* F M Buss Foundation, 1971

Camden History Society. *Streets of Camden Town* 2003; *Streets of St Pancras* 2002

Cherry, Bridget & Pevsner, Nikolaus. *London 4: North (The buildings of England).* Penguin, 1999

Claudius Ash, Sons & Co. *A centenary memoir, 1820-1921.* The company, 1921

Clinch, George. *Marylebone and St Pancras.* Truslove & Shirley, 1890

Colloms, Marianne & Weindling, Dick. *Camden Town and Kentish Town.* Tempus, 2003 (Images of London)

Denyer, C H (ed.). *St Pancras through the centuries.* Le Play House Press, 1935

Dorling, William. *Henry Vincent: a biographical sketch.* Williams & Norgate, 1881

Elliott, W. *Some Account of Kentish Town.* J Bennett, 1821

Evinson, Denis. *Catholic Churches of London.* Sheffield Academic Press, 1998

Fairfield, S. *The streets of London: a dictionary...* Macmillan, 1983

Foster, D. *Alehouses [etc.]* (at Westminster Archives)

Goslin, Geoff. *The London extension to the Midland Railway, St Pancras to Bedford.* Irwell Press, 1994

Graves, Algernon. *The Royal Academy of Arts: a complete dictionary of contributors ... 1769-1904.* Henry Graves, 1905-6

H Brooks, Peel & Co. *Company catalogue 1885*

Herbert, Cicely. *87 Holmes Road ... London Board School to Camden Institute*. The Institute, 1989

Holmes, Malcolm J. *Housing is not enough...St Pancras Housing Assoc.*, 1999

Jones, Dave. *Hampstead and Highgate tramways*. Middleton Press, 1995

Kibby, Bill. [Extracts relating to Camden from database of piano makers]. Website: www.uk-piano.org/piano-gen

King, James Frederick. *Kentish Town Panorama* [c.1848-55]. (Facsimile ed.) London Topographical Society, 1986

Lee, Charles E. *St Pancras Church and Parish*. St Pancras PCC, 1955

Le Faye, Deirdre. *Medieval Camden*. Camden History Society, 1974

Lewis, C L Mrs. *Dr Southwood Smith: a retrospect*. William Blackwood & Sons, 1898

London County Council. *Survey of London*, Vol.19. LCC, 1938

Lovett, Dennis. *London's own railway: the North London Line 1846-2001*. Irwell Press, 2001

Maple & Co. *The house of Maple*. The company, 1964

Marshall, Lesley (comp.). *Kentish Town: its past in pictures*. Camden Leisure Services, 1993

Miller, Frederick. *St Pancras past and present*. Abel Heywood, 1874

Newman, Teresa & Watkinson, Ray. *Ford Madox Brown and the Pre-Raphaelite circle*. Chatto & Windus, 1993

Oakley, E R. *The London County Council Tramways, Vol 2: North London*. London Tramways History Group, 1991

Patmore, Derek. *The life and times of Coventry Patmore*. Constable, 1949

Pevsner, Nikolaus. *London, except the Cities of London and Westminster*. (The buildings of England) Penguin, 1952

Richardson, John. *A history of Camden*. Historical Publications, 1999

Richardson, John. *Highgate*. Historical Publications, 1983

Richardson, John. *Highgate past*. Historical Publications, 1989

Richardson, John. *Kentish Town past*. Historical Publications, 1997

Robeson, Paul Jr. *The undiscovered Paul Robeson*. Wiley, 2001

St Pancras Met. Borough. *The end of one story: a souvenir of the Borough...*1965

St Pancras Chamber of Commerce. *Introducing industrial St Pancras and its many industries*. 1938?

Scholey, K. A. *The railways of Camden*. Camden History Society, 2002

Sinclair, Frederick comp.. *St Pancras through the ages: catalogue of an exhibition*. MB of St Pancras, 1928

Surtees, Virginia (ed.). *The diary of Ford Madox Brown*. Paul Mellon Centre for Studies in British Art, 1981

Palmer, Samuel. *St Pancras...* The author, 1870

Thompson, John. *Orwell's London*. Fourth Estate, 1984

Tindall, Gillian. *The fields beneath: the history of one London village*. Temple Smith, 1977

Wainwright, David. *The piano makers*. Hutchinson, 1975

Walford, Edward. *Old and new London, 1872* reprinted as *London recollected*. Alderman Press, 1987

Weinreb, B & Hibbert, C (eds.). *The London encyclopaedia*. Macmillan, 1992

Whitley, W T. *The Baptists of London, 1612–1928*. Kingsgate Press, 1928

Maps

Thompson 1801/1804 & Terrier Book; St John' College estate 1829; Davies 1834; Greenwood 1834; Britton 1834; parish 1849 & 1861; Stanford 1862; Cassell 1862; Ordnance Survey 1869 & later; Bacon 1888; Booth's poverty maps 1889–98; Goad insurance plans; LCC bomb damage maps.

Other sources

Chambers biographical dictionary
Dictionary of national biography
Who was who

Newspapers

Camden Citizen
Camden Journal
Camden New Journal, including *2004 Directions, a guide to services in and around Camden*
Hampstead & Highgate Express
St Pancras Journal, 1947-1965

Periodicals

Camden History Review. Vols 13 1985, pp 11-15 [Brecknock Arms]; 19 1995, p 31 [The Retreat]; 20 1996, pp 29-31 [butchers]; 22 1998, pp 2-6 [Jews' Free School]; 23 1999, pp 19-21 [synagogue], pp 26-30 [Bower Cottage]; 24 2000, pp 12-17 [Governesses' Asylum], pp 45-49 [Congregational Church]; 27 2003, pp 2-6 [Septimus Buss]; 28 2004, pp 2-6 [Eleanor Palmer]

Camden History Society. *Newsletters*. (The H.G. Panorama *A sketch of the line of road from Castle Tavern to Old Chapel Row, Kentish Town*, noted in Route 1, is reproduced in *Newsletter* No.200)

Greater London Industrial Archaeology Society, *Newsletters* 105 & 111

Kentish Town Parish Church. *Parish magazines* c.1914

Willesden Local History Society Journal, No.20: article by Margaret Pratt, *Mother Emily Ayckburn*

Other records

Camden & Kentish Town directories

Census returns, 1841–1901

Camden Estate – Terrier Book CLSAC

Hawley–Buck Estate: papers and deeds CLSAC and LMA

Adam Hilger – company records CLSAC

LCC/GLC street lists

Post Office London directories (Kelly's)

Registers of Electors St Pancras and Camden

St Pancras Met. Borough: rate books

St Pancras Vestry: Minutes

St Pancras Vestry: Poor Rate books

Conservation Statements

Camden Council: Inkerman Road; Kelly Street; Rochester; Dartmouth Park; Bartholomew Estate.

Websites

Numerous Internet resources, including:
cindex.camden.gov.uk
www.camden.gov.uk/planning
www.camdenbus.co.uk
www.oldbaileyonline.org
Charles Booth Online Archive
Times Digital Archive
Oxford DNB

Archive centres

Camden Local Studies & Archives Centre including Ambrose Heal Collection

London Metropolitan Archives

Guildhall Library

St Dunstan's Archive

Westminster Archives

Index

Streets included in the survey are indicated in boldface, as are the main entries for these and other selected subjects; * = illustration.

A

A&A Self Storage 35
Abbey National 95
Abbey Tavern, The 27
ABC cinema 32
Academy Projects 41
Acland Burghley School 41, 43, 138, 139, **147-148**
Acland Central School 134, 148
Acquisitions House 98
Acton, Harriet & Rose 73
Acton Housing Assoc. 98
Admiral Mann, The 114-115
Aged Governesses' Asylum 91-92*
Air Raid Precautions 123, 129
air raids, see World War Two
Air Training Corps 112
Albanian refugees 127
Albany, The 27
Albert Villa 78
Aldenham Boys' Club 38
Aldrich Road 104
Aldrich Yard 104
Aldwinckle, Thomas W 91
Ali, Tariq 37
Allam (gardener) 27
Allen, Rev. Alfred 134

Allen, Richard Jones 97
Allies & Morrison 77, 78
Allison & Allison 118
allotments 41, 116
Alma Cottage 86
Alma Press 88
Alma Road 86
Alma Street 86, **88**
Alpha Court 85
Alpha House 99
Alpha Jewels Ltd 99
Alpha Mosaic Co. 107
Alpha Place 85
Amalgamated Dental Co. 86
Amis, Kingsley 118
Anchor Care Alternatives 36
Ancient Order of Foresters 32
Andrews, Harry 99
Anglers, The (Jolly) 23, 85
Anglers Lane 13, 22-23, **85-86**, 87*, **89-90**, 91, 95
Anglo-Italian Motor Service 111
Ann Stephenson House 61
Ansell, Thomas 93
Antelope Cycle Works 78
Antonym Bookshop 145
Apollo Studios 118
Apollo Works 118
Appleford 103
Apps, John 36
Arborfield 103
Arcadian Cottages 73
Archworks 119
Argyle Villa 111
Arlington, Countess of 14
Armstrong family 50, 51
Arnold, George 24
Artesian Well Water Works 52

Arthur Street 76
Ascham Street 130
Ascham Works 130
Ash, Claudius (Sons & Co.) 36, **86**, 90, 144; works 87*
Ash Court 117, 130
Asphaltic Ltd 99
Assembly House, The 31, 45, 55, 117, 123, **124**, 125*, 126
Assembly Row 125
Associated Omnibus Co. 89
Athlone Street 95
Atkinson, Rowan 69
Atunbi House 26, 68
Auld, Patrick Campbell 75
Auntie Annie's 29
Austin, Edward 53
Autograph Sound 96
AV Laundry 119
Avanti Architects 144
Avenues Publishing 37
Avington 103
Ayckburn, Emily 132
Azania Mews **88**, 97

B

Back Lane 65
Bailie, Robert 48
Baker, Henry 42
Baker's Nursery 85
Bakewell, Joan 42
ballooning 30, 113
Bamberg, Rudolf, Ernest & Son 34
Bananarama 108
Bandung Studios 37
Baptists 58, 69, 70, 72, 126, 136, 145
Barclays Bank 30, 132
Barker, Tom 106, 108
Barko, Julius 49
Barling (flats) 75

Barling Bros 70
Barn Close 119
Barn Field 67
Barnes, Edmund 104
Barnes, Julian 140
barrage balloons 120
Bartholomew estate; St Bartholomew's Hospital 14, 27, **109-111**, 122
Bartholomew Place 27-28
Bartholomew Road 11*, **103-104**, **106**, **109-111**, 117
Bartholomew Road North 109
Bartholomew Villas 111
Bartholomew Works 111
Barwell, Eve 77
Bassett family 74, 75, 77
Bastian Meter Co. 111
Bateman, Gregory 54, 124
Bateman's Folly 54
Bates, Henry Walter 110
baths & washhouses 89, **91**
Bathurst House 48
Bayes, Gilbert 147; finials 146*
Baylis, Frances 67
Beadle, M 116
Beard, Kate 57
Beard, John Stanley 25, 32
Beardmore Motors 98
Beardsmore Gallery 91
Beaufort House 112
Becket & Sons 112
Beckford Society 76
Beddall, Herbert 21
Beedon 103
Bell Piano & Organ Co. 103
Bellgate Mews 145

Bellina House 43
Bellina Mews 44
Bellina Villas 43-44
Bennett, W R 32
Bentley, Edmund Clerihew 141*
Bernard Shaw Court 60
Bertrand, Henry 98
Bessemer, Henry 54
Betjeman, Sir John **12**, 21, 25, **31**, 32, 34, 47, **50**, 53
Better Sound 88, 89
Betts, Barbara 116
Bickerdike, Rev. John 46
Bi-Gum Adhesives 90
Binder, J & Co. 26
Birch, Eugenius 62
Birch, John Manley 88
Birch, Walter de Gray 142
Birch Bros Ltd **88**, 97, 98
Bird, Thomas 25
Bird & Davies 98
Bish, Vadnie 107
Bishop, George 107
Bishop & Hamilton 21
Black Bull, The 124
Black Horse, The 65, 66
blacking factory 84
Blanchard (balloonist) 30
Blandford Place 137
Blenheim Terrace 39*
Bluck, John 21
Blunt, Edward 141
Blur 69
Blustons 24
Board Schools, see School Board for London
Boddy, T 143
Boekbinder, J M 84
bollards 49, 63, 85, 89, 119, 145
Boma Garden Centre 102

bomb damage, see World War Two
Bon Marché 21
Bonny Street 59
Booth, Charles 12, 35, 36, 43, 63, 68, 73, 74, 75, 77, 78, 81, 84, 86, 88, 89, 102, 118, 119, 130, 139, 144
Boris the Cat 86
Borthwick, Captain 125
Boscastle (house) 143
Boscastle Road 143
Boston Hotel 138, 141
Boucher, William 53
Bowell, Charles 145
Bower Cottage (Holmes Rd) 99 (Leighton Rd) 67, **127**
Bowman, Thomas 122
Boys' Public Day School 134
Bradfield Court 72
Bramshill Gardens 142
Bramshill Mansions 141
Brandon, David 74, 91
Brandon Centre 91
Branson, Richard 30
Brearley, Mike 63
Brearley, Richard 112
Brecknock Arms, The 113*-114
Brecknock Crescent 60
Brecknock Place 60
Brecknock Road 113*, **114**, **115-116**, **132**, 138
Brecknock Street 59
Brecon Mews 114
breweries 96, 98
Brick Field 96
brickfields 74, 75, 77, 96
Bridge House 36

Bridge Housing Assoc. 42
Bridge Project 103
Bridgman, H H 61
Bright, John 63
Brilliant, A 59
Brinsmead, John &
    Son 93, 95; works 94*
British Automobile
    Traction Co. 61
British Pianoforte
    Manufacturing Co. 84
British Rail 147
    Staff Association 41
British Reeds 93
British Restaurant 127
British Road Services 96
British School 28
British Telecom 78
British Union of
    Fascists 32
British Vacuum Flask Co. 49
Broadway Terrace 59, 70
Brook Lapping Productions
    86
Brookes, Frances 22
Brooks, Henry, Peel & Co.
    103
Browell family 55, 56
Brown, Ford Madox
    56, **135***
Brown's Dairy 100
Brown's Lane 100
Browning, Robert 52
Brownlees Trust 116
Bruges, William 8,
    23, 29*, **30**, 54
Brunel House 147
Buck family 14, 71, 73,
    74, 75, 82
Bull, Simeon Thomas 47
Bull & Gate, The 9,
    31-32, 99
Bull & Last, The **55*****-56**,
    57*, 143

Bullet, The 25, 79
Burch, Edward 65
Burdett, Lavinia 132
Burdett-Coutts, Baroness
    54, 140
Burford, Robert 64
Burghley Central
    School 148
Burghley Road 35,
    42-43, 44, 147, **148**
Burghley Road School 147
Burghley Terrace 35
Burghley Yard 43
Burlison, John 38, 106
Burlison & Grylls 106, 131
Burne-Jones, Edward
    105, 131
Burton, Richard
    (actor) 124
    (architect) 128
Burton House 137
bus depots 88-89, 128
    see also omnibus…
Busby Mews 120
Busby Place 106, **119**
Buss, Rev. Alfred J 82, 111
Buss, Arthur Edward 74
Buss, Frances Mary
    82, 92, 97, **122-123**
Buss, Robert William 82
Buss, Rev. Septimus 74,
    82, 106
butchers 10, 23,
    29, 99, 121, 145
Butler-Shloss, Dame
    Elizabeth 107
Butterfield, William 140
Buttle's 75
Byron, Lord 28

C
Cabin Café 96
Cain Place 27, 65, cover*
Caldercourt, William 99

Calver 40, 41
Camden, Lords,
    see Camden estate
Camden & St Pancras
    Chronicle 26
Camden Black Sisters 138
Camden Broadway 59
Camden Car Pound 99
Camden Cardboard Box
    Co. 84
Camden Committee for
    Community Relations
    103
Camden Community
    Law Centre 90
    Nurseries 116
Camden Cottages 60,
    63, 68
Camden Council 35,
    37, 42, 43, 49, 50, 60,
    61, 73, 77, 85, 88, 98,
    99, 101, 104, 105, 110,
    115, 116, 122, 127,
    131; Depot 97
    District Housing
    Office 107
    Social Services 61
Camden Crescent
    121, **122**
Camden estate; Pratt
    Family 14, 59-71, 109,
    113-114, 120-123
Camden Falcon, The 69
Camden Gardens 26
Camden High School
    69, 70
Camden House School 69
Camden Institute 97
Camden ITEC 129
Camden Jobtrain 97
Camden Lecture Hall 69
Camden Literary &
    Scientific Institution 80
Camden New Town 60

Camden Primary Care
    Trust 61, 103
Camden Recycling
    Centre 99
Camden Road 9,
    60-61, **113-114**, 119,
    120-122
Camden Road Depot 72
Camden Road Junction 73
Camden Road Mews 122
Camden Road Station
    (Midland) 15, **121**, 123
    (North London) 15, **59**
Camden Road Villas 121
Camden Row 27
Camden School for Girls
    61, **92**, **93**, 110, **123**
Camden Society 35, 71
Camden Street
    54, **69-70**, 92
Camden Studios 27, 66
Camden Terrace 69, 70
Camden Town Station
    (North London) 59
Candida Court 82
Cansick, Nathan 37, 41
Cantelowes (Manor)
    8, 9, **14**, 54, 59, 100,
    113, 124, 138
    Manor House 136, **137**
Cantelowes Gardens
    106, 120, **122**
Cantelowes Secondary
    School 67
Cantelupe (flats) 104
Cantelupe family
    8, 23, 104
Capper, Benjamin 21
Carker's Lane
    36-37, 49
Carleton Gardens
    115, 116
Carlton Road 96
Carmo Garage 102

Carnegie, Andrew 90
Carr & Son 84
Carrol & Sanderson
    Close Estate 37
Carrol Close 46, **38**
Carrol Place 38
Carrol Road 144-145
Carroll, James J 103
Carters Close 119
Castle, The 12, **25**,
    48, 77, 79, **80*****-81**
Castle, Barbara 116
Castle, Park, Hook
    & Partners 107
Castle Court 79
Castle Mews 75
Castle Place 25, **80-81**
Castle Road 25,
    77, **79-80**
Castle Terrace 79
Castle's Pie & Mash
    Shop 71
Castlehaven Road
    73, 75, **77-78**, 79
Casual Wards 98-99, 127
Cathcart Street
    88-89, 97
Catholic Apostolic
    Church 48, 90
Catholics, see
    Roman Catholics
cattle dock 99, 117
Caversham Centre
Caversham Family
    Centre 107
    Health Centre 110
Caversham Group
    Practice 103, 110, 128
Caversham Road
    106-107, 112
Centre for Men's
    Development 44
Chalmers, Alan 147
Chamberlaines Cycles 26

Champneys, Basil 105
Charity Organisation
    Society 107
Charles, Prince of
    Wales 122
Charlton Court 115, 117
Charlton House 54
Charlton Kings Road
    117-118
Charrington's 31, 72
Chassay, M 116
Chatto, Andrew 142
Cheeke, John 56
Cheeke's Row 56
Chepstow Villas 139
Cherry Tree Court 61
Cheshire, Frederick 69
Chester Court 50
Chestnut Row 27, **66***
Chetwynd family 41, 138
Chetwynd Road 58,
    139-140, **144**, **145**
Chetwynd Villas 144
Chew, William 115
Child, James 95
Cholmondely, Sir Hugh 58
Christ Apostolic Church
    33*, 34
Christ Church estate 14,
    29, 30, **100-108**, **112**,
    117, 119
Christchurch House 112
Christian, Ewan 27
Christian Worker 76
Church Avenue 25, 78
Church House 131
Church Lands 8, 49, 53
Church of Christ 76
Church Street 25, **78**
Churches Conservation
    Trust 106
Churchill family 138, 139
Churchill Road 138-
    139, **147**

Churchland Way 53
cinemas 21, 24-25, 27, 32, 77, 112
Circle 33 Housing Association 61, 136
City Coach Co. 128
City Motor Omnibus Co. 128
Clanfield 48
Claremont House 91
Claremont Terrace 91
Clarence, The 26, 73
Clarence Buildings 68
Clarence Grove 81
Clarence Hall 82
Clarence Road 68, 73, 74, 82
Clarence Way 73-74, 82
Estate **72-75**, 81-82
Clarendon Cottages 63
Clarendon Yard 63
Clark, John T 79
Clarke, James 22
Clarke's Farm 25
Claudius Ash, see Ash…
Clayton & Bell 59, 106, 131
Clean Break Theatre Co. 111
Cleave family 27, 109
Clevedon House 51
Clevedon Mansions 50-51
Clifton Lodge 51
Clothworkers Hall 122, 123
Club Français, Le 82
Clulow, William 22
coal depots 46, 72, 96-97
Cohen, Francis 58
Cohen, Maurice 31
Cohen, Meyer 58
Coit, Stanton 116
Collard, Samuel 66, 68

College Chapel 70
College for Civil Engineers 47
College Gardens 67
College Hall 71
College Lane 36, 40, 56, **41-42**
College Mews 36
College Street Board School 64*, 67
Mission Hall 71
College Terrace 68
College Works
College Yard 36
Collins, Sir William 76
Collumpton Place 66, 67
Colquhoun & Miller 112
Combes, Frank 90
Commercial Place 138
Common, The 53
Community Meals Service 68
Comper, Sir Ninian 140
Compleat Angler, The 23
Compton House 105
Conference of Drama Schools 77
Congregational Church Avenue 78
Congregationalists 25, 28, 72, **78-79**, 82
Conservative Land Society 139
Conservatives 128
Continental Provision Store 145
Cook, Don 128
Cook, John Henry 93
Cooke, Richard 56
Cooke, William & Co. 41
Cooper (headmaster) 47
Copestake, Sampson 38
Cork, Richard William 129
Corker's Lane 36

Corner House Hotel 120
Cornwall Terrace 71
Cornwall Villas 143
Cosprop 63, 119
Cossar, Mary 106
Cosser, Edwin 80
Cottage, The 50
Countess Road 131
Cousins, Rev. G 70
Coutts, Thomas 53
Cow & Hare, The 56
Cox, John 115, 126
Cox-Sinclair, Edward
Coxeter, James 48, 57, 58
Crane, Charles 62, 67, 101, 127
Craven House School 32
Craven Place 32, 35
Crest, The 115
Crestfield 140
Creswick, Nicholas 88
cricket 63, 71, 91, 99
Crimea, The 88
Crocker, Robert 22
Crocker's Place 22
Crocker's Yard 22
Crockett, W 143
Croft. Michael 109
Croft Lodge 55
Croftdown Road 53, 55
Crosby, A 76
Crossroads Women's Centre 112
Crowe, Edward James 30
Crown Place 22, 84, 85
Cullinan, Ted 111, 116
Cumberland, John 60
Cumberland Grove 120
Cumberland Mews 120
Cumberland Villa 57
Cundall, Joseph 44

D
D'Almaine, William F 72
Dale, Rev. Thomas 74
Dallin, Sarah 108
Daniels, Charles & Alfred 24
Daniels sisters 68
Darcars Ltd 40
Darlington, John 62, 63
Dartmouth Arms, The 145
Dartmouth estate; Legge family 14, 56, 108, 109, 122, 138, 139, 142, 144
Dartmouth House 140
Dartmouth Lodge 142
Dartmouth Park 13, **138-147**
Dartmouth Park Avenue 141-142
Dartmouth Park Hill 138, **139**, **140-141**, 142
Dartmouth Park Nurseries 145
Dartmouth Park Road 140, **144**, **145**
Dartmouth Road 140, 141
Davenport, Sir Thomas 124
Davies, Windsor 108
Dawe, George 135
Dawson & Briant 21
De Jongh, Tammo 41, 43
De Syllas, J 144
Deaconsfield 54
Deane House 35
Defoe Garage 49
Delbanco Meyer & Co. 93
Dell & Co. 95
Dent, Richard 70
Denyer House 58
Denys Holland Lodge 61

Dettmer, Charles Atto & Sons 90, 129, 131
Devonshire Villas 143
Dicas Field 54
Dillons (pub) 26
Dillow, John & Jane 122
Dixon, Charles Thomas 72
Dixon, E P 118
Dixon, Henry 145
Dodwell, Mrs 108
Donaldson, D Leverton 126
Donnington Court 73
Dorner, Jane 50
Doudney, Sarah 104, **110***
Douglas, Agnes & Alice 132
Dove Commercial Centre 104
Dowdney Close 104, 110
Down, Lesley-Anne 108
D'Oyly Carte, Richard 144
Draper, John 54
Driftway 52
drinking fountains 20, 27, 59, 67, 111
Duck, The 26
Dudley Villa 111
duelling 113-114
Duke of Cambridge, The 109
Duke of St Albans, The 53
Dunn, G A & Co. 21, 27, 66
Dunne Mews 129
Dunollie Place 130
Dunollie Road 130
Dunsbier, John 116
Dunsmore, William 70, 71
Durdans House 68
Dury, Ian 58
Dyer, Henry 34

Dyos, Harold James 128

E
Eagle, The 70
Eason, Alexander 24
East Fleet House 95
East Kentish Town Library 134
Edbrook's garage 102
Eden Place 84
Edser, Fred 141, 142
Edwards, R C 58
Eleanor House 136
Eleanor Palmer Charity 14, **123**, 132, 133, **134**, 136
Eleanor Palmer School **132**, 134, 148
Eleanor Palmer Trust 136
Electric Alhambra 21, 83
electricity 41, 93, 108
Elford, Miss E J 123
Elfrida Rathbone 104
Eliott Optical Co. 96
Elizabeth I 9
Ellen Terry Court 82
Elliott, Temple 112
Ellis, William 52
Elsfield 35
Elton Villa 111
Emergency Rest Centre 123
Emmanuel Hospital 47*-48
Emporium, The 122
Enginemen's Lodgings 40-41
English Collective of Prostitutes 112
Esther Jacobs Hall 107
Ethelbert, King
Eungblut, C & J 59
Evandoré House 35
Evangelist Road 42

152

Evans, Chris 56
Evans, D O & Sons 49
Evans, Dame Edith 52
Evans, George Joseph 62
Evans Place 126
Everet, Robert 21
Ewart, Mary Anne 93
Excelsior Welding 99
Exeter Street 72
Exhibition Works 35
Expressions Dance
 Centre 36

F
Fahey, Siobhan 108
Fairfax Meadow 99
Falcon, The 69
Falkland Arms, The 130
Falkland Hall **126**, 136
Falkland House 137
Falkland House Mews 137
**Falkland Place
 125-126**
**Falkland Road
 126, 130, 137-138**
Family & Youth
 Resource Centre 104
Family Policy Studies
 Centre 35
Faraday House 147
**Farrier Street
 26, 67-68, 82**
fascists 32
Father Ted's 60
Fawcett, Lt-Col. 113
Fifty Taxis 98
Finch, Captain 125
Fink, B 31
fire stations 34
First Express Dairies 21
First House 144
Fitzpatrick, Mark 49
Fitzroy family, see
 Southampton estate

Fitzroy Place 37, 38
Fitzroy Terrace 39
Flask, The 124
Fleet, River 8, 9, 10, **13**,
 25, 26, 35-36, 39, 42,
 54, 68, 71, 72, 76, 80,
 81, 83, 85, 89, **90**, 91,
 97, 98, 139, 140, 142,
 144
Fleet House 36
Fletcher, Maj. George 41
Fletcher Court 41
Flint, W 137
Florence Court 119
Ford, Maggie 144
Ford Motor Co. 104
Forest Healthcare Co. 130
Foresters' Hall 32
Forrest, Bill 35
Forster, Rev. William
 78, 82
Forsyth, George
Fortess, see also Fortys
Fortess Grove 126,
 134, **136**, 137
Fortess Mews 136
Fortess Road 9, 32, 40,
 43-44, 123-124, 126,
 132-134, **134-136**,
 136-137, **138**, 148
Fortess Terrace 131,
 135-136, 137
Fortess Walk 32,
 34, **44-45**, 136-137
Fortess Yard 44
Forties, The 103
Fortys Field 103,
 123, 131, 132, 134
 Housing Assoc. 134
Fortys Lane 132
Forum, The 32
Foster Court 70
Francis, William 67
Francis Terrace 35

Fred's Dining Rooms 31
Free Christian
 Church 82, 83*
Freedex House 95
French academy 58
Frideswide Place 100
Frost, Shirley 43
Frost Road 131
Fullotone Gramophones
 44
Fuzzock & Firkin, The 75

G
Gaisford cinema 112
Gaisford Garage 108
Gaisford House 108
**Gaisford Street
 107-108, 112**
Gale & Ubsdell 112
Gambee, Mr 22
Gambee's Cottage 25
Garden Cinema 25, **77**
Garden of Eden
 Statues 104
Garibaldi, The 103
Gates, The 92
Gaumont cinema 25
gavelkind 8
Gay family 98
General Roadways 96
Geographia Ltd 129
George III 28, 82
George IV, The 96
George's store 145
German Evangelical
 Lutheran Church 116
Gertler, Mark 57
Gilfoy, John 70
Gillies Street 90
Gillis, Mary & Margaret 136
Glenhurst Avenue 48, **50**
Gloag, Julian 145
Gloucester, Duchess of 123
Gloucester Arms, The 129

Gloucester Gardens
 Terrace 118
Gloucester Place
 115, 117, 126
Gloucester Villas 115
Glover, Thomas 52
Goalen, Martin 41
Goldsmith, Oliver 65
Gordon House 47
 Academy 47*
 Business Estate 49
Gordon House Lane 48
Gordon House Road
 13, **48-49**
Gordon House Works 48
Gorman-Sickert,
 Joseph 95
Gospel Oak, tree
 46, 48, 96
Gospel Oak Schools 52
Gospel Oak Station 15,
 38, 49
Gospel Terrace **39-40**, 44
Gothic, The 52
Gothic Hall 52
Gottfried, Philipp 134;
 shop 133*
Gottfried Mews 134
Gottlieb, Stephen 50
Governesses' Benevolent
 Institution 74, 91-92*
Gow, Ian 141
Grafton, Dukes of 14
Grafton Arms, The 91
Grafton Crescent 77
Grafton Cricket Club 91
Grafton Hall 91
Grafton Lodge 77
Grafton Mews 90
Grafton Place 25,
 76, 77, **90**, 91
Grafton Road 91,
 95-96
Grafton Villas 76

Grafton Works 94*, 95
Grafton Yard 90
Graigian Society 43
Grand Banks, The 132
Grange Road 71, 73
Grangemill 41
Grape Place 98
Grayson, George 75
Great College Street
 59, 68, 70
 School 67
Great Field 104
Great Green Street 23
Great Paddock 134
Greater London
 Council 69, 74
 Pensioners Assoc. 34
Greatfield (flats) 104
Greek Cypriots 61, 145
Greek Orthodox
 Church 27, 48
Green, Anthony 51
Green, Charles 113
Green, Leslie 15, 25
Green, Theodore K 35
Green Dragon, The 22
Green Street 9, 32,
 40, 47, 48, 58, 71
Green Street Chapel 46
Green Street Races 39
Greenwood (flats) 104
Greenwood family
 31, 32, 35, 60
Greenwood Centre 35
Greenwood Place 35
Grignion, Charles 56-57
Grisdale, Misses 108
Grobb, John Ernest 54
Grose, W E 118
Grossmith brothers 10
Grosvenor House 141
Grove, The **46-48**,
 47*, 51, 57, 67, 81
Grove End 57

Grove End House **57-
 58**, 144
Grove End Lodge 58
Grove End Villa 58
Grove Farm 52
Grove Farm Lane 52
Grove House 46
Grove Nursery
Grove Place 46
Grove Road 143
Grove Terrace 52,
 56-57, 135, 144
Grove Terrace Mews 57
Grover, Francis 102
Grylls, Thomas 106
Gulliver Service Station 68
Gulliver Telephone
 Exchange 25

H
Hacker, Edward
 & Arthur 62
Haddo House 48
Haddo House Estate 48
Hadley Street 75
Haedy, Christopher 20
Hakewill, J H 34
Hale family 23
Hall, William 144
Hall Field 67
Hambrook, Sgt Stephen 41
Hambrook Court 41
Hamer, William Heath 141
Hamilton, Emma
 25, 27, 66, 81
Hamilton, Ian 147
Hamilton & Chambers 72
Hammond, Charles 96
Hammond, Margaret 107
Hammond & Miles 116
Hammond House 108
Hammond Street 102,
 107
Hampshire Grove 119

153

Hampshire Street 119
Studios 119
Hampstead Gates 92, 93
Hampstead Heath 49,
52, 57
Hampstead Junction Railway
15, 38, 40, 72, 73-74, 91
Hampstead Tube,
see Underground
Handeford Bridge 36
Hanley, James 51
Hannam, Rev. E P 68
Hanwell, Miss 52
Haraszti, Eva 144
Harbar Works 41
Hardwick, Charles 21
Hardwick, Philip 101
Hardy, William 70
Hare, Cecil G 131
Hargrave Place 114, 119
Hargrave Street 114
Harmonic Society 55
Harris, Pedestrian 113
Hartland Grove 74
Hartland Road 74
Havering 75
Haward, Birkin 43, 143
Hawkshead Retail 49
Hawley-Buck estate 14,
25, 26, **71-83**
Hawley family 14, 68,
71, 73
Hawley Place 25
Hawley Road 13,
71-72, 72-73
Open Space 73
Hayes, Reginald 108
Hayman's Row 124
Haywood, Ian,
Partnership 119
Hazel, Henry 112
Healey, Francis 76
Healey Street 76
Hearing Eye press 117

Heath Works 49
Heathview 49
Heaviside, Oliver 69
Hellenic Book Service 44
Hemingway & Thomas 75
Henry III 8, 40
Heppenstall, Rayner 109
Hercules Works 93
Hewett family 30, 100
Hewitt, Patricia 89
Heybridge 75
Heycroft 55
HG: panorama 23
Hickling, George 31
Hicks, Misses 139
Hicks, Leonard 134
Hicks, Robin 42
'High Street', *see*
Kentish Town Road
Highcroft 55
Highfields Terrace 118
Highfields Villas 115
Highfields Works 114, 115*
Highgate Business Centre 35
Highgate Children's
Centre 37
Highgate Centre 35
Highgate Road 9, 13, 23,
32-40, 33*, 45, **46-48**,
51-55, 51*, 56, 137, 138
Chapel/Baptist Church
48, **58**, 126, 145
Enginemen's Lodgings
40-41
Stations 15 , **40**
Highgate Studios 37
Hilger & Watts 60, 61,
63, 70
Hill & Hey 111
Hillside 55
Hirst, John 144
Hiview House 37
Hodge & Butler 78
Hogg, Phoebe 70
Holborn Metal Works 111

Holdsworth, Francis 71
Holiday, Henry 105
Holland, Frances 117
Holland & Sons 111
'Holloway Road' 60
Holmes family 14,
21, 83, 96, 97, 126
Holmes Road 9, 21,
83-84, 96, **97-99**, 127
Board School 89, **97**
Depot 97
Holmes Terrace 82
Holy Trinity & St Silas
School 74
Holy Trinity Church
72, **74**, 75
Home for Working
Boys 48
Home Zone 132
Hope Chapel 76
Hope Cottage
(Clarence Road) 82
(College Lane) 41
Hope Cottages 127
Hopeful Monsters, The 82
Horne, Edward Henry 59
Horner, Thomas 64
Horseman, Walter 28
Housing Corporation 122
Howdens Joinery 99
Howe, Darcus 37
Howe, John G 69
Howell, Killick,
Partridge & Amis 148
Hudson, Edward 21
Hunt, Leigh 46
Hurd, Philip 54

I
Iceland supermarket 21
Idris, Thomas 54;
works 61
Ifor Evans Hall 61
Image House 21
Immisch, Moritz 117
Imperial Laundry 147
Imperial Organ &
Piano Co. 93
Imperial Works 93
Ingestre, Lord 41, 138
Ingestre Community
Centre 41
Ingestre Road 40-41,
139, **147-148**
Estate 39, **40-41**, 42, 147
School 52, **148**
Inkerman Road 88, 89
Inner London Education
Authority 97
Interchange, The 99
International Oriental
Carpet Centre 37
Inwards, Jabez 27, 111
Inwood, William 57, 93
Inwood Terrace 30
Irish Centre Housing 36
Irvingites 48, 90
Islip Mini Store 103
Islip Street 30, 67,
100-102, 103
Islip Street Gardens 103
Ive family 23, 54
Ivers, Rev. Hardinge
Fiorenze **39-40**, 44
Ives, Thomas 40
Ivor Street 70
Ivy Court 117
Ivy House 51
Ivy Lodge 43
Ivybridge Court 82

J
James, William & Co. 89
James Street 114, 119
James Wigg Practice 110
Janner, Greville 108
Jarman, W E 118
Jazzy B 63
Jeans, William P 110
Jefferson Sheard 122
Jeffrey's Place 70
Jeffrey's Street 26, 69
Jeffrey's Terrace 26
Jeffreys family 14,
26, 59, 60, 69, 70
Jegers, P J 144
Jennings, Walter 22
Jepson, Miss 68
Jerrold, Douglas 35
Jersey Milk Co. 133
Jestico & Whiles 125
Jews' Free School
120, **121**, 122
Jim Faulkner Community
Room 147
Job Centres 28, 68, 111
Johnson, John 105
Johnston, Frederick 76
Jollie, Monsieur 58
Jolly Anglers, The 23, 85
Jones, A W 108
Jones, Miss C E 109
Jones, Frederick & Co 93
Jones, Henry Kimbre 80
Jones, Mike 111
Jones & Broadbent 93
Jorene Celeste, The **30**, 100
JT Coachworks 96
Junction Place 32, 34
Junction Road 9, 32, 43,
44, 123, **132**, **136-137**
Junction Street 77
Junction Tavern, The 43

K
Kay, Joseph 60
Keats, John 46
Keith, Prowse & Co. 75
Kellaway, Kate
Kelly, John 78, 80, 81
Kelly Street 25, **78-79**
Kemble family 55
Kemble Piano Group 59
Kenbrook House 129
Kennistoun House 128
Kent, Richard Jr 108
Kentish Town
Act 60
'Alps' **41**, 147
& Camden Town
National School 67
& East Hampstead Inst. 97
Bridge 35, 36
British School 28
Business Park 97, **99**
Camera Club 97
Catholic Social Club
Cattle Dock 99, 117
Chapel [of Ease] 8, 9,
10, **23**, 24*, 34, 57
CofE Primary
School 100-101*
Cinema 112
Coal Depot **96-97**, 99
Congregational Church
25, 28, **78**, 79*, 82
Day Nursery 93
Delivery Office 99
District Housing
Office 107
Evening Institute 97
Fire Station 34
Green 9, 47
Health Centre 110-111
House 54
Junior Men's Inst. 97
Library 30
Literary Society 28

Loco Depot 37, 38
Men's Institute 97
Methodist Church 44
Milk Depot 102
Panorama, see
King, James F
Parish Church, *see*
St John the Baptist …
Police Stations **83**,
88, 124
Post Office 25, 30
Residences 65
Kentish Town Road
10, 12, **20-30**, **31-
32**, 65, 66, 68, 72, 76,
77, 85, 99, 106, 112,
124, 137, **138**, *cover**
Kentish Town
Snooker & Pool Club 83
Sports Centre 91
Stations 20, 30, 100,
102
Weightlifting Club 97
West Station 15, 75, 91
Kettle, Mr 109
Key Productions 70
Kimber, George 21
King, Eliza 77
King, Haynes 77
King, James F; *Kentish
Town Panorama* **12**,
20, 22, 25, 26, 31, 32,
36, 38, 40, 45, 47, 48,
52, 55, 56, 58, 66, 67,
72, 81, 124, 125
King, Thomas 12, 80, 81
King's Arms, The 22
King's Road 60, 61,
63, 65, 67, 68
Kingsbridge Court 82
Kingsley, Henry 135
Kingston House 137
Kingsway College 97
Kinross, Robin 104

Knaggs, Henry 120
Knight, Stephen 95
Knippenberg, Rev.
K H 116
Knowles, James S 124
Kramer, Duncan 104
Kroenig-Ryan, Rev. A S 52
KT Auto Services 106
Kulubi Centre 138
Kwikfit garage 49

L
LA Fitness 37
La Sainte Union **54**, 55
La Swap 6th Form
Consortium 148
Labour Exchange 68
Lady Margaret Road
44, 126, 127, **128**, **131**
Lady Somerset Road
38, **42**, **43**
Lafargue, Paul & Laura 114
Laing, Rev. David 74, 91
Lambourn Close 131
Lamorna 144
Lampton House 137
Landley Field 119
Landor Cottage 135
Lane, Ronnie 106
Lapping, Anne & Brian 86
Larn, Kate & Louise 145
Last, Ye 55
Latter Day Saints 75
Launer, Louis 116
Laurel Villas 139
Laurier Court 143
Laurier Road 142, **143**
Lavinia, Princess 29, **82**
Lawford, John Eeles
78, 79, 80, 81, 109
Lawford Road 109
Lawrence, Frederick 72
Lee, J T 122

Legge family, *see*
Dartmouth estate
Legge House 142
Leighton, Sir David
115, 117, 126
Leighton Arms, The 115
Leighton Crescent 116
**Leighton Grove
116-117**
Leighton Halls 116
Leighton House
(36B Leighton Rd) 129
(37 Leighton Rd) 128
Leighton Place 129
Leighton Project 104
Leighton Road 67, 99,
103, 115, **117**, **118**, 123-
124,**126-128**, **128-129**
Leighton Villas 115
Lensham House 35
Lever, George 64, 67, 69
Leverton & Sons 25, 79
Leverton Place 125, 138
Leverton Street 126,
130, 131
Lewis, Mrs C L 135
Lewis Street 74-75, 81
Lewisham Road 124
Lexow, Adolphe 106
Leys, The 62
libraries 30, 90, 134
Liddon Memorial
High School 131-132
Light Rescue Service 119
Lilia Ltd 103
Lincoln, Frances, Ltd 117
Linden House 48
'Linden Road' 142
Line, John & Sons 49
Ling, M G 27
Linton House 36
Lion & Unicorn, The 107
Lissenden Gardens 49-51
Tenants Association 50

Lissenden Mansions 51
Lissenden Motors 49
Lissenden Works 49
Little Green Street
39, **40**, 41
Little Paddock 45
Lloyds TSB 22
Loach, Ken 56
Locket & Judkins 72
Loeffler, Sabine 50
London and
North Western Rly 15, 74
South Western Bank 30
London Baptist Assoc. 58
London Centre for
Psychotherapy 128
London County Council
49, 53, 67, 70, 85, 99,
107, 118, 119, 121,
122, 127, 134, 141
London Fan & Motor Co. 43
London General Omnibus
Co. 32, 43, 89, 133
London Lorries Ltd 96
London, Midland &
Scottish Rly 41, 102, 147
London Passenger
Transport Board 88, 128
London Piano Co. 84
London School Board, *see*
School Board for London
London Skills Institute 111
London Street Tramways,
see tramways
London Wildlife Trust 49
London Youth Advisory
Centre 91
Long Meadow 108
(flats) 119
Lord Palmerston, The 140*
Lorraine Court 81
Lowe, Mr 47
Lower Barn Field 67
Lower Craven Place 35

Lower Mansfield Place 97
Lower Meadow 109
Lowes, James H 77
Ludovici, Albert 68
Lunardi, Vincent 30
Lupton Street 131-132
Luther Tyndale Church 116
Luzmore, Philip 130
Lynton Villa 57
Lyons, J & Co. 21, 24

M
M&A Coachworks 40
McBurney, Simon 86
McCarthy, Henry 139
MacClaren, William 22
McCormack, T W 90
McCoy, Sylvester 42
McCrone Scientific
Research 117
McDonalds 21
McDonogh, Mr 40
MacGibbon, James 88
MacGibbon, Jean 88
Mckay, Charles 60
McNab, John 130
McVay, Charles 90
Madness 38, 58, 101, 103
Madox Brown, Ford
56, **135***
'Magic Land, The' 41
Magnet Joinery 97
Maiden Lane 114,
126, 132, **138**
Mainstone, Angelica
& Sophie 56
Malt & Hops, The 98
Malvern Cottages 72
Mann, James H 22, **114**
Mann & Sargon 119;
works 115*
Manning, Henry 106
Manor Cottages 137
Manpower Services

Commission 131
Mansell, Ernest 77
Mansfield Arms, The 98
Mansfield Bowling Club 53
Mansfield Crescent 97
Mansfield estate 15, 49, 53
Mansfield Place 9,
21, **83**, 84, **96**
School 97
Mansfield Rifle Club 53
Manville Terrace 114
Manville Yard 114
Maple, Sir Blundell 91
Maple & Co. **35-36**,
84, 106, 120
Margaret House 129
Marie Auxiliatrice,
Sisters of 43-44
Mario's Café 79
Marks & Spencer 21
Markson Music Centre 44
Marshall, David 114
Mary Webster House 141
Mather, Rick 42
Maud Wilkes Close 127
Max Rayne House 61
Mazzarello, Marie D 44
Media House 39
Medical & Surgical
Nursing Home 48
Medical Care Home 121
Meers Engineering Co. 127
Mellon, Harriet 53
Memorial Hall 72
Mensal, Andrew 32, 47
Merritt, George 51
Merry, James 22
Methodists; Wesleyans 34,
44, 46, 95, 119, 127, 128,
130; chapel 47*
Metropolitan Board of
Works 49, 65, 66, 76
Metropolitan Memorial
Co. 98

Metropolitan Police 12, **83**, 88, 124, 141
Midland Railway **15**, 20, 30, 31, 35, 37, 38, 40, 41, 96, 98, 99, 102, 105, 106, 117, 121, 122, 123, 124, 127
Miller, Terence 76
Milligan, Robert 54
Minshull, William 58
mission halls 84, 90, 102, 119, 127, 132, 136, 138
Mivart, Miss 112
Moggach, Deborah 70
Molesworth Place 69
Monant, William 114
Monck, Dan 104
Monk, William 98
Monmouth House 84, 85
Montague House 110
Montague Place 12, 20
Monte Video Place 52, **65-67**, 66*, 101, 127, cover*
Montessori Nursery 62
Montpelier 116
Montpelier Cottage 116
Montpelier Gardens 116
Montpelier Grove 130
Montpelier House 116
Montpelier Nursery 116
Montpelier Road 130
Moore, Gary 56
Moore, Temple 140
Morant, John 100, 104, 124
Moreton Arms, The 26
Moreton Street 73, 77
Moreton Terrace **26**, 72
Moreton Villas 26
Morgan family 9, 23, 24, 30, 102
Morgan's Farm 30, 102, 112

Mormons 75
Mornington Building Society **51**, 129
Morris, H 31
Morris & Co. 105
Mortimer, Richard 14, 38, 46, 71
Mortimer Terrace 38, **46**, 49
Mortimer's Farm 46
Mosley, Oswald 32
Mothers in Action 43
Motorway Box 69
Mullaly & Co. 123
Munden, Joseph S 55, 57
Munro, Lieutenant 114
Murphy, J & Sons Ltd 37
Murray, Harriet 62
Murray, John (piano-key maker) 34

N
Nag's Head, The 65*
Nando's restaurant 23, 85
National Schools 67, 101
Neave, Mrs 65
Neighbourhood Guild 116
Neil Sharp Block 61
Nelson, The 77
Nelson, Horatio 9, **25**, 48, **81***
Nelson Terrace 77
Nerli, Girolamo Piero 143
Neuberger, Rabbi Julia 126
New Chapel Place 31
New Empress Saloons 128
New Hampstead Road 77
New River Company 52, 141
Newbury & Fowler 116
Newcomen House 147
Newton, Henry C 96
Nicholls & Hale 122
Nkrumah, Kwame 42

Noakes & Co. 34
Nordoff Robbins Music Therapy **51**, 129
Norfolk Laundry 65, 68
North Camden Housing Co-operative 147
North London Collegiate School 82, 120, **122**
North London Colour Works 96
North London Emergency Secondary School 52
North London Railway/Line 10, **15**, 26, 59, 72, 93
North Point 122
North West London Synagogue 106-107
North Western Polytechnic 25, **76**, 78
Northern Line, see Underground
Northumberland House 112
nursery gardens 49, 61, 85, 93, 145
NW5 Theatre School 137

O
Oak Court 54
Oakford Road 43
Oakley, Rev. Frank 132
Ocean Furniture 37
Old Chapel House 23
Old Chapel Path 22
Old Chapel Place 22
Old Chapel Row 21, 23
Old Dairy Mews 21
Old Dolls Workshop 112
Old Eagle, The 70
Old Engine House 34
Old Farm House, The 21
Olive, Princess 28-29
omnibus operators 32, 43, 44,80, 89, 97, 98, 128, 133

Omnibus Proprietors Co. 44
One One Five Behaviour Support ... Base 116
Orchard Place 81
Orchard Street 81-82
O'Reilly's 21
organ builders 34, 43, 62, 64, 93, 103, 106, 118, 129
Orientalist, The 37
Orwell, George 98, **109**
Osborne House 111
Osborne House Business Centre 104
Oseney Crescent 90, **104-106**, 120
Ospringe Road 131
Oughton, Edward 72, 74, 81
Our Lady Help of Christians 44, 45*, 128
Our Lady's Hall 130
Owl Bookshop 24
Oxford House 111
Oxford Tavern/Vaults, The 30, 100
Oxford Villa 111

P
Paddock Lodge 134
Page, William 22
Pain's Place 65-66, 68
Palace Cinema **24**, 77, 91
Palgrave, Sir Francis 58
Palmer, Eleanor 123
Palmer, John 123
Palmer House 134
Pank, Philip 118
Paradise Row 98
Parents & Co. 104
Park, James 120
Parkyn, W & Sons 98
Parliament Hill Fields 31, **49**, 52, 53

Parliament Hill Lawn Tennis Club 50
Parliament Hill Lido 49
Parliament Hill Mansions 50
Parliament Hill School **52**, 53*, 148
Paternoster (balloonist) 113
Paterson, Edward 75
Patmore, Coventry 51-52
Patmore, Emily 52
Patshull Place 109
Patshull Road 29, **108**, **111-112**
Patterson, James 46
Paul, Winifrede 147
Payne, Joseph 20
Payne, T G & Co. 44, 136, 137
Payne's Place 65
Peacock, Joseph 131
Pearcy, Mary 70
Peckwater Centre 103
Peckwater Estate 102-103, 104
Peckwater House 105
Peckwater Street 102-103, 129
Peel & Co. 103
Penrhyn Villa 110
Pentecostals 71
Perren, Richard 93
Perren Street 93, 94*
Petit Prince, Le 83
Phelps, Frederick 44
Phelps (builders' mcht) 72
Phelps Pianos 44
Philia House 68, 69
piano industry 9, 24, 28, 32, 34-35, 36, 44, 59, 75, 84, 90, 93-95, 103, 106, 118, 129, 31, 136, 137
Piano Workers' Guild 34
Piano Works Co. 35
Piccadilly Press 79

Pickard, Tom 48
Pike (barrister) 127
Pineapple, The 130
Pinter, Harold 42
Pizza Express 25
Platt family 42
Pleasant Row 38, 46
Plouviez, Peter 108
Plymouth Brethren 71
police, see Metropolitan...
Pollyrodgers, Mrs 56
Polytechnic of North London 76, 103
Poor Relief Station 127
Porritt, Jonathan 143
Portland House 93
Positive Movement 43
post offices 25, 30, 39, 109, 129, 138
postal sorting/delivery offices 99, 128
pounds (parish) 30, **78**
Powe, F W 122
Powers, Michael 57
Pratt family, see Camden estate
Presbyterians 127, 130
Priddle, Rev. Charles J 90
Primitive Methodists 95
Primrose Laundry 99
Prince of Wales Road 25, 48, 67, **75-77**, **90**, **91-92**, 123
Baths 89, **91**
Print-in-Time 95
Priory Mews 70
Priory Place 70
Priory Street 70
Priory Works 70
Prospect Place 35
Prospect Row 35
Prout, John Skinner 116
Providence Place 26, 73
Prowse, Capt. William 70

Prowse Place **70**
Psycho-Geriatric Day
  Centre 85
Pugh, Charles Ltd 96, 98
Pugin, E W 44, 45
Pull & Field 129

Q
Quinn's 26
Quirey, Belinda 103

R
Race Fields 39, 41
Radice, Giles & Lisanne 144
Ragged Schools 20, 67, 125
Raglan Cottages 86
Raglan Day Centre 85
Raglan Estate 85
Raglan House 85
Raglan Place 84
Raglan Street 84-85, 86
Railey Mews 130-131
Railey Works Co. 131
Railway Cottage 41
Railway Tavern, The 122
Rakish Hill 43
Raleigh House 137
Randall, James 144
Randall, P Litten 43
Raphael's optical
  works 118
Raveley Street 134
Ravenswood (flats) 48
Ravenswood (house) 48
Read Bros Ltd **35**, 36*, 37
Red Lion, The 22
Redan, The 84
Reed, William 67
Reed's Place 63, 67
Reform Club 75, 77
Regent's Canal 9, 116
Regis family 100
Regis Road 13, **99**

Registered Care Homes
  Association 122
Regnart, Horace G
  90, **120***
Reise, Barbara 99
rent strike 128
Retreat, The **38**, 49
Richards, Frederick 25
Richards, Joseph 28
Richardson, A 98
Richardson, John 12,
  23, 124, 137
Riley, W E 76
Ringley's 27
Rintoul, John 111
Robeson, Paul 54
Robins, E C 93, 122, 123
Robinson, Jethro T 107
Robinson, Kenneth 57
Robson, E R 97
Rochester Cottage 65
Rochester Hall 27, 65
Rochester Mews 61, 63
Rochester Place 60,
  62, **63-64**
Rochester Road 61,
  62, 64-65
  Conservation Area 62, 63
Rochester Road Mews 61
Rochester Terrace 62, 63
Rodgers, Bill 108
Roman Catholics 39-40,
  44, 54, 128, 130, 135
Rose, John 48
Roseman Cottages 68
Rosemary House 129
Rosmer, Milton 115
Rose-Morris 49
Ross, Nick 89
Rossetti, Dante G 135
Rossiter, Charles 46
Rotunda, The 64*
Rowley, Dr William
  116, 123, **137**

Rowstock 105
Roxwell 75
Royal Air Force 55
Royal Arms, The 107
Royal College Street
  27, 54, 59, **65-67**,
  68, 69, **70-71**
Royal Exchange, The 74
Royal Mail 99, 128
Royal Mail Yard **88**, 98
Ruskin, John 52
Russell, Rev. Frederick 75
Ryland House 95
Ryland Road 93-95*
Ryland Secondary School 92
Ryves, Lavinia 82

S
St Albans, Duke &
  Duchess of 53
St Alban's Road 53, 54
St Alban's Villas 53, **54**
St Alexis RC Chapel 39
St Anargyre Church 48
St Anargyre House 48
St Andrew & St
  Barnabas Cathedral 27
St Andrew's Greek School
  64
St Anne Brookfield
  Church 140
St Barnabas Church 27
St Barnabas Parish Room 90
St Bartholomew's Hospital,
  see Bartholomew estate
St Benet & All Saints
  Church 106, **131**, 138
St Catherine's Convent 135
St Dunstan's Works 84-85*
St John the Baptist Church
  33*, **34**, 35, 38, 48,
  58, 131
  National Schools 101*
  Vicarage 42

St John the Evangelist
  Road 42
St John's College estate
  14, 34, 39, 41, 42, 58,
  123-124, 126, 128, 129,
  130, 131, 134, 148
St John's College Park 132
St John's Farm 41, 58
St John's Park House 58
St Luke's Church 62,
  105*-**106**, 111
St Luke's Hall 119
St Luke's Institute 103
St Luke's Vicarage **105***,
  119
St Margaret's Hospital 127
St Margaret's Nursery 127
St Mary Brookfield
  Church 140
  Church Hall 143
St Mary's RC Chapel 135
St Pancras (parish) 8, 14, 34
St Pancras
  Baths/Washhouses 89, **91**
  Board of Guardians
    98,127
  Borough Council 10,12,
    41, 48, 54, 56, 81, 90,
    91, 95, 98, 102, 103,
    105, 107,116, 119, 120,
    121, 122, 128, 129,
    139, 142, 243, 147
  Church Lands 8, 49, 53
  Day Nursery 107
  Ethical Society 139
St Pancras Gazette 59
St Pancras
  Hostel 98-99
  Housing Assoc. 127, 147
  Maternity …Centre 85
  North Relief Station 99
  North Unionist Club 128
  New Church 9
  Old Church 8, 23

Reform Club 75, 77
Rent Strike 128
Schools Treatment
  Centre 91
  Vestry 9, 22, 30, 57,
    76, 78, 81, 104, 114
St Pancras Way 60,
  63, **68-69**
St Patrick's School 84, **99**
St Paul's Cathedral 14, 138
St Paul's Chapel 72
St Paul's Church 105
St Richard of Chichester
  School 67, 92
St Thomas's Church 71
Salcombe Lodge 49
Salisbury Plain 49
Salmon, J & Son 5, 31
Salmon & Glickstein 24
Salter, Joseph 31, 67
Salter Rex 22, 31, 67
Salvation Army 44, 65
Sams, Sarah 23
Samuel, Jaques 32
Samuel & Spencer 48
Sandall Mews 122
Sandall Road 92,
  109, 121, **122-123**
Sanderson Close 37
Sargent & Petts 90
Sargon, James 114
SAS Martial Arts
  Academy 49
Sassie, Victor 89
Satchell, F C 58
Sayers, Michael 109
Sayers, Tom 32
Scar Studios 73
Schonfield, A 106
School Board for London;
  Board Schools 67, 97,
  134, 147, 148
School House 100
Scott, Booth 121

Scottish Fisheries 95
Scouts 119
Sears, Frances 46
Section House 83
Seddon, Thomas 56, 135
Seguier, John 69
Selway, Richard 145
Serres, Olivia 28-29
Seven O'Clock Club 104
Sewell, Rufus 130
Sewell, Samuel 20
Shand Kydd family
  37, 55, 110
Shand Kydd Ltd 37
Shaw, George Bernard
  81, 82
Shaw, Martin Fallas 50
Shaw, Richard Norman 83
Shelley, Mary 28
Sheltered Workshops 98
Sickert, Joseph 95
Sickert, Walter 61, 95
Sibthorpe, Thomas 104
Siddal, Lizzie 135
Sidney House 55
Sigismund, Emperor 8, 30
Silver Lodge 38
Silverlink 37, 46, 91
Silverside, Giles 102
Silveyra, Louisa 143
Simpson, Glenda 145
Simpson, W B & Sons 61
Sinclair, Henry 112
Sir William Collins
  School 61, 67
Sisters of
  the Church 132
  Marie Auxiliatrice 43-44
Slack, Thomas C 52, 67
Smerdon, Robert 56,
  138, 139, 140, 142, 145
Smith, Rev. Samuel 72
Smith, Dr Thomas
  Southwood 135-136*

Smith & Walton 111
Snooker & Pool Club 83
Snow, Jon 130
Social Villagers 23, 31, **124**
Society for Organising
Charitable Relief 40
Somali Youth Centre 104
Somerfields 24
Somerset House 139
Soul II Soul Studios 63
South, Rev. Robert
100, 106, 107
South Grove 57
South Kentish Town
Station **25**, 81
South Terrace 57
Southampton Arms,
The 46
Southampton estate;
Fitzroy family 10, 14,
21, 31, 46, 48, 49, 74,
76, 91
Southampton House
(Academy) 46
Southampton Terrace 25
Spectrum House 49
Spencer Rise 139, **145**
Spencer Road 139
Spring Fields 83
Spring Garden 85
Spring House 96
Spring Place 9, **96-97**
Spring Row 84
Springett, Kate 143
Stalbridge, Mr 114
Stallard, Jock 35, 73, 110
Stanhope Press 95
Stanley, Lyulph 148
Star & Garter, The 21
Stephens, Rev. James 145
Stephenson House 147
Stern, David &
Partners 107
Stevens, R F 129

Stillman & Eastwick
-Field 123
Stokes, Telfer 43
Stott, Ken 130
Straub, Peter 42
Strawberry Place 22
Street, W G 140
Stukeley, Dr William 27*-28
Suckling, J 48
Suckling, William 48, 81
Sunning Lodge 111
Surrey Ice Creamery 107
Sussex Arms, The 69
Sussex Cottages 63, 68
Sussex House **67**, 127
Sussex Place 69
Sussex Terrace 68
Suter, Clara 104
Sutton, Mr 31
Swains Lane 53
Swingler, Margaret 110
Symonds, Miss E R 145
synagogue 106

T
Tabor, P 116
Tadpole Nursery 58
Tally Ho, The 32, **45**
'Tammoland' 41
Tan Pill Field 97
TANC 147
Tanhouse Close 104
Tanhouse Field (flats) 119
Tarring, John 128
Tate, Phyllis 86
Tattenham House 68
Tavern Inn The Town 75
Tawney, Richard Henry 50
Taylor, A J P 144
Taylor, James 72, 73, 74
telephone exchange 25
Temple, Bp Frederick 27
Temple Wright 43

Tenants Association
of North Camden 147
Tennyson, Lord 52
Terry, Ellen 82, 114
Thameslink 20, 30
Théâtre de Complicité 86
Thomas, A J 103, 119
Thomas, William 49
Thompson, Lee 103
Thompson, Peter 34
Thorpe & Furniss 124
Thurston, Robert 27
Tideswell 41
Tindall, Gillian 12
Tiptree 74
Toledo Steel Co. 93
tollhouses; turnpikes
9, 21, 114
Tomkin, Inspector 12, 35,
63, 68, 75, 84, 102, 144
Top to Toe 31
Topham, Frank 134
Torbay Court 72, 82
Torbay Street 72, 75, 82
Torriano Arms, The 118
Torriano Avenue 115,
117, **118-119**, **120**
Torriano Cottages 118
Torriano family & estate
113, **115-120**, 123, 126
Torriano Gardens 118
Torriano Gardens Estate
119
Torriano Infants School 119
Torriano Junior School
28, **118**
Torriano Meeting
House 117
Torriano Mews 117
Torriano Project 117
Torriano Terrace 117
Torriano Villas 117
Torriano Yard 117

Tottenhall (Manor) 10,
14-15, 66, 68, 76
Tottenham & Hampstead
Junction Railway 15,
37-38, 40, 41, 49, 139,
147
Tottenham North Curve
15, 38
Tough, Rev. Thomas 46
Tower House 61
Towers, The 142
Town & Country Club 34
Toye, Samuel 68
Tozer, John Smith 36, 90
Trafalgar, The 75
Trafalgar Cottage 111
Trafalgar Chapel 28
Trafalgar Place 28
tramways 10, 31,
39*, 50, 60, 113, 121
Trapeze Learning 37
Tresco Car Hire 120
Trevithick House 147
Tuckwell, Barry 109
Tudor Mansions 139
Tufnell, George Foster 115
Tufnell Park Station 15
Tuke, G 112
Tweddle family 134
Tweedsyde 145
Twisden Road 144
Two Running Horses,
The 39

U
Ujima Housing Assoc. 122
Una House 90
Underground 10, 15,
25, 30
Unicorn, The 113
Unionist Club 128
Unitarians 78, 82;
chapel 83*
United Collieries 26

United Parcel Services 99
University College 61
University of London
Training Corps 119
of North London 76
Upper Barn Field 67
Upper Craven Place 7
Upper Hartland Road 74
Upper Mansfield Place
97-98
Upper Meadow 109
Upper Spring Garden 85
Utting, Robert Brooke 108

V
Vadnie Bish House 107
Van Heyningen,
Joanna 43, 143
Varley, Cornelius 20
Varley, Samuel 21
Venus Cinema 27
Vicarage Farm Dairies 21
Vicarage Place 83
Vicarage Row 22
Victoria Road 73, **77**
Victoria Terrace 75
Victoria Villa 78
Victory, The 73
Village House 125
Vincent, Henry 108
Vincent, Thomas 104
Vine, The **38-39**, 41
Vulture's Perch, The 30

W
Wages Due Lesbians 112
Wall to Wall 96
Walter (dairyman) 27
Walton, Hassell &
Port 30, 96
Walton, Thomas 34
War Child 86
war memorial 41
Ward, Rowland 129

Wardlow 41
Warner, Robert 23
Water Lane 26, 65
Watson (telescope mfr) 66
Watson's Syphon 111
Watts, E R 60
Weatherhead, William
Harris 72
Webb, David 77
Webb, Philip 105
Webster, Rev. Mary 141
Weldon, Fay 93
Welford Court 73
Wesley, John 9, **22**
Wesleyan Place 46
Nature Reserve 49
Wesleyans, see Methodists
Westlea Children's
Home 142
Westminster Kingsway
College 97
Weston, Edward 38
Weston's Retreat 38
Wheatley House 48
Whish, Rev. Albert E 90
Whitbread plc 99
Whitcher, John 61
Whitcher & Searles 61
Whitcher Place 54, 61, 62
White, Edward 72
White Horse, The 38
White Lion & Bell, The 22
Whitehead, Philip 108
Whitewater Graphics 44
Whittington, Dick
(fl.1900) 130
Whittington & Cat, The 39
Wiber, Lewis 52
Wiblin, John 39
Widford 75, 77
Wigg family 27, 110
Wild, David 63
Wilkes, Maud 127
Wilkin Street 95

Willes Road **89**, **96**, 106
William Ellis School 52
Williams, Sir James 52
Williams, Jane 28
Willingham Close 130
**Willingham Terrace
  129-130**
Willis, Henry 62, 64, 105,
  111; works 64*
Willis, John 42
Willow Walk 32,
  44-45, 136-137
Wills, Robert 81
Wilmot, James 28
Wilmot Cottages 63
Wilmot Place 62, **63**,
  68, 69
Wilson, Elizabeth 103
Wilson, Philip 63
Winchester Place 137
Winifrede Paul House 147
Winsor & Newton 96
Wiseman, Cardinal 40
Woffendale, Rev. Z B 112
Wolsey House 105, 119
Wolsey Mews 112
Wolsey Tavern, The 29
Wolsey Terrace 29, 30
Wombles (squatters) 132
Women Against Rape 112
Women's Evening Inst. 67
Wood, Edward 116
Wood, Haydn 50
Wood, Thomas 124
Wood, Walter 50
Wood, William 140, 145
Woodentots Nursery 62
Woodfall family 58
Woodland Cottages 36
Woodland House 36
Woodland Place 34
Woodsome Road 56, **143**
Woodward, Keren 108
Woodward, S Pickworth 90

Woolworth's 21
Workplace Co-operative
  11*, 104
World War One 10,
  25, 41, 116, 148
World War Two 10, 26, 20,
  41, 42, 43, 52, 54, 55, 63,
  71, 73, 74, 75, 77, 78, 81,
  82, 84, 88, 92, 95, 96,
  101, 102, 104, 110, 119,
  120, 122, 123, 126, 127,
  130, 132, 133, 139, 140,
  142, 143, 148
Wright, Robert 124
Wurlitzer Cinema
  Organs 118
Wyatt, James 34, 35
Wyatt, Thomas
  Henry 74, 91

Y
Yard, The 43
Yates, W 31
Yearwood, Rev.
  Randolph 22
York Mews 99
York Place 20-21
York Rise 13,
  142-143, 145-147
York Rise Estate 146*, 147
York Road 138, 142
York Villas 139
Yorke, Rosenberg
  & Mardall 37
YWCA Home &
  Institute 58

Z
Zierler Media 39
Zimmern, Alice 50
Zuni Southwest
  restaurant 134
Zwanziger, Albert 31

The Camden History Society

has published historical street surveys of the following parts of the London Borough of Camden

All are obtainable on application to:

CHS Publications Manager: Roger Cline, Flat 13, 13 Tavistock Place, London WC1H 9SH, tel 020 7388 9889 (with answerphone)

or to the:

Camden Local Studies and Archives Centre, 32-38 Theobalds Road, London WC1X 8PA, tel 020 7974 6342 (closed Wednesdays and Sundays)

The Streets of Hampstead, 3rd edition (2001)

The Streets of Belsize (1991)

The Streets of West Hampstead (1992)

From Primrose Hill to Euston Road (1995)

Streets of Bloomsbury and Fitzrovia (1997)

East of Bloomsbury (1998)

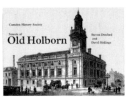

Streets of Old Holborn (1999)

Streets of St Giles (2000)

Streets of St Pancras (Somers Town and the Railway Lands) (2002)

Streets of Camden Town (2003)